D1252743

"In this readable and intellectually exciting synthesis of science and Christian faith, Laurie Brink shows how communities of religious women may fruitfully integrate the new scientific cosmic story into their spiritual lives. I hope, however, that many other Christian readers also may take this scientifically and theologically informed and inspiring work with them on their own religious journeys."

—John Haught, Distinguished Research Professor Emeritus, Georgetown University

"Laurie Brink's well-researched and thoughtful book is a much-needed contribution to the conversation regarding the present and future of religious life in the twenty-first century. As a middleton who is also a newer vocation, now serving in elected leadership, I discovered pathways to deeper understanding of the experiences and ecclesiologies of my sisters of all generations. Brink deftly weaves Scripture, theology, and science to explore an intercultural, unitive, evolutionary, and integrative vision of wholeness for formation, vows, and mission in apostolic religious life."

—Susan Francois, CSJP, Assistant Congregation Leader, Sisters of St. Joseph of Peace

"Religious life has been in flux since the close of the Second Vatican Council. What was once a static and fixed life has become an open system of emerging communities and ministries. Laurie Brink's new book brings the heart of religious life into deep dialogue with the sciences in a scholarly and thoughtful way. By weaving together new life in God with new life in the universe, we can begin to appreciate the value of the Gospels with new depth and breadth. This is an important book, as religious communities diminish in size, yet expand with new possibilities of communal and intercommunal life. Framing religious life with a scientific worldview will not detract from the life but expand it in creative and novel ways. The Spirit who calls us into new life in God is breathing through a dynamic and vibrant universe; indeed, God is doing new things throughout the entire cosmos."

—Ilia Delio, OSF, Josephine C. Connelly Endowed Chair in Theology, Villanova University

# The Heavens Are Telling
# the Glory of God

*An Emerging Chapter for Religious Life
Science, Theology, and Mission*

Laurie Brink, OP

LITURGICAL PRESS
Collegeville, Minnesota

www.litpress.org

| 1 | 2 | 3 | 4 | 5 | 6 | 7 | 8 | 9 |
| --- | --- | --- | --- | --- | --- | --- | --- | --- |

Library of Congress Cataloging-in-Publication Data

Names: Brink, Laurie, 1961– author.
Title: The heavens are telling the glory of God : an emerging chapter for religious life : science, theology, and mission / Laurie Brink, OP.
Description: Collegeville, Minnesota : Liturgical Press, [2022] | Includes bibliographical references and index. | Summary: "Beginning with the experiences of women religious and their encounter with the New Cosmology or Universe Story, The Heavens Are Telling the Glory of God seeks to mediate among the various perspectives and proposes how informed and reflective engagement with science, tradition, and theology can bridge the generational divides and foster a spirituality that is both emergent and incarnational. Access to online discussion and reflection questions is included"— Provided by publisher.
Identifiers: LCCN 2021040260 (print) | LCCN 2021040261 (ebook) | ISBN 9780814667248 (paperback) | ISBN 9780814667255 (epub) | ISBN 9780814667255 (pdf)
Subjects: LCSH: Monastic and religious life of women. | Creation. | Teilhard de Chardin, Pierre. | Science and religion. | Cosmology. | Ecotheology.
Classification: LCC BX4210 .B735 2022 (print) | LCC BX4210 (ebook) | DDC 255/.9—dc23
LC record available at https://lccn.loc.gov/2021040260
LC ebook record available at https://lccn.loc.gov/2021040261

*To the Dominican Sisters of Sinsinawa*
*Past, Present, and Future*
*and most especially*
*to Evie and Julie*
*who asked The Question.*

# Contents

Discussion and Reflection Questions are available at
https://litpress.org/discussion/the-heavens.

# Foreword

We are all shaped by our histories and the cultures of which we are a part. This applies also to our theological questions and answers, and to the spirituality that flows from them. We can be instructed and inspired by the insights and perspectives of the past, but they will really only genuinely convert us if we examine them through contemporary lenses. This has been done frequently in the recent past when social justice, gender equality, or cultural diversity have overwhelmed us with their challenge. From such interpretations, theologies and spiritualties of liberation, feminism, and interculturality have been born. Today another concern is pressing to be heard, a concern that touches every aspect of our existence on Earth. That concern is ecological integrity. Insights gained in this area have come to be known as the New Cosmology.

For many people, the New Cosmology is anything but new. Some might say that it can be traced as far back as 1543, when Copernicus published his thesis claiming that the universe was heliocentric and not geocentric. Building on his revolutionary findings, astronomers down through the centuries have discovered an amazing universe of which we are a part, and people of every way of life have become fascinated by their discoveries. Modern cosmology is based on Einstein's 1905 theory of relativity. Elements of this cosmological awareness took religious shape in the thinking of Teilhard de Chardin when, in the 1950s, he advanced the theory that the universe has not yet finished evolving but is emerging toward what he called the Omega Point. Though silenced by his religious superiors, his thinking has kindled a fire in the minds and hearts of people today.

While many people are aflame with this New Cosmology and the possible theologies and spiritualities it might generate, most of the population know very little about the scientific theory and even less about its religious potential. Still, just as social concerns such as social justice, gender equality, or cultural diversity demand that we address the bigotry they have uncovered and remedy any evil that yet remains, so the New Cosmology can no longer be seen as the pastime of stargazers. Instead, it must be acknowledged as a mapping of the world of which we are a part, a mapping that will influence how we comprehend ourselves as children of Earth and as citizens of the universe. It will expand our perception of the dazzling magnificence of the Creator-God through this awe-inspiring creation. In so many ways, the New Cosmology will "blow our minds."

What better way to forge forward in opening this worldview to a broader population than to engage women religious in a study of the possibilities such a worldview offers in the area of spirituality. Much of the groundwork for such a study of women religious has already been done, for in the recent past they have been called to examine their religious values and the reasons they have espoused them, the ministries to which they have committed themselves, and the life style that has developed to support those ministries. An examination of spirituality could certainly be seen as the next step in personal and communal inventory. Women religious might be diminishing, but they are not floundering; they might be aging, but they are not brittle. Rather, they continue to be the vanguard that they were called to be by the Second Vatican Council.

Such a study was undertaken by Laurie Brink. Limiting the scope of participation to women religious who share a certain worldview and hold various values in common, she maintained that authentic differences in spirituality would still be easily detected. Brink came to this venture with more questions than answers. While she brought a vast amount of information regarding various aspects of the issues under consideration, she did not presume that the reader was interested in or willing to be open to being spiritually formed by that information. If the reader was interested, Brink wanted to know why; if the reader was not interested, why not? Finally, the question of the age of the participants was addressed. Brink sought to determine if what is frequently referred to as the New Cosmology or Universe Story is attractive to one age cohort more than another.

This book grew out of that study. It treats the topics under three rubrics: "Chapter of Faults," which offers a summary of the study in which the participants speak candidly about the struggles they faced in trying to be faithful to their religious values and aspirations during radically changing times; "Chapter of Affairs," where features of the reality of contemporary cosmology are discussed; and "Chapter of Elections," which looks to the future, envisioning how these new insights might take root in the reader's consciousness and thus reshape her life.

One cannot easily classify this book as a work on ecospirituality. It has a very different goal than a reflection of relevant religious topics, as meaningful as such reflection might be. It seeks to discover which participants consider themselves enriched by embracing a spirituality emerging from the theological reflection on cosmology, and which do not, and why this might be the case. It includes the findings of a social scientific study, but it is not content with simply offering the findings of the study. Brink is in favor of the spirituality emerging from the New Cosmology and uses the findings of the study to encourage those of like mind to continue in their search for such spirituality, and those of a different mind to open themselves to the possibilities that it offers.

Brink deals with very heavy matters here—the depths of personal spirituality, cosmology, the formation of mind and heart—but it is not a heavy read. Without wearying the reader with repetitive scientific calculations or attenuating the complexity of cosmological explanations, she unfolds her discourse with remarkable ease, employing a conversational style. The quantity and quality of her footnotes indicate the scope of her own reading in the areas she treats. Her genuine admiration for women religious, her profound respect for the spiritualties they espouse, and her enduring commitment to offering ways of deepening that spirituality for the future are transparent throughout the book.

For several years Laurie Brink has been a colleague of mine here at Catholic Theological Union. I stand in awe of the work she has done in this book, bringing the New Cosmology to bear on the fashioning of a contemporary spirituality. She has laid down a challenge. It is for the reader to pick it up.

Dianne Bergant, CSA

# Acknowledgments

From the original and abiding question, to the preparation of a grant to fund the research, to the construction of a survey, to the compilation of data, to the arduous work of research, writing, and rewriting, to the endless bumps in the road to publishing—this book before you is directly and indirectly the work of an entire community.

First and foremost, I am indebted to the Dominican Sisters of Sinsinawa, who remain my inspiration, my primary support, and my lodestar. While I could name each sister for her contribution to the charism and mission, I want particularly to acknowledge my local community—Patricia Mulcahey, OP, and Betsy Pawlicki, OP—who supported my efforts and offered constructive critique throughout the two-and-a-half-year research project.

In addition to the support of my own congregation members, other women religious have provided significant assistance, direction, and wisdom, including Dianne Bergant, CSA, Ellen Dauwer, SC, Ilia Delio, OSF, Susan Francois, CSJP, Elizabeth Johnson, CSJ, Jean McSweeney, OP, and Katarina Schuth, OSF. Additionally, I am grateful to the preliminary survey-takers: Regina Siegfried, ASC, Maria Cimperman, RSCJ, Didi Madden, OP, Katarina Schuth, OSF, and Mary Ann Zollman, BVM.

My academic community, Catholic Theological Union (CTU), remains an oasis for the conversation, construction, and critique of emerging theology and praxis. I would have written a very different book if it were not for the challenge of Carmen Nanko-Fernández, Professor of Hispanic Theology and Ministry, who encouraged me to "exegete" the varied comments and concerns of women religious found in the survey results. In this monograph, I draw from the research and publications of many of my colleagues, including Nanko-Fernández, Maria Cimperman, RSCJ, Joanne (Jaruko) Doi,

MM, Daniel Horan, OFM, Dawn Nothwehr, OSF, Barbara Reid, OP, Robin Ryan, CP, Robert Schreiter, CPPS, and former faculty—Dianne Bergant, CSA, Barbara Bowe, RSCJ, Mary Frohlich, RSCJ, Anthony Gittins, CSSp, and Zachary Hayes, OFM. I am indebted to the Paul Bechtold Library at CTU, especially the Director of the Library, Kristine Veldheer, and Electronic Resources and Instruction Librarian, Deborah Winarski, who truly went the extra mile in securing the resources I required. Particular thanks go to the former president of CTU, Mark Francis, CSV, who granted me an academic sabbatical in 2019–2020 during which the bulk of the research occurred. The former Interim Dean Gina Wolfe, Vice President for Advancement Colleen Kennedy, and Director of Development Rachel Kuhn assisted in the preparation of the project budget and the writing and administration of the grant.

The Louisville Institute awarded me a Sabbatical Grant for Researchers, which allowed for a more robust investigation of the topic. Hats off to Edwin Aponte, Jessica Bowman, Pam Collins, Keri Liechty and Don Richter for their financial and professional support. The participants of the Winter Seminar provided helpful feedback on how to process and organize the data.

As the proverb goes, many hands make work light. And it is true with this project. William Becerra, DMin, constructed the survey and organized the data. The project's research assistant, Rhonda Miska, was tireless in her efforts to disseminate the survey, even taking the extra steps to translate the survey into Spanish. She prepared the glossary of terms that appears at the end of the book, with the hope of stimulating a more fulsome conversation on the topic. Associate Professor of Systematic Theology Robin Ryan, CP, read and commented on the theological sections in the "Chapter of Affairs," while Dr. Allan Wirth, of Massachusetts Institute of Technology Lincoln Laboratory, reviewed the presentation of the science. Dianne Bergant, CSA, Sarah Kohles, OSF, and I represent the three age cohorts discussed in the book. Sisters Dianne and Sarah offer their insights in the foreword and afterword as bookends to my own reflections. The generous Sullivan Grant, administered by Catholic Theological Union, enabled me to make this work more accessible by including an index. Kris Veldheer and Jen Carlson worked tirelessly to copyedit and index this volume. However, any errors, awkward statements, or misplaced modifiers are all on me.

Finally, I was fortunate to find a publisher who recognized this book's potential and valued the contribution it could make to religious life. I am immensely grateful to Hans Christoffersen, Editorial Director, and Peter Dwyer, Director of Liturgical Press, who advocated for its publication.

Indeed, in the case of this book, the proverb rings true: "Two are better than one, because they have a good reward for their toil" (Eccl 4:9). How much more so when a whole community joins in the effort!

Laurie Brink, OP
February 23, 2021

# Preface

Bear with me. This isn't so much a work of theology as it is a labor of love. Because I am writing about religious life and I am a finally-professed sister, I have a particular take on the topic. I'm personally invested. That means that in no way am I objective. At the beginning, it seems fitting to acknowledge that personal location matters. We are all from some place and that place (or places) has a claim on us. Anthony Gittins describes this as "social geography."

> People do not simply inhabit the world—they live in a particular world, where certain features like this mountain, this lake, this ocean, or this forest have a particular importance in their lives.[1]

For example, the Maori of Aotearoa (New Zealand) include in their personal introduction the name of their mountain, river/lake/sea, founding ancestor, tribe, marae (meeting place), home location, parents, and finally their name. Closer to home, ask a Chicagoan where they live and they will most often name their parish, even if they are not Catholic!

The particular feature that has marked my identity and sense of self is that of being a cradle Catholic, emphasis on the cradle. I was adopted as an infant, and for the first fifty years of my life the only information I had about my biological mother was that she was Catholic. My adoptive father had been raised Catholic, my adoptive mother a convert, and my religious education marked by intermittent attendance at CCD (Confraternity of Christian Doctrine) classes, much of which I hated. And yet, I clung to being "catholic"

---

1. Anthony J. Gittins, *Living Mission Interculturally: Faith, Culture, and the Renewal of Praxis* (Collegeville, MN: Liturgical Press, 2015), 67.

though I knew little about what that meant until adulthood. My father's career in the US Navy meant that we moved frequently. I was baptized in Norfolk, Virginia, received First Communion in San Francisco, and was confirmed in Virginia Beach. My earliest church memories are kneeling behind a pew I could not see over and listening to words I did not understand from a priest whose name I never knew on a naval base I don't remember. Having not attended Catholic school, my early education in the faith consisted of making God's eyes with orange yarn, singing Bible camp songs, and constructing felt banners. I was the generation between the *Baltimore Catechism* and the *Catechism of the Catholic Church*.

What forged my Catholic identity was being the "other." During much of my childhood, my father was stationed in the Southern United States where Catholics made up less than 1 percent of the population. In Henderson, North Carolina, in the mid-1970s, my brother and I were altar servers in the tiny Catholic church. The priest wasn't "before his time" in allowing girl altar servers; we were literally the only children in the parish. In high school, I was invited to join my Protestant friends on their youth group's outing to an amusement park—on Good Friday. I may not have been well-catechized, but I sensed that riding a roller-coaster was not quite the appropriate Triduum activity. And when I was fourteen, my parents, new to Knoxville, Tennessee, hosted the church choir's Christmas party. During the party, I discovered a six-foot wooden cross ablaze on our front lawn. These experiences forged in me a deep sense of affection for my faith, and I daresay an apologetic tendency. Truly, as a Catholic in the 1970s Southern United States, you had to defend both your faith and yourself.

Yet my religious vocation did not emerge from an experience of the institutional church, but from an encounter with tragedy. The 1980 martyrdoms of Maryknoll Sisters Ita Ford and Maura Clarke, Ursuline Sister Dorothy Kazel, and lay missionary Jean Donovan struck a profound chord in me. In college, I worked as a "copy girl" for a morning newspaper. It was December 4, 1980. I still remember walking to the Associated Press wire photo machine and watching as the images of the burial site and their lifeless bodies slowly emerged. I was nineteen years old, and at that point more interested in personal success than spirituality pursuits. If I had known more Scripture then, I would have quoted John's Gospel: "unless a grain of wheat falls into the earth and dies, it remains just a single grain; but if it dies, it bears much fruit" (John 12:24). Very truly, their deaths produced the fruit of my vocation. I became radicalized by their witness. I began exploring vocation and service. I graduated early from college, so that I could spend two years as a lay volunteer in Jamaica. Every step of my discernment finds its roots in the lives and martyrdom of these four women.

A winding road finally brought me to the Dominican Sisters of Sinsinawa. Recognizing that you might have a call to religious life[2] is particularly difficult when you've never met any sisters. It's compounded when you know nothing of charism or call or discernment. And it seems almost hopeless when others—even sisters—argue that the life is dying, a sentiment seemingly based on more than anecdotal evidence. The 1992 report on religious life by David Nygren and Miriam Ukeritis was published the same year I entered my religious congregation.[3] By the time I made perpetual profession in 1998, ten of my age peers had left the community. For the next decade, I would be the youngest member of the congregation. The Nygren and Ukeritis report felt like prophecy. I turned from hope in a future of vowed life to a personal commitment to the Dominican charism of study. If I was going to be the last to turn out the lights, I wasn't going to go meekly.

And somewhere along the way to my doctorate in Scripture, something happened. Through the combined efforts of an excellent vocation director and the Holy Spirit, young women began discerning, entering, and staying. I felt a little bit like the Grinch when his

---

2. Religious life is composed of those who "express their dedication [of a way of life in the Church] through the profession of the public vows of poverty, chastity, and obedience within a canonically established religious institute." See Mary Johnson, SNDdeN, Patricia Wittberg, SC, and Mary L. Gautier, *New Generations of Catholic Sisters: The Challenge of Diversity* (Oxford: Oxford University Press, 2014), 32.

3. David Nygren and Miriam Ukeritis, "Future of Religious Orders in the United States," *Origins* 22, no. 15 (September 24, 1992): 257–92. For the full report, see David Nygren and Miriam Ukeritis, *The Future of Religious Orders in the United States: Transformation and Commitment* (Westport, CT: Praeger, 1993).

too-small heart "grows three sizes that day." Without any help on my part, without many sponsored institutions, hardly any convent buildings, and a median age of seventy-five, the Dominicans of Sinsinawa had young religious vocations. Accomplished. Talented. Thoughtful. Prayerful. Ministry-centered and community-minded. And confident.

All of this is to say that I write as an insider who has one particular perspective, a perspective that is broadened and deepened by research, critical reading, and innumerable conversations. But mine is only one take on the larger picture of religious life in the twenty-first century. I'm a member of what I call the straddle generation. I was a bit too late to be a Baby Boomer, and I barely make the statistical cut off for Generation X. This sense of betweenness has followed me throughout my life, so that now I find myself again between generations. There is the majority generation of religious: women and men who entered right before or just after the Council, sometimes referred to as Vatican II religious. And then there is the new minority generation whose faith-identity took shape under Pope John Paul II's outward reach and liturgical reform. This is also the church-in-chaos generation who came to young adulthood during the early days of the clergy abuse crisis. Chapter 3, "Orienting Ecclesiologies," will explore these categories more fully.

As I begin this monograph, I am celebrating my silver jubilee. Ironically, many of the questions about the future of consecrated religious life that I had as a novice have not substantially changed in twenty-five years. What does it mean to be a woman who vows poverty, chastity, and obedience in a capitalist country and a global world? How does one who upholds the value of all persons—female and male—participate in an institutional church where access to sacramental leadership is limited to men? After years of trying to become an anti-racist congregation, why do we still struggle so with accepting diversity among us?

But to these, I add a new question: as a middleton between the majority generation and the one yet emerging, what is mine to do? How do I revere the accomplishments of the past, appreciate the wisdom of elders, and acknowledge that this generation is passing? While at the same time, how do I respond to the queries of the next generation? How do I engage their theological questions and liturgical preferences without judgement and ridicule? And perhaps most importantly, how do I bridge the distance between the two?

As Carmen Nanko-Fernández recognizes, "The jarring admission that theologies emerge from within complex matrices of lived experiences refocuses attention on communities of interpretation and calls for reflection from embedded theologians."[4] I write as one such "embedded theologian." This book is a small attempt to create a crossing-over point, a place of encounter and conversation that takes the generations within religious life seriously. While there are many topics around which this conversation could begin, I have chosen one: What are implications of the New Cosmology, the theological reflection on the science of the universe, for religious life? And throughout this book, I'll explain why this question of theology and science first fueled my concern, then captured my imagination, and finally created a new lens through which I view the future of religious life.

# Introduction

## Why This Topic Now?

### A Turbulent Time

In the decades since Vatican II opened the windows of the church, the breezes have blown through every aspect of our faith and life. One of the more noticeable changes that has left some of the faithful still pining for the old days is the change in dress for women religious. Convents, once the home for sisters who taught in the school, have become parish offices. Institutions run by sisters are now under the capable direction of lay leadership. Without distinctive dress or established homes and institutions, sisters are no longer "seen" in public and ecclesial circles. This, coupled with the decline in membership—through aging and lessening of vocations—has created an atmosphere in which one person asked, "Do they even have sisters anymore?" Just when the cloak of public invisibility had almost settled over the nation's then fifty thousand women religious, three very different, very significant events reminded everyone that women religious remain a force to be recognized and reckoned with: the Women of Spirit exhibition, the Vatican-initiated visitation of the US women's congregations featured in the exhibit, and the doctrinal assessment of Leadership Conference of Women Religious (LCWR), the sponsors of the exhibit.

In 2009, the "Women of Spirit: Catholic Sisters in America" exhibition, initiated by the LCWR, shone a spotlight on the innumerable works of charity, the hundreds of institutions established, the thousands of people educated—all at the hands of women religious in the United States.

Meanwhile, while the exhibit was under development, the Congregation for Consecrated Life and Societies of Apostolic Life (CICLSAL)—the Vatican office charged with overseeing the congregations of men and women religious—initiated an apostolic visitation of sisters in the United States in order to "look at the quality of life of apostolic Congregations of women religious." Under its then prefect Cardinal Franc Rodé, CICLSAL announced the visitation on December 22, 2008. In a later radio address, the cardinal noted concerns for the diminishing number of vocations as well as "some irregularities or omissions in American religious life. Most of all, you could say, it involves a certain secular mentality that has spread in these religious families and perhaps, also a certain 'feminist' spirit."[1]

Just two months prior to the opening of the "Women of Spirit" exhibit, its sponsors, LCWR received a letter from Cardinal William Levada, then prefect of the Vatican's Congregation for the Doctrine of the Faith (CDF), announcing that CDF would conduct a doctrinal assessment of the activities and initiatives of LCWR with the purpose of reviewing "the work of the LCWR in supporting its membership as communities of faith and witness to Christ in today's Church, and to offer any useful assistance." The letter named the following as concerns: addresses at LCWR assemblies, policies of Corporate Dissent (in particular as it is related to women's ordination and ministry to the homosexual community), and finally radical feminist themes in some LCWR programs and presentations.[2]

Under the direction of Mother Clare Millea, ASCJ, the visitation process began with an appeal to superiors general for financial support, followed by a request for documentation from US major superiors of four hundred apostolic women's congregations, and finally concluded with on-site visitations. In 2012, CICLSAL released its final report.

---

1. Cindy Wooden, "Cardinal Rodé Defends Apostolic Visitation of U.S. Nuns," Catholic News Service (November 3, 2009), https://www.ncronline.org/news/vatican/cardinal-rod-defends-apostolic-visitation-us-nuns.

2. See the "Doctrinal Assessment of the Leadership Conference of Women Religious," http://www.vatican.va/roman_curia//congregations/cfaith/documents/rc_con_cfaith_doc_20120418_assessment-lcwr_en.html.

The tone of the report was laudatory—it used some form of the word "gratitude" eight times over its 12 pages, and the few criticisms it contained were carefully couched—and there was effusive praise from the head of CICLSAL, Cardinal João Bráz de Aviz.[3]

The distrustful tenor of the original announcement had abated, replaced now by one of respect. Reflecting on the experience, management consultant, Margaret J. Wheatley, noted:

> The Vatican's report has entrusted the congregations to discern their way forward rather than impose a more traditional and hierarchical approach. This feels like real progress and wisdom to me; it signifies a new quality of trust and possibility to what had been a very troubling and troubled relationship. And the sisters are ready to assume this responsibility because they have emerged from this crisis with renewed clarity about who they are and what their true values and mission are. They have led so well through these years that the conditions are present for them to work with the report wisely and well.[4]

The doctrinal assessment concluded some three years later. LCWR officers issued a statement about the process and its conclusion.[5]

> Our hope is that the positive outcome of the assessment and mandate will lead to the creation of additional spaces within the Catholic Church where the church leadership and membership can speak together regularly about the critical matters before all of us. The collective exploration of the meaning and application of key theological, spiritual, social, moral, and ethical concepts must be an ongoing

---

3. Dan Stockman, "Apostolic Visitation Brought Dialogue with Rome, New Unity of Women Religious with Laity," *Global Sisters Report* (February 14, 2017), https://www.globalsistersreport.org/news/trends/apostolic-visitation-brought-dialogue-rome-new-unity-women-religious-laity-44941.

4. Margaret J. Wheatley, "Leadership Lessons from Besieged Nuns," *Global Sisters Report* (January 22, 2014), https://www.globalsistersreport.org/column/trends/leadership-lessons-besieged-nuns-17311.

5. For a more thorough account of the experience, see Annmarie Sanders, ed., *However Long the Night: Making Meaning in a Time of Crisis; A Spiritual Journey of the Leadership Conference of Women Religious (LCWR)* (Silver Spring, MD: Leadership Conference of Women Religious, 2018).

effort for all of us in the world today. Admittedly, entering into a commitment to regular and consistent dialogue about core matters that have the potential to divide us can be arduous, demanding work, but work that is ultimately transformative. However, challenging these efforts are, in a world marked by polarities and intolerance of difference, perhaps no work is more important.[6]

The Women of Spirit exhibition celebrated the outward accomplishments of a unique subset of American women; the visitation questioned the vitality—and some would say the fidelity—of the inner life of those same communities, and the doctrinal assessment questioned the doctrinal faithfulness of its leadership. No reflection on the future of religious life can proceed without acknowledging the profound costs the visitation and the doctrinal assessment leveled on religious congregations. I remember sitting with our vocation director just after the interviewers had come and gone. Through tears, she described the reports that were required, the hours it took to prepare them, and the fear that no matter how honest and faithful we were, we would be found wanting by those in the Vatican who had never even met us. Other sisters also acknowledged the personal pain of the process but found that the experience led to a sense of renewed commitment.

> We recall how we combed Vatican documents on consecrated life seeking common language to answer questions in the canonical Visitation document, *Instrumentum Laboris*, about identity, governance, formation, spirituality life, community life, and mission. We tap into our sense of validation as historical paper letters and encyclicals mirrored back to us evidence of our fidelity. And, we linger even now with the joy of being returned by these documents to the inspirational beauty of our congregational constitutions.[7]

6. Statement of the LCWR Officers on the CDF Doctrinal Assessment and Conclusion of the Mandate, https://lcwr.org/media/statement-lcwr-officers-cdf-doctrinal-assessment-and-conclusion-mandate.

7. Margaret Cain McCarthy and Mary Ann Zollmann, eds., *Power of Sisterhood: Women Religious Tell the Story of the Apostolic Visitation* (Lanham, MD: University Press of America, 2014), 182.

Having spoken and written on religious life prior to the visitation and assessment,[8] I had named concerns about how we attract and incorporate new members, to what degree our theological diversity is sustainable, and how we can relate to church hierarchy. The Vatican investigations into the lives of US women religious interrupted our asking and seeking answers to our own questions. Now that the investigations have subsided, we can return to pondering, revivifying, and responding to the call of the Spirit as the women of faith we have always been.

## In Search of Jesus

Long before the intervention of the Vatican, the 1992 Nygren and Ukeritis report had acknowledged the "restraining forces" limiting the growth of religious life. It named individualism, work absorption, materialism, and parochial assimilation, but it also noted avenues of potential growth. The forces that could open a way to a future included reclaiming the vocation to religious life, excellence in leadership, recognition of the charism of religious life, role clarity, and greater corporate identity. "Those (religious orders) that are most responsive to pressing human need and motivated by the love of Christ will be vitalized as long as their efforts are consistent with their tradition."[9]

More recently, Seán Sammon proposed that religious congregations that choose to open themselves to a future "must first be courageous in responding to the real challenges facing our world and church today; second, have a membership willing to allow itself the

---

8. "Living with the Poor as Formative for Christian Mission," and "Risking Commitment in an Age of Relativism," *Vocations and Prayer Magazine*, 1997–98; "Another Woman Religious Breaks Camp," *National Catholic Reporter* (February 18, 2000); "Can We Allow a New Generation to Shape Religious Life?," *Horizons* 32 (2007): 16–31; "Pursing a Dream, Finding a Vocation," *Vision* (2007): 98–103; "A Marginal Life: Pursing Holiness in the 21st Century," *Horizons* 33 (2008): 4–9; "Walking in the Footsteps of Christ: Religious Orders as Followers, Disciples, and Apostles," *New Theology Review* 22 (2009): 56–65; "U.S. Sisters: Accolades and Admonitions," *New Theology Review* (2011): 51–60.

9. David Nygren and Miriam Ukeritis, *The Future of Religious Orders in the United States: Transformation and Commitment* (Westport, CT: Praeger, 1993), 235.

experience of personal and congregational conversion; and third, rediscover the spirit of their founding charism." Sammon calls on the Holy Spirit to aid us in this difficult work, but cautions:

> A spirituality [of renewal] does not come cheaply. It demands a habit of prayer that helps us come to know who Jesus is and how he acts and decides. So, too, contemplation of Jesus in the Gospels is the essential discipline that makes this type of decision-making possible. For contemplation of this nature schools our hearts and guides us to decisions that bring us closer to God.[10]

Loan Le makes a similar statement: "Religious Life is a charism of the Holy Spirit, at the heart of which lies the faith relationship between a person and Christ Jesus lived in the context of a particular state of life in the Church."[11]

It is precisely this Jesus-focus that sparks my current research. Twenty-eight years after the Nygren and Ukeritis report, a new potential "restraining force" has appeared. This new force requires attention because it has the potential to upset the traditional paradigm of the role of Jesus as Christ and Redeemer. Though a biblical cosmology remains an active metaphor for describing the originating work of God, theologians recognize that Judeo-Christian cosmology must now integrate scientific findings into the work of theology. "Christian theology no longer has an effective cosmology that enables believers to relate to the world in its physical character in a way that is consistent with their religious symbols," writes Ilia Delio.[12] The "New Cosmology" integrates scientific facts, including discoveries about the expanding universe and evolution, and proposes that creation is ongoing and—building on the work of Teilhard de Chardin—emerging into greater complexity. This developing cosmology has been called the "universe story," and has

---

10. Seán D. Sammon, FMS, "What Is the Future of Religious Life in the Vocation Crisis?," *America* 216 (September 14, 2015), https://www.americamagazine.org/issue /religious-life-reimagined.

11. Loan Le, *Religious Life: A Reflective Examination of Its Charism and Mission for Today* (Newcastle upon Tyne, UK: Cambridge Scholars Publishing, 2016), 197.

12. Ilia Delio, *Christ in Evolution* (Maryknoll, NY: Orbis Books, 2008), 22.

profound implications not only for Catholic religious life but for all Christian organizations. J. Matthew Ashley well notes the potential difficulties for Christian believers.

> Both evolutionary biology and Scripture present narratives that bear on human origins and subsequent history, narratives that alternatively generate, sustain, or destabilize the ways we understand ourselves in relationship to one another, to the natural world, and to God.[13]

The future-oriented cosmology embraces creation as an ongoing process for which concepts like "original sin" and "redemption" must be re-envisioned or jettisoned altogether. How does one "retrofit" religious tradition and Scripture into this scenario? Is there room for the historical Jesus in the New Cosmology? How does the Cosmic Christ relate to Jesus Christ? While a ready concern for all Christians, these questions have unique implications for us women religious whose constitutions are centered on the person and mission of Jesus Christ. How are we to understand our vows of poverty, chastity, and obedience in light of a cosmology in which the need for redemption and the role of Jesus are either absent or significantly redefined?

These questions do not emerge from a stance of hostility toward science or from a defense of traditional Christology. Rather, they are an outgrowth of our commitment to education and study. After Vatican II (1962–65), women religious were challenged to return to their congregation's foundational charism and renew that gift for the modern world. This led to serious study of the signs of the times and updating in theology. As a result, women religious are often on the forefront of new ideas about how to live the faith in an ever-changing world. In the last two decades, many women religious have engaged in the growing conversation between theology and science. For some Catholic sisters, discoveries in science, evolutionary theory, and cosmology have provided new lenses through which

13. J. Matthew Ashley, "Reading the Universe Story Theologically: The Contribution of a Biblical Narrative Imagination," *Theological Studies* 71 (2010): 876.

to view and understand their religious vocation in a twenty-first century context. Many of the proponents and authors writing on evolution and the New Cosmology are women and men religious (e.g., Bergant, Delio, Johnson, O'Murchu, Wessels). Orbis Publisher Robert Ellsberg suggests that women religious are advancing this new horizon because it speaks to themes that resonate with their values, such as:

> an appreciation for mystery, evolution, and change; a much larger idea of God than the traditional androcentric model; a perspective that is more ecologically sound; a recovery of the cosmic Christology of the early church; a perspective on salvation that extends to all of creation, not so human-centered; a departure from a more judging, juridical model of salvation.[14]

In the twentieth century, the conversation between science and theology gained notable support in Catholic circles.

> If the cosmologies of the ancient Near Eastern world could be purified and assimilated into the first chapters of Genesis, might not contemporary cosmology have something to offer to our reflections upon creation? Does an evolutionary perspective bring any light to bear upon theological anthropology, the meaning of the human person as the *imago Dei*, the problem of Christology—and even upon the development of doctrine itself? What, if any, are the eschatological implications of contemporary cosmology, especially in light of the vast future of our universe? Can theological method fruitfully appropriate insights from scientific methodology and the philosophy of science?
>
> Questions of this kind can be suggested in abundance. Pursuing them further would require the sort of intense dialogue with contemporary science that has, on the whole, been lacking among those engaged in theological research and teaching. It would entail that some theologians, at least, should be sufficiently well-versed in the sciences to make authentic and creative use of the resources that the best-established theories may offer them. Such an expertise would prevent them from making uncritical and overhasty use for

14. Robert Ellsberg, email to author, October 23, 2018.

apologetic purposes of such recent theories as that of the "Big Bang" in cosmology. Yet it would equally keep them from discounting altogether the potential relevance of such theories to the deepening of understanding in traditional areas of theological inquiry.[15]

It would seem that Pope John Paul II in his Letter to Reverend George V. Coyne, SJ, director of the Vatican Observatory, not only tread along this path before me but encouraged me and others to follow.

## Ask and You Shall Receive: Assumptions and Method

According to the Code of Canon Law, Canon 717:

> §3 Those entrusted with the governance of the institute are to ensure that its unity of spirit is maintained, and that the active participation of the members is developed.

Far from leaving the full responsibility for the quality of life in the hands of elected leadership, the canon invites the members to exercise their rights to "active participation." My own congregation's constitution frames this "active participation" within our Dominican tradition of subsidiarity.[16] In order for subsidiarity and mutuality to frame this investigation, the first step was to ask those for whom these questions mattered the most: US women religious. Anecdotally I had gathered a fair bit of evidence that suggested that

---

15. His Holiness John Paul II, letter to Reverend George V. Coyne, SJ, director of the Vatican Observatory, June 1, 1988, https://w2.vatican.va/content/john-paul-ii/en/letters/1988/documents/hf_jp-ii_let_19880601_padre-coyne.html.

16. "The principle of subsidiarity prevails within all areas of government. To be effective, subsidiarity calls for a sense of mutuality. This mutuality in turn shows itself in the firm coordination of the various levels of decision-making (¶ 47)" (Dominican Sisters of Sinsinawa, *Rule, Constitution, Statues, and Enactments* [Sinsinawa, WI: Sinsinawa Dominicans, 2012], 53). For an interesting review of the principle and practice of subsidiarity, see Patrick McKinley Brennan, "Subsidiarity in the Tradition of Catholic Social Doctrine," in *Global Perspectives on Subsidiarity*, ed. Michelle Evans and Augusto Zimmermann, 37 vols., Ius Gentium: Comparative Perspectives on Law and Justice (Dordrecht: Springer, 2014), 29–48.

the New Cosmology was of interest to a particular group among US women religious, and that a different group felt they were being "force-fed" this new theology. Some sisters loved the New Cosmology; some sisters loathed the New Cosmology. I needed to test my suppositions.

With a grant from the Louisville Institute, I began an eighteen-month research project to test the following assumptions:

1. Some women religious find the New Cosmology an attractive and engaging theology and spirituality.

2. The New Cosmology challenges the traditional paradigm of how Jesus functions, which has implications for women religious and all Christians.

3. Women religious adherents of the New Cosmology may question Scripture as a continued source of revelation, since the books of Bible were composed under a different cosmology.

4. A hermeneutical strategy developed from the principles of the New Cosmology can create a corrective lens for reading to the Bible, despite its cosmology of origin.

Spoiler alert: The response to assumption 4 is the content for another time and hopefully another book. While my preliminary concern focused on the Bible and its relevance in light of the New Cosmology, that interest has taken a backseat in light of the findings of my research, the process and outcome of which I will summarize.

### Survey and Results

My first step was to assess assumption 1— that some women religious find the New Cosmology an attractive and engaging theology and spirituality. With the aid of a research assistant, Rhonda Miska, and a survey consultant, William Becerra, I compiled a series of twenty-six questions to address the topic of the New Cosmology and theology. The survey was available in English and Spanish and followed the Institutional Review Board guidelines established at Catholic Theological Union. Katarina Schuth, OSF, Professor Emerita/Endowed Chair for Social Scientific Study of Religion, Dianne Bergant, CSA, Carroll Stuhlmueller, CP, Distinguished Professor Emerita of Old Testament Studies, and Elizabeth Johnson, CSJ, Distinguished Professor Emerita of Theology at Fordham University, reviewed the drafts and made substantive suggestions for revisions. Several sisters took a "test drive" of the survey and assisted in rounding off its rough edges.[17]

Often when surveys are conducted among women religious, they are distributed to members of elected leadership only or broadly to all members. Since the vast majority of religious women in the United States are seventy years or older, I wanted to create a way to amplify the voices of sisters of color and younger members. To balance the scales so to speak, the survey was sent to select groups of sisters so as to get a general feel of their interest in the topic. These included the Asociación de Hermanas Latinas Misioneras en América (AHLMA), the Conference of Major Superiors of Women Religious (CMSWR), Giving Voice, the Leadership Conference of Women Religious (LCWR), the National Black Sisters Conference (NBSC), and the Religious Formation Conference (RFC). These distinct groups represent Black Sisters, Latina Sisters, Leadership from both conferences of Superiors, Sisters in or training for formation ministry, and younger members (under fifty years of age). In order to respect the sisters' privacy, we asked the director of each organization to disseminate the survey.

Since I was not directly responsible for the survey's distribution, I could not estimate the total number to whom it was sent. We did receive 215 completed responses from members of the above listed organizations. Because of the low response rate from AHLMA and the Spanish-language survey, I have combined the results of these cohorts together. For each question, a participant could choose not to respond. The majority of responses came from LCWR (36.6 percent), followed by Giving Voice (24 percent) and RFC (18 percent). Fewer members of CMSWR (6 percent), NBSC (3 percent), and AHLMA (2 percent) responded.

---

17. We remain grateful to the preliminary survey-takers: Regina Siegfried, ASC, Maria Cimperman, RSCJ, Didi Madden, OP, Katarina Schuth, OSF, and Mary Ann Zollman, BVM.

In addition to general questions of age, ethnicity/race, education, ministry, and date of profession, the survey asked participants about their level of familiarity with the New Cosmology (or the Universe Story), its impact on their faith as a religious sister, the relationship of the New Cosmology to eco-feminism and social justice efforts, their sources of theological knowledge, their definitions of various terms related to the New Cosmology, their descriptions of God, the Holy Spirit, and Jesus, and finally how the New Cosmology impacted their understanding of Jesus Christ. Since the level of familiarity and potential impact of the New Cosmology directed or redirected my research efforts, we will begin with a summary of these results.[18]

### Familiarity with the New Cosmology

More than 90 percent of those surveyed who answered the question have knowledge (somewhat, familiar, well-read) about the New Cosmology, though most had varying understandings of the elements. Only 7.2 percent had no familiarity with the concepts. Of those who answered, 33.6 percent were somewhat familiar, and 38.8 percent were familiar with the topic. More than 20 percent were well-read in the concepts.

Familiarity with the concepts of the New Cosmology differed among those in various groups. The Religious Formation Conference had the highest percentage of members who were familiar with the New Cosmology (53 percent), followed by members of LCWR (47 percent) and Giving Voice (44.2 percent). CMSWR participants had the highest level of unfamiliarity (45.5 percent).

### Impact on Faith as a Religious Sister

Almost 70 percent of all survey participants who answered the question responded that the New Cosmology and its related concepts enhanced their faith as a vowed religious sister. Two areas in which the New Cosmology and related concepts have enhanced

---

18. For a fuller presentation of the data, see Laurie Brink, "The Differences Among Us: The Results of a Survey on the New Cosmology and Women Religious," *Review for Religious* 1.2 (2021): 257–72.

their Catholic faith are their understanding of Scripture (71.7 percent) and that of Religious Life (74.3 percent). For 22.9 percent of the participants, the New Cosmology does not impact their faith as vowed religious. Only 7.2 percent responded that "the New Cosmology and related concepts are in conflict with my faith as a vowed religious sister." Of those respondents, an equal number (40.5 percent) held that the New Cosmology was in conflict with their understanding of tradition and their understanding of the church. Less than 30 percent said the New Cosmology was in conflict with their understanding of Scripture, and less than 14 percent said it conflicted with their understanding of religious life.

Sisters over the age of 65 were more interested and well-read on the topic, and a higher percentage of this age group finds that the New Cosmology enhances their faith as a vowed religious sister. The youngest cohort of sisters were more likely to respond that the New Cosmology and its related concepts were in conflict with their faith. Chapter 1, "Whence Comes Wisdom? (Job 28:20): Differences among Age Cohorts" explores the responses according to the three age cohorts: youngest (25–44 years of age), middle (45–64 years of age), and oldest (65 plus).

As the survey results indicate, the New Cosmology does not pose a difficulty for the reading of Scripture or the experience of religious life for the majority of sisters surveyed. For those for whom the New Cosmology is problematic for their faith, the areas in conflict are their understanding of tradition and their understanding of church.

### Direction Forward

Pondering the survey results leads to three conclusions. First, the problem doesn't seem to be the concept per se but the uneven knowledge of the actual findings of science and their import for theological thinking. Younger survey participants in general were less familiar with the concepts and tended to see the New Cosmology as being in conflict with their faith. Second, taking science seriously has profound implications for ethics and ministry. The response of one cohort member that "this isn't of interest to our sisters. We are busy in ministry," demonstrates the potential disconnect between emerging theology and praxis. Third, and perhaps most concerning for the future of religious life, there appears to be a theological generation gap between the Vatican II religious and the emerging generation. Some newer members report that they feel obliged to "believe" the New Cosmology, and that failure to do so has implications on their membership.

In light of these findings, I propose that the New Cosmology may provide a novel theological lens with which to view the future of religious life, but we must first all agree on what that theology is and then explore the implications for the whole of our vowed religious life: community, prayer, study, and ministry. That begins with acknowledging that we do not all start on the same page, and that perhaps our failure to recognize that has created some of the confusion and indifference we experience.

My first attempt to create common ground is to format this book within the context of our religious lives. This isn't meant to retrieve lost practice so much as it is to use our unique history as a touchstone for our considerations of our future. Three sections are thus divided as "Chapter of Faults," "Chapter of Affairs," and "Chapter of Elections."

The section "Chapter of Faults" discusses our differences, not as a penance, but as an attempt to reconcile misunderstandings. The first chapter, "Whence Comes Wisdom? (Job 28:20): Differences among Age Cohorts," reviews the survey results according to specific age groups. Of the 215 sisters who completed the survey, 54 were 25–44 years of age, 55 were 45–64 years of age, and 68 were 65 years of age and older. These three age groups each make up roughly a third of the total, allowing for the amplification of what are normally minority voices among the younger cohorts.

In order to understand why the age cohorts responded as they did, chapter 2, "There Is a Season and a Time (Eccl 3:1): Exploring American Generations" reviews the four living generations present in women religious congregations in the United States. The "Silent Generation or Lucky Few" are generally those sisters who came of age following the Depression and during World War II. These sisters make up the majority of women religious in the United States today. "The Baby Boomers" include those born after World War II and shortly before the tumultuous period of the 1960s. Approximately

32 percent of women religious hail from the Baby Boomer generation. What could be called the "Forgotten Generation," Generation
X, are a smaller cohort born between 1960s and 1980s. They came
of age just as a wave of conservatism ushered in Ronald Reagan and
the Moral Majority. Only 5.4 percent of US Catholic sisters are from
Generation X. Finally, the fourth generation explored were born in
the decades of the 1980s–1990s. In many respects, the Millennials
mirror the Greatest Generation in their civic-mindedness and rival
the Baby Boomers for their size. Millennials make up only 4 percent
of US women religious.

Once we set the stage of the sociological distinctiveness of each
generation, we return to the survey's three age cohorts in chapter 3,
"Orienting Ecclesiologies: The Formative Experience of Church for
Cohort Identity." These age cohorts represent three distinct periods
in recent church history: Vatican II, post-Vatican II, and the church
experiencing the clergy abuse crisis. Our age cohort's formative
experience of the church helped shape their religious identity and
their understanding of their vocation. I argue that each group's
ecclesiology also impacts how they perceive and respond to the
New Cosmology.

In section 2, "Chapter of Affairs," we find the content of the New
Cosmology or Universe Story and ponder its implications for our
lives as women religious. In many respects, the trio of cosmology,
quantum mechanics, and evolution form a new trinity that challenges our way of thinking about God's actions in creation and
our response as evolving creatures. This section will explore the
discoveries and theories of science with regard to the origins of the
cosmos, quantum mechanics, and evolution, before turning to the
theological reflection on those discoveries. Chapter 4, "The Cosmos
and Creation," traces the origins of the universe first through the
lens of astronomy and then with the eyes of faith. Chapter 5, "The
Quantum World of the Spirit," presents the interconnectedness of
all matter at the subatomic, quantum level, and envisions a new
pneumatology in light of the science. Chapter 6, "Evolution and
the Jesus Singularity," in many respects, is the heart of our investigation. How do we understand Jesus as Christ in our expanding,
evolving world?

Finally, section 3, "Chapter of Elections," proposes that theological reflection on science offers new avenues for understanding and pursuing a future of religious life in "light of the signs of the times." And in the spirit of subsidiarity, on this we all get to vote. Chapter 7, "The Emergent Disciple: Formation in an Unfinished Universe," explores the historic response of religious congregations to the signs of the times and encourages a similar flexible stance toward formation. How do we envision ministry and service in light of these signs of the times? Chapter 8, "Seeking the Whole: The Vows through a Hermeneutic of Catholicity," proposes an evolutionary reinterpretation of the evangelical counsels. As we began with a question, "Where's Jesus," we conclude with one: "What is ours to do?" In light of the findings of science, the deep thinking of theology, and our faithful commitment as women religious, how are we to respond to the emergent needs of our world? Chapter 9, "'For All the Earth' (1 Cor 10:26): Mission and the Reign of God," proposes that the future of religious life is intricately connected to the well-being of God's creation.

We conclude with a proposal for the future of religious life, a proposal that many may call simplistic, some may laud as prophetic, and a few, perhaps, will be courageous enough to try. "Community as the Holy Preaching" invites us to think deeply about our lives in common witness to the emergent reality of wholeness/holiness, the power of reconciliation to heal, and our personal and communal commitment to the shalom of God.

# Section One

## *Chapter of Faults*
### *Naming Our Diversity*

As a teenager, my take on the sacrament of reconciliation was strictly utilitarian. Like a giant eraser, the sacrament disappeared whatever you had done that you oughtn't have done. I wielded this sacrament like an avenging angel when I caught my brother stealing a dollar from my room. If he went to confession, I wouldn't tell our parents. I then force-marched him to the church and sat outside the confessional. Needless to say, I was none too pleased with his rather lenient penance.

I would have hoped that my appreciation for the sacrament would have matured as I did. But growing in personal self-awareness as a woman in our church, I found it difficult to confess to a man, ordained or not. Two startlingly different experiences changed all that. First, I was tasked with leading a retreat in the Holy Land, and the majority of the participants were women and men studying to be formators. I take seriously the admonition to "not grieve the Holy Spirit" (Eph 4:30). How could I hope to guide these folks through the Holy Land, offering spiritual insight, when I hadn't taken care of my own spirit? My desire to have "a clean heart" (Ps 51:10) and my longing to truly accompany these women and men helped me to see the deeper value of the sacrament. Of course, it helps to have a confessor for whom offering the sacrament is as sacred as receiving it.

The second experience is drawn from an interreligious context. Sometimes you don't realize the gift you have until you meet someone who doesn't have it. As a Princeton Seminary doctoral student, Briana Wong, conducted research on conversion and transnational ministry among Cambodian Christians. During one of her interviews, she met a Christian who had formerly been a Buddhist. When asked why the woman was now Christian, she explained, "because of forgiveness." The experience of forgiveness is not found in Buddhism, rather karma becomes the great leveler. "For some survivors of the Cambodian genocide, then, the Christian promise of forgiveness through the breaking of karma often comes as a breath of fresh air."[1] Though the cross, the story of Jesus, and the Bible may have all been attractive to this woman, what she needed most, what was unattainable to her in her current tradition, was forgiveness. The researcher recognized that "the concept of forgiveness from sins offers a sense of victory over karma, even for those who continue to hold a space for karma in their personal views."[2] Listening to the story being retold, it occurred to me what a gift we have that I had failed to recognize.

The sacrament of reconciliation reunites us with community and, more importantly, brings us back to ourselves renewed and forgiven. Though I doubt that St. Augustine would have used this language, he certainly understood the impact of forgiveness, especially among members of a religious community:

> Bear in mind that if anyone does injure another by insult or slander or an accusation she should make amends as soon as possible, and the injured party should also be willing to forgive . . . A sister who is quick-tempered, and yet quickly asks the pardon of the one she has injured, is better than one who is seldom angered, and then is slow to ask forgiveness . . . For your sake, therefore, avoid the use

---

1. Briana Wong, "Buddhist-Christians in Cambodian America," *Studies in World Christianity* 25, no. 1 (2019): 50–70, here 64.

2. Briana Wong, "Winter Gathering: Introductory Information," Louisville Institute Winter Seminar (January 22, 2020), 1.

of harsh words; but if they fall from your lips, do not be ashamed to offer the remedy with the same tongue that caused the wound.[3]

As it would develop in monastic communities, the place of communal forgiveness became the chapter of faults.

> The expression *chapter of faults* refers to the monastic practice, in place since early times, of disclosure before the community assembled in the chapter-house of offenses against the outward order of the community, either by confession of the offender or by statement of a third party . . . and atonement for them through a penance imposed by the superior. Such chapters were held after some fashion in almost every monastery.[4]

Even into the twentieth century, this practice continued. The "techniques of monastic discipline were aimed at installing in subjects a sense of self-sacrifice and dedication to the broader aims of the institutional church, whatever these may be in various contexts."[5] The well-being of the community rested on the ability of its members to live together peaceably; the chapter of faults—at its best—created a public airing of grievances for the purpose of reconciliation. While after Vatican II such monastic practices dissipated among apostolic orders, the memory of such practices lingered.[6] In my own congregation, stories of "doing the venia" (prostrating yourself before the superior in penance) abound.

I invoke the memory of this penitential chapter not to encourage its reinstitution but rather its rehabilitation. Sometimes we are best

---

3. Barbara Beyenka, OP, "Translation of the Rule of St. Augustine," in *The Rule, Constitution, Statutes, and Enactments* (Sinsinawa, WI: Sinsinawa Dominicans, 1990, revised 2012).

4. Stephan Haering, "Chapter of Faults," *Religion Past & Present: Encyclopedia of Theology and Religion*, vol. 2 (Leiden; Boston: Brill, 2007), 490.

5. Christine Gervais and Amanda Watson, "Discipline, Resistance, Solace and the Body: Catholic Women Religious' Convent Experiences from the Late 1930s to the Late 1960s," *Religions* 5 (2014): 277–303, here 280.

6. "The sisters' experiences with corporal discipline [was] complicated, nuanced, restrictive, and sometimes even generative," write Christine Gervais and Amanda Watson in "Discipline, Resistance, Solace and the Body," 282.

served by admitting our faults; sometimes we need to receive the "mercy of God" and others. As I continue this exploration of the New Cosmology in the context of religious life, I must begin with a confession. I was a hater.

Perhaps "hate" is too strong a word. I was suspicious of the New Cosmology, and prior to this research, rather than attempt to understand the concept I simply, wholesale, ignored it. I suffered from what I now call a myopic Christology. I'm quite confident in the New Testament Christologies, but move beyond the second century, and it gets a little fuzzy. Some of my sisters were using language like "Cosmic Christ," "Christogenesis," and "Omega Point." I worried that, as one survey respondent wrote, "some concepts are in conflict with some teachings of the Church (e.g., original sin, need for redemption)." Another respondent captured my concern exactly:

> The New Cosmology itself is not in conflict with my faith, but the way it has become central to U.S. religious life spirituality leaves me wanting. We rarely speak of Jesus or Christ in community prayer outside of Mass. We forgo scripture in favor of more general cosmic material.

As a biblical scholar, I have a vested interest in keeping Scripture in the forefront of our faith and spirituality. Call it job security. When I did begin to read some of the publications on the topic, I found that, as one respondent noted, "the quality is extremely uneven." Additionally, I found I agreed wholeheartedly with a respondent who recognized that she didn't have a problem with concepts of the New Cosmology; she simply didn't know it by that name:

> The concepts of the New Cosmology have just always been a part of my world. They are truths that have always existed, but [that] I do not attribute to the New Cosmology. In fact, I did not know the term "new cosmology" until a few years ago. My understanding of creation is impacted by scientific research on evolution and the Big Bang theory, but not because of the New Cosmology, because of being taught those concepts in school.

Finally, I realized the root of my concern: I was "seeking answers about how the 'old' faith tradition fits with the Universe story," as one respondent disclosed.

Perhaps my fault doesn't rise to a grievous or even middle fault, but it does merit acknowledgment. And as I reviewed the generous written responses to the survey questions, I recognized a similar pattern of mistakes. Some of those who did not find the concepts of the New Cosmology helpful, whether as theology or hermeneutical lenses, like me, did not have a clear sense of the concepts. Others who found the New Cosmology meaningful were not always cognizant of the deep resonances with elements of our tradition. In preparing the survey and in conversation with various sisters, it has become clear that we are not all on the same page as concerns this topic, and we are not always tolerant of the differences among us. This section of the book is designed to acknowledge our limitations, frustrations, and disappointments, not so as to do penance, but as to create a reconciliation of sorts—a way forward that allows us to acknowledge and reverence our differences.

The survey data demonstrated that age cohorts generally view the New Cosmology differently, so in chapter 1, "Whence Comes Wisdom?" I will explore the responses according to these cohorts. The intent is to see more clearly the concerns, confusions, and possibilities for deeper conversation. But before delving into questions of theology, chapter 2, "There Is a Season and a Time," provides a brief introduction to the four generations to which the majority of US women religious belong: Silent, Baby Boom, Generation X, and Millennial. Chapter 3, "Orienting Ecclesiologies," reflects on those differences through a theological lens. I'll argue that how we view religious life within our congregations and how we respond to the New Cosmology is reflective of both our age cohort and the generation of religious life to which we identify. For example, someone may be a "new" member recently professed, and yet be in her 60s. Her experience of religious life is reflective of a twenty-first-century mode of formation and integration. And yet, she has seen significant changes in church and society that impact her theology and ecclesiology. I propose that the Silent Generation, Baby Boomers, Gen Xers, and Millennials not only view the world through their unique generational lens, but they encounter theology and relate to church decidedly differently as well. Holding in tension and respect our differences becomes a public witness to the value of diversity in community.

And here we return to the Rule of St. Augustine. "Since you are the temples of God, live together in peace and harmony, and recognize [God] in one another."[7]

Let's try, shall we?

7. Beyenka, "Translation of the Rule of St. Augustine."

# Chapter One

## Whence Comes Wisdom?
### (Job 28:20)

### Differences among Age Cohorts

### Introduction

"An intelligent mind acquires knowledge, / and the ear of the wise seeks knowledge" (Prov 18:15). A collection of wisdom sayings, the Book of Proverbs posits that reverence for the divine leads to wisdom, which in turn manifests itself in a successful life. The responses from all three age groups in this survey (25–44, 45–64, and 65 plus) evidenced a commitment to the search for wisdom. The question is where can wisdom be found—whether or not the so-called New Cosmology and related concepts can be a legitimate source for theological knowledge for women religious? Interestingly, the three age cohorts had differing responses to this question. Across the generations, some sisters were laudatory, concerned, or cautious. No one was complacent.

### A Snapshot of a Generation

#### The Rachels among Us: The Youngest Cohort

There are a few stories that form the foundation of any congregation. These are the legends, mythic tales, and heroic adventures of our founders and early sisters. They become a part of our formation, our sense of self as sister among these sisters. In many respects, these stories are icons that reflect back to us the presence of the Holy Spirit among our foremothers.

The story of Rachel is one such true tale for the Dominicans of Sinsinawa. In January 1849, the fledging Dominican congregation of Benton, Wisconsin, under the direction of Fr. Samuel Mazzuchelli, OP, had just four members. Fr. Samuel left it up to the sisters to decide whether they would disband or continue. The sisters gathered on retreat to consider the congregation's future and continued mission. Showing great trust in providence, the sisters choose to leave the decision to the youngest among them, Sister Rachel Conway. As the story goes, Sister Rachel announced (I like to think with great conviction!): "In the name of God, let us remain together in our present community." Early the next month, bolstered by Sister Rachel's statement of hope and faith, the community reorganized. And so today the Dominicans of Sinsinawa owe a debt to these sisters who listened to the voice of the youngest. It's a story worth repeating.

Those sisters aged 25–44 are the Rachels among the survey participants. Of the 215 sisters who took the survey, 177 identified their age. Of that number, 22 were 25–34 years of age and 32 were 35–44 years of age. This cohort represents 31 percent of the survey takers who identified their age. Ninety-five percent had made their first profession between 2001 and 2015.

### Both/And: The Middle Cohort

Full disclosure: I'm in this middle cohort, which by most standards is middle age. But according to the editors of *Encyclopaedia Britannica*, we middlers are on the precipice of decline!

> The physiological and psychological changes experienced by a middle-aged person centre on the gradual decline of physical abilities and the awareness of mortality. In middle age, the relative potencies of past, present, and future are altered as the individual increasingly directs effort to the process of reminiscence and recollection of the past, rather than anticipation of the future. If approached constructively, middle age can prepare an individual for a satisfying and productive old age.[1]

---

1. *Encyclopaedia Britannica*, s.v. "middle age," https://www.britannica.com/science /middle-age.

But in religious life, we age differently. Some in this cohort are not long ago finally professed. Some are entering a new type of ministerial life, for example in leadership or formation. Because we are in smaller numbers, in comparison with those sisters 65 plus, we are less visible in the larger congregation. Though we may be physically in middle age, we are often seen as "one of the young sisters" within congregations and local communities. And yet, the survey showed that this age cohort perceives the New Cosmology and its related concepts differently than the chronologically "younger sisters."

The second age cohort under 65 represents 31 percent of those survey takers who identified their age. Twenty-five sisters were 45–54 years old and 30 were 55–64 years old. Seventy-five percent made their first profession between 1976 and 2000, and nearly 18 percent made their profession between 2001 and 2010.

## *Let Days Speak, and Many Years Teach Wisdom (Job 32:7): The Oldest Cohort*

Enduring the rapid upheaval of their nearly cloistered lives and the turmoil of the society around them, this cohort is, in many respects, the greatest generation of modern religious life. Think Sisters Theresa Kane, RSM, Donna Quinn, OP, Simone Campbell, SSS, Elizabeth M. Johnson, CSJ, and Mother Mary Clare Millea, ASCJ. These sisters didn't watch history. They made it!

Indeed, this generation includes the US sisters whose commitment to service cost many of them their lives. We need think only of Maryknoll Sisters Ita Ford and Maura Clarke, and Ursuline Sister Dorothy Kazel martyred in El Salvador in 1980, and Mary Joel Kolmer, ASC, Shirley Kolmer, ASC, Kathleen McGuire, ASC, Agnes Mueller, ASC, and Barbara Ann Muttra, ASC martyred in Liberia in 1992. More recently Dorothy Stang, SND, was martyred in Brazil in 2005. The papal call to the missions, the post-Vatican move into and beyond the classroom, the turn toward the poor—all marked this generation of women religious with a zeal, a passion, a palpable sense of mission, little diminished over time.

This cohort represents 38 percent of those survey takers who identified their age. Seventy-eight percent made their first profession by 1975, and of that percentage the largest number made their profession between 1966 and 1970.

### Responses to the New Cosmology by Age Cohort

The survey results clearly demonstrated a demarcation among age cohorts concerning the familiarity, content, and impact of the New Cosmology on religious life. Similarly, each age cohort offered distinct comments about the New Cosmology, which reflected their knowledge and familiarity of the concepts.

The youngest age cohort was slightly less familiar with the New Cosmology than the next age cohort. More than 9 percent responded that they were unfamiliar, and 44 percent were only somewhat familiar with the topic. The next age group (44–64 years of age) reported 10.4 percent were not familiar and nearly 40 percent were somewhat familiar. The oldest cohort had the lowest percentage (3.3 percent) of sisters who were unfamiliar with the topic or only somewhat familiar (20 percent).

Likely because they reported being better versed on the subject, a higher percentage of the oldest cohort knew the general elements of the New Cosmology when compared to both younger groups. Nearly 12 percent of those aged 25–44 and 15 percent of those aged 45–64 were not familiar enough to comment on the elements of the New Cosmology, compared to 3 percent of those ages 65 plus. Drawn from the works of Teilhard de Chardin, Delio, Johnson, Haught, Edwards and others, the following are generally considered elements of the New Cosmology:

- The big bang: the universe has a beginning

- The universe is expanding

- The universe will eventually "die"

- All of creation is interrelated

- Our consciousness is evolving

- The Cosmic Christ is the Omega Point to which all creation evolves

More than three-quarters of all age cohorts recognize that the interrelatedness of creation and the evolving consciousness are elements of the New Cosmology. Though the majority note that the expansion of the universe is part of the New Cosmology, fewer included the big bang or the universe's beginning. Across the age cohorts, a lesser percentage considered the ending of the universe as an element.

The goal of this project is to assess both the familiarity and the perceived impact of the New Cosmology on religious life. Sisters were asked if the New Cosmology and its related concepts enhanced, made no difference, or were in conflict with their faith, and in which areas (Scripture, church, tradition, religious life). As the analysis showed, differences appear along generational lines. Those age cohorts with less familiarity and knowledge tended to be more concerned about its influence on their religious lives. Among the youngest cohort for whom the New Cosmology was thought to enhance their faith, the areas most affected were their understanding of religious life (75 percent) and Scripture (60 percent), followed by that of tradition (50 percent) and the church (50 percent). For those in the middle cohort for whom the New Cosmology was thought to enhance their faith, the areas most affected were their understanding of Scripture (68 percent) and religious life (65 percent), followed by that of the church (53 percent) and tradition (50 percent). For the members of the oldest cohort whose faith was enhanced by the New Cosmology, the areas most affected were their understanding of Scripture (78 percent) and religious life (76 percent), followed by that of tradition (56 percent) and the church (54 percent). Across the age cohorts, those sisters who reckoned the New Cosmology as an enhancement for faith generally agreed that their understanding of Scripture and religious life were most impacted by their knowledge of the New Cosmology.

In the youngest cohort, those who felt that the New Cosmology was in conflict with their faith reported that their understanding of the church (55 percent), Scripture (36 percent) and tradition (36 percent) was most affected. Only 18 percent thought the New Cosmology was in conflict with their understanding of religious life. For the members of the middle cohort for whom the New Cosmology was thought to be in conflict with their faith, the areas most affected were their understanding of tradition (50 percent) and church (50 percent), followed by that of Scripture (42 percent). Only 17 percent thought the New Cosmology was in conflict with their understanding of religious life. For those in the oldest cohort who thought the New Cosmology was conflictual with their faith, the areas most affected included their understating of tradition (36 percent), church (21 percent), Scripture (14 percent), and religious life (7 percent). Across the age cohorts among those who found the New Cosmology conflictual, the area of least conflict was religious life.

Regardless of their level of familiarity with the concepts and content of the New Cosmology, sisters across the age cohorts expressed clear opinions as to its potential to enliven or to diminish their faith. In the proceeding sections, the written responses that accompanied the survey questions are collected according to age cohort and theme, further demonstrating similarities and differences among the generations.

## The Youngest Cohort and the New Cosmology

The 25–44 aged cohort's lack of familiarity may partially account for its questions and concerns regarding the New Cosmology and related concepts. Collectively, their comments centered around the idea of "newness" in the New Cosmology, the role of Jesus Christ within this theology, and its potential to create division within community.

### *How Is This New?*

Where you stand affects what you see. This is very apparent when describing the youngest cohort's perspective on the conversation between science and theology. Several respondents noted, "I have trouble calling it 'New,'" "I'm not sure it's really all that NEW." One sister wrote: "As I am over 30 years old, the concept is older than I am." Respondents weren't against a conversation between science and theology, and in fact "the 'New' Cosmology seems [. . .] to be, in some ways, a rediscovery of ancient ways of understanding the interrelatedness of creation which can now be verified by modern science."

This cohort recognizes an integration between scientific findings and their faith. Their innate openness to science is a product of their education.

I feel like the New Cosmology is not new to me because I was taught from a young age in school about evolution and the earth and the universe being billions of years old. This has always been a part of my faith and does impact my faith. But the popularity of New Cosmology in recent years has not necessarily changed my faith.

## *Where's Jesus?*

The consistent theological question among these respondents was simple: "Where's Jesus?" Some perceived that the New Cosmology, with its emphasis on the Cosmic Christ, actually "decenters Jesus," "loses the particularity of Jesus," or challenges one's faith so that "I lose Jesus in this" or "I'm still trying to find the Jesus piece." Some admitted that their lack of knowledge on the topic might be part of the problem.

> Though I'm not too familiar with the specific terms of the 'new' cosmology, it does seem that Christ gets left behind. Jesus the man is acknowledged, in that a person existed that did some good things, and for some writers the Cosmic Christ is a thing. But for many other people Jesus is an historical figure but Jesus the Christ isn't acknowledged.

In general, this age cohort was particularly interested and invested in this research project. One reported: "I'm glad there is an emphasis on Jesus as I did not experience that from some of our sisters who first introduced me to this very big concept." Another was deeply concerned:

> I do not find New Cosmology attractive, especially in relationship to Jesus. I grew up with science and its implications for theology. Perhaps New Cosmology doesn't feel new . . . Also, I might intellectually understand a cosmic Jesus Christ, but that's a harder image to relate to and is not something that interests me. And I never want to see the Universe Story again.

## *A House Divided*

Beyond the question of the place of Jesus Christ in the New Cosmology, sisters in the youngest age cohort reported that this theology seemed to appeal to a specific group.

The New Cosmology is described in so many ways and usually only spoken about by religious communities and baby boomers. Most young adults and middle-age adults (scientists and theologians alike) don't use the term. Instead, they talk about astrophysics or creation theology, incarnational theology, etc.

While advocates see the New Cosmology as deeply unifying, some younger sisters worry:

The New Cosmology . . . for me speaks of great privilege. My context is always the people in the pews, the people of God, who are still grappling with their own understanding of God, who want the Bible broken down for them in a way that they can understand it and apply it in their own lives.

The enthusiasm for the New Cosmology among many in their congregations has led some younger sisters to worry that "the New Cosmology [is] being seen as a replacement for more traditional understandings of faith, which is not helpful for [them]." This concern about theological "replacement" was echoed by others in this age cohort:

I am concerned that enthusiasm for the New Cosmology among some women religious may lead to a desire to take it as a wholesale replacement for other theological interpretations, which separates us from the People of God in the Church.

There is little doubt that some of this age cohort feel strongly about the concepts and their implications for faith.

I feel completely turned off by the terminology of the "new cosmology." I'm not necessarily opposed to the concepts involved . . . but [they] seem a little too loose. I'm not sure how to articulate my problems with this trend in spirituality/theology. Sometimes when people talk about the "cosmic Christ," it doesn't even sound Christian to me. Perhaps I haven't read enough, but what I've read turns me off completely.

For one respondent the concern wasn't theological, but rather epistemological.

I'm concerned about the emphasis being placed on only one branch of science [as if] Quantum Physics is [the] only way of understanding the world. I'm concerned that other branches of science are being ignored, whether biology (except for evolution, which is only one part of biological science) or even chemistry and physics. On the other side, I'm concerned about a preference for scientific principles being put over theological understanding. Science is only one way of understanding the world, and we shouldn't forget the other important ways of understanding the world, whether from other cultures, social sciences, art or literature.

Whether Christological, theological, or epistemological, the concerns about the New Cosmology from this age cohort were clearly and consistently articulated. And while few named it outwardly, generational differences appear to have created a rift among sisters, leading one to write: "I hope language and spirituality between old and young sisters can be bridged."

### An Olive Branch

Clearly there is tension between some of the majority generation who find the New Cosmology a liberating, unifying, hopeful theology, and some of the younger generation for whom "new" is a misnomer, and the "theology" potentially dismissive of other theological perspectives. And yet, even among those sisters who question the New Cosmology, they are often open to its potential to enliven religious life.

- I hope that the connection (between Jesus Christ and the New Cosmology) can be nurtured and fleshed out robustly in ways that illuminate our charisms for the twenty-first century.

- Specifically related to my understanding of religious life, the Universe Story helps me to have hope and embrace the changes and challenges in religious life today.

- While [my knowledge is] limited, the notions of the New Cosmology have helped me grow in my relationship with Jesus, God, and creation. I am also new to religious life and I am growing into my religious skin. I have much to learn.

The New Cosmology can provide an opportunity for deeper theological conversations among sisters, since it "reflects an attempt to update our theology in order to respond (with newer knowledge, science) to the world today." But the New Cosmology also can create a conversation between scientists and theologians.

> It's a fascinating conversation to be part of. I think the Church has so much to gain from conversations with the scientific community in growing and deepening our sense of WONDER and AWE at the created universe. Likewise, I think the scientific community can grow when they find that their research doesn't "destroy" our faith, but simply enhances it. Additionally, reading some of these research questions—particular the ones I didn't answer—has opened my eyes and mind to what else is "out there" in the theological world. I see this as an invitation to deepen my own reading and reflecting.

Finally, the New Cosmology provides an opportunity to reconsider how we understand and relate to our Catholic faith. As one sister noted, "My questions about the New Cosmology compel me to seek more deeply the ancient truths within our Tradition." Another wrote, "The understanding of the new cosmology helped me to give another pair of lenses to look at Scriptures." We are encouraged to think for ourselves, as one respondent stated, "I like the way the New Cosmology opens God and the world up to the bigger, unknowable mystery even as it seeks greater understanding. I appreciate that it doesn't ask us to leave our reason at the door when we seek to engage with God and Church."

This theological thinking can be liberative for the people in the pew. "I hope that we continue to open the minds of the whole people of God in terms of knowing and understanding our Catholic faith in light of the New Cosmology. I think it will save us as humanity."

## The Middle Cohort and the New Cosmology

More so than the younger group, members of this age cohort articulated definite and diverse opinions on the topic. Some found it liberating. "I believe that the New Cosmology is a very freeing concept. How wonderful it would be if we could integrate it into daily liturgies and the official liturgical language!" Another thought quite differently. "I wish the hierarchical church would speak publicly about the new universe story." Like those aged 25–44, some of this cohort questioned the adjective "new" to describe the New Cosmology and others wondered what role Jesus played in this theological perspective. Concerned about the implications of the New Cosmology on religious life and their experience of community, some in this cohort focused on the possible conflict with church doctrine and tradition.

### Still Not New

Many in this age group were children when NASA sent spaceships to the moon and young adults when the Challenger Space Shuttle exploded on television before the eyes of millions, so they, too, question why this topic of cosmology would be called "new." As one respondent wrote, "The new cosmology was not a 'revelation' to me, having been born after the Big Bang theory, and the Apollo landing and growing up with Cosmos and Carl Sagan . . . this is the 'one story.' " For others this theology was "new" to them, but they wouldn't characterize the scientific theories behind the theology as "new." One respondent noted, "I am not familiar with the New Cosmology. Why is it called new and what are the sources and origins of its 'Newness'?"

### Finding Jesus

Unlike the responses from the younger age cohort, the comments from this group were more balanced on the question of the role of Jesus within in the New Cosmology. For some, this theological perspective was peripheral to the question of Jesus. "The relationship with Jesus Christ does not need the New Universe story! Certainly, it informs the relationship, nuances, and deepens . . . but Jesus is Jesus!" Others had not studied the concepts enough to make an informed decision. "I do not understand [the New Cosmology] but have not taken the time for a full study. The Jesus story is foundational to my faith and my vocation." For one respondent familiar with the New Cosmology, this theological perspective opened up new avenues for understanding.

There were limits on how people in the context of Jesus' birth at that time could hear the message of Jesus. I think if we realize that we only know one aspect of Christ from the scriptures and view that God may be continuing to reveal more about divine grace and love through evolution, I think there are ways to keep Jesus' story as part of learning how to live in the context of the New Cosmology.

## *The Church Is One Foundation*

Where the younger cohort was concerned about the implications of the New Cosmology within its religious life contexts, this age group focused on the relationship between the New Cosmology and their Catholic faith. In fact, several commented that "some concepts are in conflict with some teachings of the Church (e.g., original sin, need for redemption)," and "much of this is counter to traditional Church teaching." Others focused on the understanding of God in light of the New Cosmology, positing that "God does not evolve . . . He is immutable, infinite, eternal, unchanging." A question arose as to the philosophical underpinnings of the New Cosmology:

> For one who is not familiar with the concept, at first blush, the terms give the impression that the concept derives simply from science and materialism. While materialism is certainly not incompatible with the faith—I believe in the incarnation as stated in the creed—only a materialistic world view is incompatible. I am suspicious of systems of thought that have their basis in reduced views of creation as simply material or those that have Whitehead as a philosophical foundation. Both views seem reductive to me and do not seem to capture the mystery of faith. I do not believe that God who is mystery and also Pure Being evolves or changes in the way we envision change—the act of a being in potency in so far as it is in potency. God is mystery, love, Being, and this mystery is intelligible but not reducible.

The concern seems to be how to hold in tension the findings of science without diminishing holy mystery.

> All things were made through Jesus Christ. Science cannot, nor ever will be able to comprehensively explain where matter (in the beginning) comes from, what caused it to "explode," to what point it will expand or the future of how it will develop.

### *"Lift Up Your Eyes and Look to the Heavens" (Isa 40:26)*

Despite the theological and philosophical concerns named, this cohort still recognized the possibilities of a fruitful conversation between the New Cosmology and their faith. "God Created, He is the one who gave all scientific law their construction, order and meaning." While another commented on how this science and theology has expanded her "belief in a God whose imagination is infinite and marvelous." But we are also encouraged to not slip into dichotomous thinking.

> What concerns me is when [Jesus Christ and the New Cosmology] are seen as mutually exclusive. One can be very excited about the new universe story and passionate about Jesus. I hope as our awareness grows, we hold on to the core of our faith and bring that into conversation with all our new learning.

In fact, the theology emerging from critical reflection on science may provide a new way to enhance our faith. "I would hope that others would be open to Christ beyond the scriptural understanding, and experience oneness in love," offered one respondent. But another acknowledged that she was slow to see the benefits of the New Cosmology.

> I was very resistant to the New Cosmology—as recent as five years ago. It was when Ilia Delio spoke at the LCWR Assembly that I finally moved from "oh, here we go again, fairy dust spirituality"—to a sense of wonder at what this means for me as a woman religious and elected leader. I'm now open and eager to understand the New Cosmology . . . as long as I don't lose the grounding I have in the Trinity (created and uncreated).

Many in this cohort reported that the New Cosmology was popular among their sisters. But, as one noted, "I feel the New Cosmology has impacted my congregation more than me personally. I take some interest in it but it has not been life-changing for me." However, another saw great potential for religious life:

> Especially as we see the demographic changes in religious life in the US and Europe, I find it helpful and hopeful to reframe what some call diminishment into the evolution into something new.

## The Oldest Cohort and the New Cosmology

Where the youngest cohort struggled with nomenclature and pondered the relationship of the New Cosmology with their growing experience of religious life, the second age cohort posed questions about theological incompatibility and doctrine. The older cohort had what could be called a more seasoned response, only partly due to their age. This cohort is more knowledgeable in the elements of the New Cosmology and seemed better equipped to evaluate various resources on the topic. As one sister wrote, "Some ideas [about the New Cosmology] conflict; others deeply align. It depends on who you are reading." Another commented, "'the new cosmology' is, in my opinion a fluffy term—I am very much affected by reading Teilhard de Chardin, Kathy Duffy, Ilia Delio, but not everyone is as grounded as they. I have not found [author] to be as grounded, as intellectually honest as the others."

The majority of written responses indicated a cautiously hopeful attitude that integrating the tradition with emerging insights from science would lead to deeper faith. And yet many still acknowledged their experience of tension between the two. The insights and learnings from the New Cosmology and its related concepts have profound implications on how one sees oneself and comes to know one's place in the universe. Despite their various concerns, all the age cohorts saw the value of theological reflection on scientific findings. This older cohort was, perhaps, the most enthusiastic about those possibilities.

### *Integrating Old and New*

This age cohort knows something about old and new. These are the sisters, for the most part, who entered a pre-Vatican II convent and professed in the years shortly after the Council's close. The profound number and speed of changes in theology, prayer, horarium, ministry, and clothing are astounding. Many chose to leave their congregations during these years of experimentation. Those that remained had to reimagine their lives as women religious in the turbulent decades of the 1960s–1980s. It's no wonder that as one sister wrote, "the New Cosmology also challenges my faith; I am seeking answers about how the 'old' faith tradition fits with the Universe story," while another noted, "I believe that the New Creation Story can [be] both enhancing and conflicting at times in my vowed life."

The conflict comes when ancient language meets new insights. "The institutional church language used in the Eucharistic celebration is from another era and inhibits the teachings in the new cosmology," responded one participant. "The medieval theology that we came from no longer appears to have the same relevance in today's theology of the New Creation Story," offered another. But there is hope "that through the sharing of those who understand the relationship and the reconciliation of redemption theology with cosmology, we will have a better understanding of the beauty of the universe story." Indeed, the invitation is to find common ground. One sister proposed that "as we grow in understanding of the new cosmology, we can find ways to hold the tension between our belief in God and our recognition of on-going revelation." But occasionally there is a point of no return:

> The learnings and insights are stretching. I can never return to more traditional views. I know that the fullness of the Mystery of God is evolving within us, within creation. We must protect and cherish this work of God in one another and in all creation.

And we are also called to share those learnings and insights with others. "Most of the work I do is helping others see the connection of the [New Cosmology] with our faith. If we can't do that, there isn't much point in learning the [New Cosmology] except as a science lesson."

### Holding the Tension

There is a tempered impatience among some sisters of this age cohort. "I wish the Roman Catholic Church would simply 'grow-up' but like Francis of Assisi I stay within it and honor the structures while I work for deep change and live what I believe God calls me to do in the day-to-day." A tension exists between one's understanding of the New Cosmology and its related concepts and the reality of the institutional church, born of a different cosmology:

Yes, it is very difficult to try and go against the institution of the Catholic Church and its Medieval Theology, because our Order is under the Papacy. I find going to Mass difficult and even our Office of Hours difficult too. I will at times translate sayings or prayers with what the New Creation Story would be telling us to use. How much longer can we do this and continue to be stagnant? Everything evolves and the Church needs to do the same.

But some of this cohort posed the question: How far is too far? As one sister wrote, "I think there will come a point when we will deny the cross and resurrection as central. I fear that day."

### A Reason to Hope

For some sisters, the New Cosmology is reorienting and "impacts my/our understanding of my place in the universe." As a survey respondent wrote:

Actually, I feel that living within the story of an evolving universe changes everything, (enhanced faith) image of God, who God is, our relationship to God and the rest of the Universe, implications of those relationships; regarding Scriptures, Tradition and Church, concepts related to the New Cosmology have put some things into a different and perhaps more realistic perspective.

This new space is energizing, as another sister noted, "I became even MORE aware of the gift of understanding in a broader sense of these concepts and how this expanding consciousness takes me to new places spiritually and energizes me toward the future." Another stated, "I continue to pray that my heart and spirit will be open to the Living, Loving, Inviting God that is opening me/us to this new understanding of God's nearness in all that is."

Many of these sisters are finding that the New Cosmology and related concepts are opening new avenues for their own spirituality enrichment.

I just find new Cosmology very exciting. At my age I thought I would settle in and settle down. The concepts of new cosmology have made all things new for me and very hopeful. I am excited to be alive and have my consciousness expanding.

Some sisters are revivified in their religious vocation.

> My hope is that there be more sharing of ideas and possibilities for living with joy and hope as we continue to delve into Mystery. My hope is that by being inclusive and questioning, we may find the "life in abundance" that Jesus promised. This abundance is not material but relational.

Another stated, "I am left with more questions than answers . . . at the same time a deep awareness of my search for the God who gives meaning to my life!"

## Conclusion

Paying attention to the differences among the age cohorts provides a glimpse into how the New Cosmology is perceived and received. For some the integration of science with theology is astonishing, opening up new ways of viewing religious life, relationship, ministry, and prayer. Those who have found the New Cosmology and its related concepts astonishing are most often the ones who share it with others. However, as the comments demonstrate, not all sisters are equally enamored by what they have heard.

The middle cohort was most strident in its remarks about the potential conflict with tradition and the church. These sisters were also the group with the highest percentage of survey participants who had no familiarity with the topic. One sister wondered if she should bother to learn more about the topic. "Is the New Cosmology simply a passing fad or is there more to it? Is it something to which I should invest time and attention?" Another pondered whether the New Cosmology was perhaps serving as a subterfuge.

> I think our narrative on New Cosmology in religious life is somewhat stuck, not evolving. I think it is also used as an escape hatch to avoid engaging in our patriarchal structures, almost creating an alternative universe. My hope is that we can get through this stuck point and have those "so what" conversations, talk about why it might be important to figure out how to engage the "people in the pews" or even the hierarchy in this conversation. How evolved are

we really if we use the New Cosmology as our own litmus test for theological correctness? And how out of touch are we from the rest of the Church?"

In comparison, the younger cohort was generally more curious about the topic and less strident in their critical responses. Since the Religious Formation Conference cohort had the highest level of familiarity on the topic, this might suggest that the younger group, whom we could surmise have more recently been in formation, may have been introduced to the concepts by RFC members.

Sisters may have questions about the compatibility of the theology of the New Cosmology with the church and tradition, but in general they are less concerned about its effect on religious life. In fact, most thought religious life was one area in which the elements of the New Cosmology could offer a new or renewed vision. The biggest hurdle to exploring the relationship between the New Cosmology and religious life lies in the misinformation, misperceptions, and missed opportunities for conversation across the chasm of cohorts. Not surprisingly, the generational differences have led to generation gaps. In the following chapters, we will explore these three age cohorts in light of their sociological and ecclesiological orientations.

# Chapter Two

# There Is a Season and a Time (Eccl 3:1)

## Exploring American Generations

> Every generation inherits a world it never made; and, as it does
> so, it automatically becomes the trustee of that world for those
> who come after. In due course, each generation makes its own
> accounting to its children.
>
> —Robert Kennedy (1925–68)

### Introduction

It was a typical night. After evening prayer, my local community relaxed in the living room. Around the room sat four generations, one from the Silent Generation, a Baby Boomer, a Gen Xer, and a Millennial. While the older sister read the newspaper, the Baby Boomer read a news magazine. The Generation X sister flipped through the channels on the television, and the Millennial posted, tweeted, or typed something with amazing speed on her tiny phone screen. The use of different technology stands as one of the many markers that distinguish generational cohorts. Before exploring the role that the New Cosmology may have in the development of religious life, in this and the following chapter we will situate ourselves among the US generations represented in our congregations and then place ourselves along a continuum of theological and ecclesiological diversity.

Our first dilemma is deciding how to delineate generational bound-aries. For some studies, divisions are made based on birth rates. "The demographic definition of a generation is very precise: simply observe the age of a parent at a baby's birth. The years between births of parents and child give the length of the generation."[1] We know this as a "family generation." But social scientists argue that

> birth cohorts . . . do not in themselves constitute a generation: it is rather a matter of the possible relation to a common experience that marks and influences, and from which there arises evidence of something shared, despite difference of provenance, religious or ethnic affiliation. When this evidence is missing, then we are not dealing with a generation, even when the years of birth coincide.[2]

This leads to another definition that describes a cohort as a his-torical generation, "a group of birth cohort set off from other groups by strong historical boundaries."[3] This type of cohort possesses a "a generational persona recognized and determined by (1) common age location; (2) common beliefs and behavior; and (3) perceived membership in a common generation."[4] Strauss and Howe explain the relationship between family and historical cohort generations.

> Cohort generations are to societies what family generations are to families . . . the earlier generation is always older than the next and normally exercises authority over those that follow—the cohort type in a public setting, the family type in a private setting.[5]

---

1. Elwood Carlson, *The Lucky Few: Between the Greatest Generation and the Baby Boom* (Dordrecht; London: Springer, 2008), 7.

2. Heinz Bude, "Qualitative Research," in *A Companion to Qualitative Research*, ed. Uwe Flick, Ernst von Kardoff, and Ines Steinke, trans. Bryan Jenner, English (London: Sage Publications, 2004), 109.

3. Carlson, *The Lucky Few*, 8.

4. William Strauss and Neil Howe, *Generations: The History of America's Future, 1584 to 2069* (New York: HarperCollins, 1991), 64. While Strauss and Howe's methodology has been well-received, "a criticism of their work is that it does not adequately consider differences in race, socio-economic class, or other social markers" ("Strauss-Howe Generational Theory," Centre for the Critical Study of Apocalyptic and Millenarian Movements, https://censamm.org/resources/profiles/strauss-howe-generational-theory).

5. Strauss and Howe, *Generations*, 437.

For our purposes we are most interested in societal relationships, hence the focus on "social moments" as generational markers. For example, "dramatic political and economic events such as the stock market crash in 1929, the attack on Pearl Harbor in 1941, the oil shock in the mid-1970s, or the World Trade Center and Pentagon attacks of 2001 changed the ideas and lives of each new generation just coming into adulthood."[6] Such events create a "peer personality," which "distinguishes a generation as a cohesive cohort-group with its own unique biography."[7]

Two types of social moments—secular crises and spiritual awakenings—have demonstrative effects on generation members who "are socialized (during youth and, perhaps, rising adulthood) and begin to recognize the impact of historic events on their social environment."[8] Secular crises occur "when society focuses on re-ordering the outer world of institutions and public behavior; and Spiritual awakenings [occur], when society focuses on changing the inner world of values and private behavior."[9] The most recent social moments of secular crises would be the Depression – World War II Crisis (1932–1945) and the Financial Crisis – War on Terror (2001–2008). The most recent spiritual awakening occurred in 1960s–1970s and was known by various titles including the "Counter-cultural," or "Consciousness Revolution." This spiritual awakening lead Americans to experience "a reshuffling of national life, an amalgam of radical changes in attitudes toward family, language, dress, duty, community, sex, and art."[10]

These two social moments affect each generation differently depending on their life phrase. Strauss and Howe identified those phases as:

- Youth (age 0 to 21), growing, learning, accepting protection and nurture, avoiding harm, acquiring values, as part of the central role of dependence;

6. Carlson, *The Lucky Few*, 8.
7. Strauss and Howe, *Generations*, 64.
8. Strauss and Howe, 71.
9. Strauss and Howe, 71.
10. Strauss and Howe, 72.

- Rising adulthood (age 22 to 43), focusing on working, starting families and livelihoods, serving institutions, testing values as part of the central role of activity;

- Midlife (age 44 to 65), focusing on parenting, teaching, directing institutions, using values as part of leadership;

- Elderhood (age 66 to 87), focusing on supervising, mentoring, passing on value—all as part of the central role of stewardship; [11]

- And more recently some scholars propose "late elderhood" (age 88 to 109) with a central role of "life review," "preservation of self," or "vital involvement."[12]

A generation in each of these phases responds differently to social moments. "Dominant" generations are those who enter adulthood or elderhood during one social moment while "recessive" generations are those entering youth or midlife during those same social moments. These encounters with social moments have a decided effect on cohort personality. "These four generational types recur in fixed order, given one important condition: that society resolves with reasonable success each secular crisis that it encounters." If it doesn't, then the cycle effectively "skips a beat."

Strauss and Howe propose that each generation's location can be plotted on the four-type cycle:

1. A dominant, inner-fixed IDEALIST GENERATION grows up as increasingly indulged youths after a secular crisis; comes of age inspiring a spiritual awakening; fragments into narcissistic rising adults; cultivates principle as moralistic midlifers; and emerges as visionary elders guiding the next secular crisis.

2. A recessive REACTIVE GENERATION grows up as underprotected and criticized youths during a spiritual awakening;

11. Strauss and Howe, 60–61.

12. C. Joanne Grabinski, "Cohorts of the Future," *New Directions for Adult and Continuing Education* 77 (Spring 1998): 74.

matures into risk-taking, alienated rising adults; mellows into pragmatic midlife leaders during a secular crisis; and maintains respect (but less influence) as reclusive elders.

3. A dominant, outer-fixated CIVIC GENERATION grows up as increasingly protected youths after a spiritual awakening; comes of age overcoming a secular crisis; unites into a heroic and achieving cadre of rising adults; sustains that image while building institutions as powerful midlifers; and emerges as busy elders attacked by the next spiritual awakening.

4. A recessive ADAPTIVE GENERATION grows up as overprotected and suffocated youths during a secular crisis; matures into risk-averse, conformist rising adults; produces indecisive midlife arbitrator-leaders during a spiritual awakening; and maintains influence (but less respect) as sensitive elders.[13]

Idealists live "a prophetic lifecycle of vision and values," while Reactives have a "picaresque lifecycle of survival and adventure; Civics a heroic lifecycle of secular achievement and reward; and Adaptives a genteel lifecycle of expertise and amelioration."[14] We can plot our recent generations onto this four-type cycle. The Greatest Generation would be considered a civic generation by Strauss and Howe's criteria. The next cohort, the Silent Generation or Lucky Few, entered a secular crisis as children, so they would be considered adaptive. Baby Boomers were entering adulthood during a social awakening hence they would be considered idealists. By Strauss and Howe's standards, Generation X would be a reactive generation, which means Millennials would be the civic generation, coming of age in a secular crisis. This four-type cycle supports Bude's comment that "generations define themselves by their difference from other generations . . . Generations reproduce themselves in both external and internal opposition."[15]

---

13. Strauss and Howe, *Generations*, 74.
14. Strauss and Howe, 74.
15. Bude, "Qualitative Research," 110.

Six generations can be plotted on American society in the twentieth and twenty-first centuries: the Greatest Generation (those born in 1901–1924 or 1901–1927),[16] the Silent Generation/Lucky Few (1925–1942 or 1928–1945), the Baby Boomer Generation (1943–1960 or 1946–1964), Generation X (1961–1981 or 1965–1980), Millennials (1982–2004 or 1981–1996), Generation Z (born since 2005 or 1997). Of more than 44,000 women religious in the United States as of 2018, representatives can be found from all these generations. The following highlights some of the characteristics of the four generations that comprise the majority of women religious, particularly those who took part in the survey.

## The Silent Generation or the Lucky Few
## (1925–1942 or 1928–1945)

The name is a misnomer. The accomplishments of this generation demonstrate that the collective voice has left an indelible mark on American society. Among those in this generation, we find astronauts like Neil Armstrong, scientists like Carl Sagan, entrepreneurs like Thomas B. Monaghan of Domino's, H. Ross Perot, and Martha Stewart, sports stars like Bart Starr, Gayle Sayers, Joe Namath, Willie Mays, Jack Niklaus and Kathy Whitworth. Poets and authors include Maya Angelou, Alice Walker, and Mary Oliver. Elected officials include Joe Biden, Mitch McConnell, Bernie Sanders, and Nancy Pelosi. In the music and media industry, they were stars: Elvis Presley, the Beatles, Roberta Flack, Janis Joplin, Johnny Cash, Willie Nelson, Tom Brokaw, Barbara Walters, Carol Burnett, Bill Cosby, Julie Andrews, Robert DeNiro, and Leonard Nimoy. In the civil rights movement, the women's movement, and the gay rights movement, they were the leaders. Among these were Martin Luther King Jr., Andrew Young, Malcom X, Robert Kennedy, Cesar Chavez, Harvey Milk, and Gloria Steinem.

This is the generation for whom the effects of the Great Depression and World War II weighed heavily upon their youth and young

---

16. The two date ranges reflect different modes of analysis. The first set of dates is taken from Strauss and Howe, while the second is from the Pew Research Center.

adulthood. As young adults, the Korean War, McCarthyism, and anti-communist fears caused further concern. No wonder Leonard Nimoy would offer, "I'm touched by the idea that when we do things that are useful and helpful—collecting these shards of spirituality—that we may be helping to bring about a healing." To that end, this generation "created the surge of growth in the helping professions (teaching, medicine, ministry, and government) and in public-interest advocacy groups."[17]

In a 1951 *Time Magazine* article, this generation was introduced as a collection of opposites:

> What of today's youth? Some are smoking marijuana; some are dying in Korea. Some are going to college with their wives; some are making $400 a week in television. Some are sure they will be blown to bits by the atom bomb. Some pray. Some are raising the highest towers and running the fastest machines in the world. Some wear blue jeans; some wear Dior gowns. Some want to vote the straight Republican ticket. Some want to fly to the moon.[18]

Owing to the economic insecurity and the Second World War, this generation was sizably smaller than the previous one. With the ongoing Korean War, these young adults feared the draft, but did little to avoid it. The goal of this generation at the time was to find a steady job. With the financial success of this generation today, it would seem their aspirations in 1951 have been largely fulfilled.

> [This generation] came of age during a period of quiet prosperity. Its relatively small size benefited its members—companies needed entry-level workers when they were young adults and managers as they reached middle age. Achieving a middle-class lifestyle seemed easy when the economy was expanding and corporations were feeling generous. This has been the most affluent group of older Americans in history—and likely will remain so, a footnote in the history books.[19]

17. Grabinski, "Cohorts of the Future," 75.

18. "The Younger Generation," *Time* (November 5, 1951), http://content.time.com /time/subscriber/article/0,33009,856950-3,00.html.

19. New Strategist Press, *American Generations: Who They Are & How They Live* (East Patchogue, NY: New Strategist Press, 2018), 27.

While we often think of the Baby Boomers as the instigators of equal rights, the *Time Magazine* article reported that female members of the Silent Generation were actively seeking a life beyond the household.

> American young women are, in many ways, the generation's most serious problem: they are emotional D.P.s [displaced persons]. The granddaughters of the suffragettes, the daughters of the cigarette-and-short-skirt crusaders, they were raised to believe in woman's emancipation, and equality with man. Large numbers of them feel that a home and children alone would be a fate worse than death, and they invade the big cities in search of a career. They ride crowded subways on which men, enjoying equality, do not offer them seats. They compete with men in industry and the arts; and keep up with them, Martini for Martini, at the cocktail parties.[20]

This generation was the first American cohort smaller in size than the proceeding one, which left more opportunities for its members, leading Elwood Carlson to name this group the Lucky Few.[21] Men in this cohort benefited from veterans benefits but served mostly in peacetime. They had ample employment opportunities and often retired early. Women of this cohort tended to marry earlier than previous cohorts but also received more educational opportunities than earlier generations.

Of the 31,535 women religious who participated in the Retirement Fund for Religious in 2019,[22] nearly 20,000 were 75–94 years of age. In light of these numbers, we can estimate that 62 percent of women religious in the United States belong to the Silent Generation. Considering that their ranks include Sisters Thea Bowman, FSPA, Sandra Schneiders, IHM, Jeannine Gramick, SSND, Dianne Bergant, CSA, Elizabeth A. Johnson, CSJ, Joan Chittister, OSB, and Helen Prejean, CSJ, we would hardly think of this generation as "silent." Indeed, it is we who are the lucky few who have benefited from their wisdom, service, and inspiration.

20. "The Younger Generation," *Time* (November 5, 1951), http://content.time.com/time/subscriber/article/0,33009,856950-3,00.html.

21. Carlson, *The Lucky Few*

22. National Religious Retirement Office, "Statistical Report 2019" (Washington DC, 2019).

## The Baby Boomers (1943–60 or 1946–64)

Until 2019, when the Millennials surpassed it, the Baby Boomer generation was the largest in American history. At its peak, more than 78 million comprised the cohort between the Silent Generation/ Lucky Few and Generation X.[23] Its sheer size made it a formidable group, but coupled with its corporate personality, Baby Boomers have greatly outshone the generational cohorts on either side of them. This was the first generation to grow up nurtured by Dr. Spock (published in 1946), safe from polio (the vaccine was discovered in 1954) and entertained by television in their homes.

While the Pew Research Center among others begins the "boom" with the first wave of post-World War II babies, Strauss and Howe begin with 1943, the turning point of the World War II, since it fits with their generational theory of social moments.

> They started out as feed-on-demand Dr. Spock babies, then grew into the indulged Beaver Cleavers of the '50s, then the college and inner-city rioters of the late '60s, and finally ended up as the young family-values moms and dads of the '80s.[24]

Their size and the widespread access to television made them the focus of much economic attention.

> Baby Boomers were the first to be raised in front of the TV during the Cold War and Vietnam. They remember the deaths of JFK, RFK and MLK Jr. Images and memories of protests against the war and for Civil Rights, Watergate, *M\*A\*S\*H*, *All in the Family* and Elvis have been burned upon their collective consciousness. Boomers have been driving the engine of the American economy since they came

---

23. "The Baby Boomer label is drawn from the great spike in fertility that began in 1946, right after the end of World War II, and ended almost as abruptly in 1964, around the time the birth control pill went on the market. It's a classic example of a demography-driven name" (Paul Taylor and Scott Keeter, "Millennials: Confident. Connected. Open to Change," *Pew Research Center* [February 2010], 4, https://assets.pewresearch.org/wp-content/uploads/sites/3/2010/10/millennials-confident-connected-open-to-change.pdf).

24. Neil Howe, "The Boom Generation, 'What a Long Strange Trip' (Part 4 of 7)," *Forbes* (August 20, 2014), https://www.forbes.com/sites/neilhowe/2014/08/20/the-boom-generation-what-a-long-strange-trip-part-4-of-7/#584f978f6197.

of age in the 1970s. Since they made up the bulk of the 18–49 year old demographic group, they have been the focus of practically everything, including virtually all marketing and advertising as well as books, movies, and TV shows. It truly was all about them.[25]

Indeed, many of this generation shared a particular idyllic experience of the American dream in their youth followed by a young adult upheaval, much of their own making.[26]

The year was 1969. Across the nation in upstate New York, the Woodstock Festival would make history, and, in New York City, the Stonewall Rebellion marked the beginning of the gay rights movement. A year earlier, Dr. Martin Luther King Jr. and Robert Kennedy had been assassinated. Riots, protests, and images of war flooded television screens.

> The sense of unrest was pervasive in many parts of the world. Nearly three hundred thousand boat people fled Vietnam; the Cultural Revolution was underway in the People's Republic of China; there was rioting in France, Germany, and Italy and a revolution in Czechoslovakia. Not surprisingly, growing up amid these events caused many Boomers, regardless of political persuasion, to conclude that the world was not working all that well—that it needed to be changed.[27]

All was not right. And this generation protested that out loud. They "remained a deliberate antithesis to everything G.I.: spiritualism over science, gratification over patience, negativism over positivism, fractiousness over conformity, rage over friendliness, self over community."[28] Henri Nouwen would comment on this generational angst.

25. Matt Thornhill and John Martin, *Boomer Consumer: Ten New Rules for Marketing to America's Largest, Wealthiest and Most Influential Group* (Great Falls, VA: Linx Corp, 2007), 13.

26. Much of the writing and research on the Baby Boom generation pays little attention to the experience of Black and Latinx Boomers for whom access to education, jobs, and now retirement lagged significantly behind White Boomers. See Melvin Delgado, *Baby Boomers of Color: Implications for Social Work Policy and Practice* (New York: Columbia University Press, 2015).

27. Tamara J. Erickson, *What's Next, Gen X? Keeping Up, Moving Ahead, and Getting the Career You Want* (Boston: Harvard Business Review Press, 2010), 50.

28. Strauss and Howe, *Generations*, 302.

No authority, no institution, no outer concrete reality has the power to relieve them of their anxiety and loneliness and make them free. Therefore, the only way is the inward way. If there is nothing "out there" or "up there," perhaps there is something meaningful, something solid "in there."[29]

But as Delgado writes in *Baby Boomers of Color*, many of this generation may have been called by the same name, but they were often vastly different as individuals.

> Variations within the boomer generation are greater than the variations between generations, making broad generalizations difficult, if not dangerous to make . . . There may be an extreme, for example, between a boomer who served in the Vietnam War and the one who protested America's military engagement there.[30]

As this generation aged, the hot ideals of youth met the cool reality of adulthood. Fast forward to 1984. Ronald Reagan is running for re-election as president, and the average boomer is now in midlife. According to *New York Times* polls at the time, it is these Boomers who will re-elect Reagan, largely based on their economic concerns. The article reported one boomer as stating, "I guess I have more to lose now. I've gotten attached to my creature comforts. I've started having a vested interest in the status quo, because I am the status quo."[31] It would seem the hippie was dead; long live the yuppie (young urban professional): "The rise of the original Yuppies in the early eighties coincided with the exact point at which the Boomers decided to throw in the towel on saving the world and began, instead, doing lucrative consulting work for Union Carbide."[32] The Boomer had become "the Man"!

Indeed, Boomers became titans of technology, politics, finance, sports, and the arts. Think Steve Jobs, Bill Gates, Donald Trump, Amy Klobuchar, Oprah Winfrey, Meryl Streep, Denzel Washington,

---

29. Henri J. M. Nouwen, *The Wound Healer: Ministry in Contemporary Society* (New York: Doubleday, 1972), 28.

30. Delgado, *Baby Boomers of Color*, 8.

31. Steven V. Roberts, "Making Mark on Politics, 'Baby Boomers' Appear to Rally Round Reagan," *New York Times* (November 5, 1984), 18.

32. Erickson, *What's Next, Gen X?*, 51.

Douglas Adams, Tim O'Brian, Walter Payton, Johnny Bench, Bruce Springsteen, James Taylor, and Carly Simon. But being part of a large, talented cohort has its disadvantages. As this generation has entered retirement age, "millions have postponed retirement because the Great Recession devastated their savings."[33] A 2008 Pew Research study reported that members of the Baby Boom generation were much more likely to be "in a funk" about the quality of their life.

> It's . . . possible that the seeds of the boomers' discontent were planted long ago—back when they were young and their generation reveled in the culture of youth. Boomers are a big, complicated generation, but one thing can be said about them without fear of contradiction: They are no longer young.[34]

Of the women religious in the United States, approximately 32 percent are from the Boomer Generation. Unlike many of their generational peers who have capitulated, these sisters continue to work toward a better, more equal world and church. Many are social activists, theologians, and environmentalists, including Sisters Simone Campbell, SSS, Maureen Fiedler, SL, Barbara E. Reid, OP, Ilia Delio, OSF, Christine Schenk, CSJ, Nancy Sylvester, IHM, and Sharon Zayac, OP.

## Generation X (1961–1981 or 1965–1980)

Though its members argue that "X is more a sensibility than a rigidly confined demographic," demographers proposed a range of dates.[35] Following Strauss and Howe's cohort boundaries, this generation begins in 1961 and concludes in 1981. Pew Research studies start the cohort in 1965 when birth control became more

---

33. New Strategist Press, *American Generations*, 22.

34. "Baby Boomers: The Gloomiest Generation," *Pew Research Center Social and Demographic Trends* (June 25, 2008), https://www.pewsocialtrends.org/2008/06/25/baby-boomers-the-gloomiest-generation.

35. Jeff Gordinier, *X Saves the World: How Generation X Got the Shaft but Can Still Keep Everything from Sucking* (New York: Penguin Books, 2008), 22.

readily available, thus effectively ending the Baby Boom. The New Strategist reports a rather positive picture of this generation:

> This is a well-educated, media-savvy generation. The small size of Generation X has made it relatively easy to overlook—and it is painfully aware of this fact. When Gen Xers were teenagers, attention focused on the Baby Boom. Businesses retailored youth-oriented offerings to suit the tastes of Boomer families. Now that Generation X has entered middle age, businesses are focusing on young adults to capture the spending of the large Millennial generation.[36]

Others have a decidedly different take. Nancy Smith of the Washington Post described this cohort as "the generation born after. Born after 1960, after you, after it all happened."[37] *New York Times* reporter Felicity Barringer called it "the lost generation, an army of aging Bart Simpsons, possibly armed and dangerous."[38] It was a generation marked by "low test scores, high rates of crime, suicide, and substance abuse."[39]

> These were the babies of 1961, 8-year-olds of Woodstock, 13-year-olds of Watergate, 18-year-olds of energy crisis and hostage humiliation—and 29-year-olds when a 1990 Time cover story defined this generation as post-Boom "twenty-somethings."[40]

The moniker "Generation X" had been variously used since the 1950s. "Social commentators have recycled the term Generation X every ten or fifteen years to express their anxieties about the younger generation."[41] It seems it was this generation itself that should have been anxious. At the time of Strauss and Howe's book, this cohort

---

36. New Strategist Press, *American Generations*, 5.

37. Quoted in Strauss and Howe, *Generations*, 317.

38. Felicity Barringer, "Ideas & Trends; What IS Youth Coming To?," *New York Times*, August 19, 1990, 4.

39. New Strategist Press, *American Generations*, 317.

40. Strauss and Howe, *Generations*, 317.

41. Jon C. Pennington, PhD, "A Guide to Marketing Issues Related to Generation X," https://www.scribd.com/document/96989995/Generation-X-Marketing-Report.

was "the most aborted generation in American history. After rising sharply during the late 1960s and 1970s, the abortion rate climbed by another 80 percent during the first six years (1973–1979) after the Supreme Court's *Roe v. Wade* decision."[42]

Sandwiched between two huge cohorts on either side, the sixty-five million American Gen Xers seemed "doomed to suffer a shared case of middle-child syndrome, an eight-figure-strong army of Jan Bradys."[43] But the corporate portrait of this generation is one of resilience and adaptability. Drawn from various reports, Gen Xers have been described as

- more tolerant of diversity than the previous generations;

- the first generation of Americans whom other people took pills not to have;

- the grown-up "latchkey kids" who delayed life commitments and looked for a world and church that was stable;

- those who took on adult responsibilities at an early age because of absent parents;

- those who define family without relying on blood ties, because of the high experience of divorce;

- those who trust friendship over all other relationships;

- those who are slow to commit;

- those who long for institutions to live up to their claims;

- those who are often considered a cynical generation, growing out of their distrust of institutions, particularly marriage and government.

In his book, *X Saves the World: How Generation X Got the Shaft but Can Still Keep Everything from Sucking*, Jeff Gordinier muses that "Xers have to contend with: a playing field that has not only

---

42. Strauss and Howe, *Generations*, 324.

43. Alex Williams, "Actually, Gen X Did Sell Out, Invent All Things Millennial, and Cause Everything," *New York Times (online)* (May 14, 2019).

shifted beyond recognition but has also taken on shifting as its very business model."[44]

With at least one television in their homes, world events became personal in a very different way than for previous generations. As Michael Kruse reports in "Contemplating the Intersection of Work, the Global Economy, and Ethics":

> In an effort to interest children in science and technology, NASA teamed up the education leaders to put a school teacher in space. Teachers around the nation had their classes follow the preparation of educator Crista McAuliffe, the first private citizen to go into space, as she prepared for the January 1986 lift off. Generation X occupied all grade levels from high school down through kindergarten, with kindergarten being the trailing edge of the generation. When the 28th came, televisions in schools all around the nation were tuned in to watch the historic accomplishment. Instead, they witnessed the horrifying explosion of the spacecraft shortly after lift off. Most Baby Boomers can point to the assassination of President Kennedy as a defining moment in their lives. For most Generation Xers it was the Challenger explosion which they probably experienced more intensely than did most adults. It was just one more reminder of how everything from families to federal governments was an unsafe place for your hopes.[45]

The live broadcast of the Challenger disaster devasted viewers, particularly the young. As Jessica Mesman reflects:

> You were, as a child in the mid-'80s, encouraged to be invested in McAuliffe's space odyssey. She was going to teach us from space! A woman was ushering in the promised era of civilian space travel. The future was upon us. Instead, the Challenger tragedy resulted in widespread NASA layoffs and a chilling of the space program in general. The promised future didn't arrive—or rather, it didn't look anything like they promised.[46]

---

44. Gordinier, *X Saves the World*, xxix.

45. *Kruse Kronicle*, "Contemplating the Intersection of Work, the Global Economy, and Ethics," blog entry by Michael Kruse, December 2, 2005, https://krusekronicle .typepad.com/kruse_kronicle/2005/12/generation_x_19.html#.XrG8uy-ZOlE.

46. Jessica Mesman, "Reality Bites Again: The Dashed Dreams of Gen X Women: For Gen X Women, There's a Disconnect between Expectations and Reality," *U.S. Catholic*

As they became young adults, "Generation X also bridged pre-digital and digital cultures, liberal and neo-conservative political swings, material abundance and economic hardship, social engagement and cynical withdrawal, and class-based and non-class-based radicalism (e.g., environmental issues, LGBT rights)."[47] In addition, as Strauss and Howe noted, "No previous American generation has arrived in the workforce paying such high tax rates on their first dollar of earnings, bearing such large high-interest student loans, facing so many anti-youth 'two-tier' wage and benefit scales, or encountering such high housing costs relative to income."[48] This would be the first modern American generation that at age forty had a lower standard of living than their parents had enjoyed at that age.[49]

But as they moved into mid-life, prospects looked more hopeful. Despite the crises and economic uncertainties, Gen Xers have done alright for themselves. Look at Elon Musk, Sergey Brin and Larry Page of Google, and Jack Dorsey of Twitter. Not to mention Jay-Z, P. Diddy, Missy Elliot, Elizabeth Wurtzel, Lin-Manuel Miranda, Kamala Harris, Andrew Yang, Paul Ryan, and Beto O'Rourke. If you adhere to the Strauss and Howe timeline, then we get Barack Obama, Michael J. Fox, Tom Cruise, Eddie Murphy, and Whitney Houston. Not bad for a "lame" generation.

Before "woke" was a thing, Gen Xers were on their way to "woke."

> We did feel like we had imbibed the civil rights, and feminist and gay rights changes from our earliest experience, and were able to try putting the theory into practice with less of the self-consciousness of a generation for whom these were very definitely changes. To those of us who had been carefully and deliberately educated in those traditions, they could seem like self-evident truths, solid gains we might be able to take for granted, a reality that was ours to build

---

(April 27, 2020), https://www.uscatholic.org/articles/202004/reality-bites-again-dashed-dreams-gen-x-women-32042.

47. Stephen Katz, "Generation X: A Critical Sociological Perspective," *Generations: Journal of the American Society on Aging* 41 (Fall 2017): 16.

48. Strauss and Howe, *Generations*, 409.

49. New Strategist Press, *American Generations*, 410.

on. I think Gen X liberals felt a special pride and ownership in the legalization of gay marriage and the election of the first black president—and now feel a particular horror that it might all be getting dismantled in a way we never foresaw.[50]

Their Boomer parents may have marched for Civil Rights, but these were the children to desegregate classrooms. Like the generation before them, some Gen Xers saw the power imbalances and fought against them.

Generation X may be socially active, but most of their activism is done outside a religious context. A 2012 Pew Forum on Religion and Public Life reported that a third of Gen-Xers described themselves as "nones," not fitting any religious category. The early Catholic members of Generation X were poorly catechized; the later informed more on social justice than on church doctrine. Gen Xer Kaya Oakes described:

> Some Catholics of my generation grew up believing that twirling scarves around the altar was a sanctioned part of the liturgy. Bay Area Boomers were not interested in orthodoxy, and they raised a generation of kids who, eventually, were not even interested in faith.[51]

Despite that, the Spirit still calls. About 5.4 percent of Catholic sisters today are Gen Xers including Deborah Marie Borneman, SSCM, Maria Cimperman, RSCJ, Kristin Matthes, SNDdeN, and Teresa Maya, CCVI.

## Millennials (1982–2004 or 1981–1996)

Unlike the generation before them, "Millennials are children their parents wanted to have!"[52] In fact, this is the generation whose parents were dubbed "helicopter" for their constant hovering. By the

---

50. Katz, "Generation X," 18.

51. Kaya Oakes, "Faithless Generation? In Search of Other Gen-X Catholics," *Commonweal* (October 10, 2013), https://www.commonwealmagazine.org/faithless-generation.

52. Grabinski, "Cohorts of the Future," 81.

Strauss and Howe criteria, those born between 1982 and 2004 are part of this cohort. The Pew Research Center dates this generation between 1981 and 1996. Strauss and Howe named the group "millennial" since it would be the first cohort to come of age in the new millennium.[53] In their 1991 publication, *Generations: The History of America's Future, 1584 to 2069*, the authors anticipated that this cohort would be decidedly different than the previous Gen Xers.

> Meet the Millennials, born in or after 1982—the "Babies on Board" of the early Reagan years, the "Have You Hugged Your Child Today?" sixth graders of the early Clinton years, the teens of Columbine, and . . . the much-touted high school Class of 2000.[54]

And in the first month of their sophomore year of college, terrorists hijacked airplanes and struck the World Trade Towers and the Pentagon. Their lives and ours would never be the same.

Despite the tragedies that marked their childhood and early adulthood, including the Gulf Wars and the Recession of 2008, this generation demonstrates a remarkable affability. "Not as selfish or narcissistic, eschewing risk-taking and profanity, Millennials were more cohesive and hopeful. Not apathetic or antisocial, they were comfortable as team players. Participation and engagement were rewarded. They respected the rules laid out before them, they trusted their parents, and they looked down on disruptive behavior."[55]

As many of this generation grew from adored children to overprotected adolescents, some negative aspects of its corporate personality made for media fodder.[56] In a May 2013 *Time Magazine*

---

53. A 1993 editorial in *Ad Age* called this cohort "Generation Y," since it followed Generation X, but the name didn't stick.

54. Neil Howe and William Strauss, *Millennials Rising: The Next Great Generation* (New York: Random House, 2000), 4.

55. Reid Cramer, "Millennials Rising: Coming of Age in the Wake of the Great Recession," New America (2014): 11–12, https://d1y8sb8igg2f8e.cloudfront.net/documents/Millennials_Rising_Coming_of_Age_in_the_Wake_of_the_Great_Recession_hPH6qs7.pdf.

56. Some scholars "have suggested that discussion of 'Millennials' tends to focus on mostly white youth from suburban areas, ignoring the unique experience of immigrants

cover story, the Millennials were described as narcissistic, lazy, and fame obsessed.[57]

However, Millennials are not a monolith. Multiple cohorts can be found within the standard category, including what one author called the "Internet Pioneers," those born between 1991 and 1995. These are the folks who have experienced global economic collapse, the war on terror, and tremendous developments in technology. Myers describes another side of some Millennials:

- They are confidently empowered, but do not consider themselves to be entitled.

- They are focused on themselves, but care deeply about their families and their friends, which is sometimes an imposing responsibility.

- They have opinions and respect the opinions of others, and have little patience or tolerance for uninformed viewpoints.

- They expect to be given the freedom and power to manage their lives, yet seek out and consider the advice of others.

- They are perfectionists who strive to achieve, assuming they have the ability and potential.

- They question the rules but mostly live within them.

- They accept and embrace diversity, not as an aspiration, but as an accepted reality.[58]

---

and minorities" (Douglas Main, "Who Are the Millennials?," *Live Science* [September 8, 2017], https://www.livescience.com/38061-millennials-generation-y.html).

57. "Millennials got so many participation trophies growing up that a recent study showed that 40 percent believe they should be promoted every two years, regardless of performance. . . . They're so convinced of their own greatness that the National Study of Youth and Religion found the guiding morality of 60 percent of millennials in any situation is that they'll just be able to feel what's right" (Joel Stein, "Millennials: The Me Me Me Generation," *Time Magazine* [May 20, 2013], https://time.com/247/millennials-the-me-me-me-generation).

58. See Jack Myers, *Hooked Up: A New Generation's Surprising Take on Sex, Politics and Saving the World* (Stamford, CT: York House Press, 2012).

As others have noted, millennials, in many ways, mirror their G.I. generation great grandparents. "They will be the working-together scouts, warriors, and heroes in rising adulthood who, as powerful civic leaders in their midlife and later years, will build and restructure societal institutions."[59] But this generation has some marked differences from that of the G.I. cohort, Silent Generation, and Baby Boomers that proceeded them. Millennials are more racially diverse than previous generations. "Racial and ethnic minorities make up 39 percent of Millennials and 38 percent of Gen Xers, compared with just 27 percent of Baby Boomers and 20 percent of the Silent generation."[60] Additionally, this generation is more tolerant of difference.

> Whether the topic is religious affiliation, gay marriage, or political leanings, Millennial attitudes are distinctly more liberal than those of older generations. . . . If the attitudes of Millennials continue into middle and old age, then American society will become more scientifically oriented, politically liberal, and socially tolerant in the years ahead.[61]

Another striking difference between this generation and previous ones is its use of technology. This is the first generation to grow up in a globally-connected world community via the Internet, the cell phone, and social media. The availability of digital communication tools and the rise of social media have led some to dub this cohort "Digital Natives."

But post-graduation, the job market hasn't been very welcoming, only partially due to the Millennial corporate personality. An MTV poll, "No Collar Workers," reported that employed Millennials "want flexible work schedules, more 'me time' on the job, and nearly nonstop feedback and career advice from managers."[62] The

---

59. Grabinski, "Cohorts of the Future," 82.
60. Taylor and Keeter, "Millennials."
61. New Strategist Press, *American Generations*, 23.
62. Dan Schawbel, "Millennials vs. Baby Boomers: Who Would You Rather Hire?," *Time Business* (March 29, 2012), https://business.time.com/2012/03/29/millennials-vs-baby-boomers-who-would-you-rather-hire/#ixzz1rpO8inUE.

sheer size of the Millennial generation meant increased competition for jobs, and many "embarked on their careers in the midst of the Great Recession and its aftermath. They are struggling to get ahead and burdened by student loan debt. Because of their financial problems, Millennials have postponed marriage, delayed childbearing, and resisted buying homes."[63] The economic insecurity has spurred many Millennials to return to their parents' home.[64]

This return to the nest doesn't seem to bother Millennials who are supportive of multigenerational living.[65] Millennials go along and get along, especially with their elders. "For a nation whose population is rapidly going gray, that could prove to be a most welcome character trait."[66]

Millennials grew up surrounded by environmental advocacy, which may partially explain why they "are supportive of stricter environmental laws, more likely to attribute global warming to human activity, and likely to favor environmentally friendly policies such as green energy development and economic incentives for sustainability."[67]

Millennials are making their mark in business, sports, the arts, and politics. Here are some noteworthy members of this cohort: Alexandria Ocasio-Cortez, Jared Kushner, Priscilla Chan, Mark Zuckerberg, LeBron James, Edward Snowden, LeAnn Rimes, Jason Reynolds, Serena Williams, Peter Buttigieg, Chance the Rapper, and Eli Manning.

Though some of the older generations accuse Millennials of worshipping at the altar of social media, in reality their religious sensibilities are more complex. While almost a quarter of young

---

63. New Strategist Press, *American Generations*, 5.

64. "Thanks to student loan debt, rising rents and stagnant wages, more millennials are living at home with their parents than at any other point this century. More than one in five adults, or 22 percent of millennial Americans, are either staying home or returning to childhood bedrooms," writes Sarah Min. "More millennials are living at home than at any other time this century," CBS News (May 10, 2019), https://www.cbsnews.com/news/more-millennials-are-living-at-home-than-at-any-other-time-this-century.

65. New Strategist Press, *American Generations*, 57.

66. Taylor and Keeter, "Millennials."

67. Iman Naderi and Eric Van Steenburg, "Me First, Then the Environment: Young Millennials as Green Consumers," *Young Consumers* 19 (2018): 6.

adults surveyed report the religious affiliation as "none," more than 50 percent of Millennials believe in the existence of God.[68] Interestingly, more than half of Catholic Millennials surveyed said that their religion was important to them. But though fewer Millennials may affiliate with organized religion, those that do commit fully. This intensity of religious commitment is evident in the growing number of Millennial Catholics who are entering religious life. According to the 2020 survey by the Center for Applied Research in the Apostolate (CARA) on "Recent Vocations to Religious Life: A Report for the National Religious Vocation Conference,"

> Almost half of those in initial formation are under age 30, an increase from the 43 percent who were under age 30 in 2009. Nearly three-fourths of those in initial formation are part of the Millennial Generation (born in the 1980s or 1990s) and another 6 percent, born in 2000 or later, could be considered part of the emerging next generation of young adults.[69]

Unlike the few Gen Xers in community with them, Millennial sisters are much more likely to be fully participative in congregational life, whether soloing in the choir, speaking up at assembly, or freely disagreeing with their Silent Generation sisters. As the authors of a *New Generation of Catholic Sisters* note of this cohort:

> [They] are more likely to exhibit high self-esteem, whether or not it is warranted. The *average* millennial woman scored higher on a self-esteem scale than *three-fourths* of women did a generation ago.[70]

Part of the self-confidence demonstrated by these sisters likely finds its roots in Giving Voice, the self-initiated organization of sisters under fifty years of age. Not only did the Gen X and millen-

---

68. Taylor and Keeter, "Millennials," 9.

69. "Recent Vocations to Religious Life: A Report for the National Religious Vocation Conference: Executive Report" (Washington, DC: Center for Applied Research in the Apostolate, 2020), 4.

70. Mary Johnson, SNDdeN, Patricia Wittberg, SC, and Mary L. Gautier, *New Generations of Catholic Sisters: The Challenge of Diversity* (Oxford: Oxford University Press, 2014), 134.

nial members of Giving Voice prepare the publication *In Our Own Words: Religious Life in a Changing World* (Collegeville, MN: Liturgical Press, 2018), but authors and editors then went on a public tour engaging with sisters and communities about their emerging vision of religious life. At a time when the future of religious life seems uncertain, the Millennial sisters among us deserve a trophy for showing up. They make up less than 4 percent of women religious in the United States whose median age is over seventy-five years. To paraphrase an expression likely familiar only to Gen Xers and Millennials, "the force is strong in these ones."

## Conclusion

> Each of us moves with the men [and women] of our generation, submerged in the great anonymous multitude, and save for the final individual nucleus of our life, to ask ourselves to which generation we belong is, in large measure, to ask who we are.
>
> —Julián Marías (1914–2005)[71]

In generational terms, we know where we belong. And we have definite opinions about what makes us different from the cohorts on our left and our right. The differences among generations are likely, as Strauss and Howe proposed, the result of the life stage of each generation at moments of a secular crisis and a spiritual awakening. A 2016 Pew Research Center study, "Americans Name the 10 Most Significant Historic Events in Their Lifetimes," seems to confirm this.

> The survey finds that Americans are primarily bound together by their generation and the major events that occurred during their formative years. For the oldest Americans, the Silent and Greatest generations, that unifying event is World War II. For Baby Boomers, the assassination of John F. Kennedy and the Vietnam War are defining moments. For Millennials and Gen Xers, the 9/11 terror attacks

---

71. Julián Marías, *Generations: A Historical Method*, trans. Harold C. Raley (Tuscaloosa, AL: University of Alabama Press, 1970), 106.

and the Obama election leads the list by a greater margin than for other generations.[72]

The timing of the event is only one aspect considered. If the cohort identifies with the event it is ranked more significantly. "Millennials also are unique in that five of their top 10 events—the Sandy Hook and Orlando/Pulse nightclub shootings, the death of Osama bin Laden, the Boston Marathon bombing and the Great Recession—appear in no other generation's top 10 list."[73] African Americans were the only group to rank Obama's election higher than the September 11 terrorist attacks. Among the racial cohorts of Whites, Blacks, and Hispanics, Blacks were also the only cohort to rank the civil rights movement and the assassination of Dr. Martin Luther King Jr. in their top ten. Hispanics were the only racial cohort to list the Orland Pulse Night Club massacre and Hurricane Katrina in their top ten significant events.[74]

As Marías recognized, our identity is born out of the life events that surround us. To ask an individual where he or she was when . . . (fill in the blank) happened is to gain a good sense of the generation to which he or she belongs. But cohort identity can stretch beyond the general corporate personality of a group informed by life-changing events in their young adulthood. Much of the generational analysis discussed in this chapter reflects only the United States context and often only the experience of middle-income white folks. As discussed above, Black Americans rate historical events differently because some of those events impacted them personally. Ninety percent of the victims in the Pulse Night Club massacre

72. Claudia Deane, Maeve Duggan, and Rich Morin, "Americans Name the 10 Most Significant Historic Events in Their Lifetimes: 9/11, Obama Election and the Tech Revolution among Those with Greatest Impact on the Country," *Pew Research Center* (December 2016), 3.

73. "While these data cannot explain why Latinos disproportionately see the Orlando/Pulse mass shooting as historically significant, the circumstances of the attack provide some clues. The attack occurred on the night that Pulse, a popular nightclub, was hosting a 'Latin Night' celebration, and counts immediately after the tragedy indicate that 90% of the 49 murder victims were Latino," explained Deane, Duggan, and Morin, "Americans Name," 3.

74. Deane, Duggan, and Morin, "Americans Name," 9.

were Latinx, so it is not surprising that that horror is ranked as more significant by Hispanic survey participants than members of other groups.

Generational generalities give us a broad portrait of the age cohort to which we belong, but it's more like a Picasso painting than an Annie Leibovitz photograph. In the context of our religious life, what these generational differences do is remind us that, while we may all be members of our congregations, we do not all come from the same experience, speaking a familiar life vocabulary, or holding as self-evident the same truths. This is especially the case when we speak about our visions and hopes for the church. In the next chapter, we will explore the orienting ecclesiologies evident among the different age cohorts as culled from the survey responses.

# Chapter Three

## *Orienting Ecclesiologies*

## The Formative Experience of Church for Cohort Identity

### Introduction

> I do not think, sir, you have any right to command me, merely because you are older than I, or because you have seen more of the world than I have; your claim to superiority depends on the use you have made of your time and experience.
>
> —Charlotte Brontë, *Jane Eyre*

Members of each age cohort surveyed brought their experience of the church and religious life to bear on their survey answers. In order to contextualize their answers, in this chapter, we will explore the ecclesial backdrops of the three age cohorts—elders, middletons, and youngers—which likely impacted how they envisioned God and understood their faith. As Strauss and Howe noted, our sense of self is affected by the secular crises and spiritual awakenings that we encounter, particularly in young adulthood. For those in the oldest cohort, 78 percent made their profession before 1975 having experienced both a pre- and post-Second Vatican Council church. Three-quarters of those aged 45–64 made their first profession between 1976 and 2000, a span of time that covers the majority of the pontificate of John Paul II. Nearly all of those ages 25–44 made their first profession between 2001 and 2015, in a church scarred by the clergy abuse crisis and longing for the balm of Pope

Francis. A brief description of the church in which the majority of each cohort "came of age" provides a context in which to ponder their responses to the survey questions.

## In Which Church?

In *New Wineskins*, Sandra Schneiders describes religious profession as a formal, solemn, and public act. "By making public profession the religious assumes the responsibility to live religious life in the Church and to be held accountable for how he or she carries out that responsibility."[1] "In the Church"—and therein lies some of the conflict among sisters of different age cohorts in community.

> There are real generational differences in perception and attitude between millennial and post-Vatican II entrants and older entrants, differences that manifest themselves most readily to vocation and formation personnel. But they soon become apparent in community living, communal prayer, and ministry settings as well, and must be faced.[2]

Different ecclesiologies are at work today. For some, the growing obstinacy of the church hierarchy when it comes to any issues dealing with women and their voice and power in the church, coupled with the actual experience of abuse and oppression by pastors, has left the once hopeful committed Vatican II religious alienated and angry. The church that for a bright moment was "the people of God" has been entrenched and fortified into a renewed bastion of patriarchy.

But for many professed in the last thirty years, the church has been our only access to spiritual growth. Most have never experienced a Catholic culture as it existed prior to Vatican II. We didn't have practices such as adoration, first Fridays, and novenas. The

---

1. Sandra Schneiders, *New Wineskins: Re-Imaging Religious Life Today* (Mahwah, NJ: Paulist Press, 1986), 59.

2. Mary Johnson, SNDdeN, Patricia Wittberg, SC, and Mary L. Gautier, *New Generations of Catholic Sisters: The Challenge of Diversity* (Oxford: Oxford University Press, 2014), 76.

prayers, practices, obligations and celebrations experienced by the vast majority of older religious are unknown to most of us professed in the last few decades.

> Variations in Catholics' identification with the faith and their commitment to the Church are rooted in a number of conditions. Chief among these is the generation (or birth cohort) to which a Catholic belongs . . . Catholics who are born at different points in history learn to approach the faith and the Church in different ways.[3]

In what follows, we briefly highlight three periods of the US Catholic Church—immediately following Vatican II, under Pope John Paul II, and a half century after the Second Vatican Council—so as to situate each of the age cohorts' descriptions of the Divine within their orienting ecclesiology. But first, a portrait of the Catholic Church on the eve of Vatican II as painted by Sandra Schneiders:

> In the United States [the ever-widening gulf between the Church and the world] was expressed in the construction of a quasi-ghetto which was intended to protect Catholics, from birth in a Catholic hospital to burial in a Catholic cemetery, from persecution and contagion but which also isolated them from full participation in society. Public school kids, false worship with Protestant heretics, contaminating contacts with faithless Jews and pagans, mixed marriages, forbidden books and movies, and much else that was part of modern American culture was to be sedulously avoided by good Catholics. We were recruited early for the Army of Youth flying the standard of truth and inducted into the ranks of a Church militant at war with the rest of the world. We bought pagan babies and said the family rosary to convert the rest of the world to the truth possessed only by the Catholic Church outside of which there was no salvation. But by the 1950s, not co- incidentally the high point of the influx of young women into Religious Life, it was becoming increasingly clear that the Church was not winning its war against the modern world, even in the hearts of many of the faithful who were as modern as they were Catholic . . . Not quite a hundred years after Pius IX had slammed

---

3. William V. D'Antonio et al., *American Catholics Today: New Realities of Their Faith and Their Church* (Lanham, MD: Rowman & Littlefield, 2007), 11.

the Church's door on modernity, John XXIII threw open the windows of the Church on the modern world by calling the second Vatican Council.[4]

## The Church in the Modern World: Vatican II Sisters

I listened with rapt attention as Sr. Nora retold her experience of unintended civil disobedience. It was the late 60s, and Nora was the local superior. She was still in the habit and still trying to figure out the implications of Vatican II as the documents slowly made their way to the rank and file. She had returned from school one day to learn that two of the other sisters had gone downtown to a civil rights rally. Fearing they would meet with trouble, she hurried after them. She paints a vivid picture of her five-foot two inch habited-self running into the fray. Just as she arrived, the police began sweeping up the protesters and loading them onto awaiting school buses. Having been caught up in the crowd, poor Nora suddenly found herself amidst the protesters being herded onto the bus. Now what would she do? Absolutely bewildered, she sat down on the bus and turned to look at the window. There across the street stood her sisters whose shock at seeing their superior under arrest was likely only slightly less than Nora's own shock at being arrested.

### A Time to Experiment

Such was the 1960s. Immediately after Vatican II, civil unrest rocked the United States and elsewhere. Institutions of education, industry, government, and religion were all undergoing their own crucible. For religious congregations, the provocation was *Perfectae Caritatis* (Decree on the Adaptation and Renewal of Religious Life). Pope Paul VI had mandated the norms for implementation of the document, encouraging religious congregations to speedily adopt the recommendations of the Council, particularly through their general chapters.

4. Sandra Schneiders, "Vowed Religious Life," Presentation to the IHM Congregation (June 14, 2009), 16, https://anunslife.org/sites/www.anunslife.org/files/assets/blogimages/SSchneidersLecture2009.pdf.

This general chapter has the right to alter certain norms of the constitutions . . . as an experiment, as long as the purpose, nature and character of the institute are preserved. Experiments contrary to the common law, provided they are to be undertaken prudently, will be willingly permitted by the Holy See as the occasions call for them.

These experiments can be prolonged until the next Ordinary general chapter, which will have the faculty to continue them further but not beyond the chapter immediately following.[5]

For those of us who have come after, it's hard to imagine that it took a chapter enactment to enable sisters to wear wristwatches! Even small changes had large implications. Vatican II removed the special status of religious who now no longer had "a higher calling." Young women who had been raised on the *Baltimore Catechism*, who had entered to "save their souls," who had been forbidden to witness their sibling's marriage, or to hold an infant, or to attend a parent's funeral were now told: "Never mind." As Fr. Thomas Reese, SJ, a seminarian during Vatican II explained, "One week, if you eat meat on Friday, you're going to go to hell. The following week, you can have meat on Friday. The church changed."[6]

Congregations were to return to the spirit of their founders and modernize in light of the signs of the times. For many the changes were simply much too quickly. They feared that the greater inclusivity in decision-making "allowed groups who may not have represented the viewpoints of the majority to have an inordinate voice in promoting radical change."[7] In some congregations this led to schisms. "A strange dichotomy arose in many religious institutes, as evidenced in the United States: there was a concerted effort both to distance the religious institute from the institutional Church, and, at the same time, to demand jurisdictional powers proper only to the hierarchy."[8]

5. Pope Paul VI, *Ecclesiae Sanctae* II (August 6, 1966), II.i.6.

6. Quoted in Sylvia Poggioli, "Vatican II: A Half-Century Later, A Mixed Legacy," National Public Radio (October 11, 2012), https://www.npr.org/2012/10/11/162594956/vatican-ii-a-half-century-later-a-mixed-legacy.

7. Sister Mary Judith O'Brien, RSM, and Sister Mary Nika Schaumber, RSM, "Conclusion," in *The Foundations of Religious Life: Revisiting the Vision*, ed. Council of Major Superiors of Women Religious (Notre Dame, IN: Ava Maria Press, 2009), 186.

8. O'Brien and Schaumber, "Conclusion," 187.

But many Vatican II sisters look back fondly on those years of experimentation. "The changes to religious life prompted by Vatican II were met with considerable enthusiasm, despite the inertia and inefficiency that may have slowed their implementation in some instances and locations."[9] Eventually, the tidal wave of change passed, leaving those who remained to adapt to the new landscape. Congregations were "to evaluate objectively and humbly the years of experimentation so as to recognize their positive elements and their deviations," as Pope John Paul II directed to the Union of Superiors General in 1979. With the newly formulated Code of Canon Law of 1983, the period of experimentation ended. "This was the context for tension within religious congregations between the two approaches, one referred to as 'traditional' and the other as 'progressive.' "[10]

These sisters, who make up the majority cohort today, "experienced religious life before the Second Vatican Council," and "their worldviews, theological perspectives, and spiritualities evolved over time in tandem, particularly their shared response to the spirit of Vatican II and from expanded educational and ministerial experiences."[11] Renewal was offered, hope abounded, experimentation encouraged. Until it wasn't.

> While the nuns were central to the story of American Catholicism and were key in showing the nation's women the possibilities of assuming leadership positions in society, they have been largely overlooked or ignored by historians and journalists. In part, this neglect has been the result of the nuns' exclusion from positions of power within the Church. Their subjugation to a male clerical order, I believe, not only kept them out of the public eye but also ultimately crushed their efforts to refashion themselves boldly and creatively. Much of the demise of religious orders at the dawn of the twenty-first century can

9. Christine L. M. Gervais, *Beyond the Altar: Women Religious, Patriarchal Power, and the Church* (Waterloo, ON: Wilfrid Laurier University Press, 2019), 158.

10. William Cleary, *The Spiritan Life and Mission Since Vatican II* (Eugene, OR: Wipf & Stock, 2018), 243.

11. Susan Rose Francois, CSJP, "Religious Life in a Time of Fog," in *In Our Own Words: Religious Life in a Changing World*, ed. Juliet Mousseau and Sarah Kohles (Collegeville, MN: Liturgical Press, 2018), 194.

be traced to the hierarchy's refusal to make good on the promise of renewal made by the Vatican forty years before.[12]

There are those who would argue that the effects of renewal actually moved beyond the bounds anticipated by Vatican II. In a spirit of inclusivity, many women's congregations moved toward collaborative models of leadership, though the Sacred Congregation of Religious and Secular Institutes countered that "purely democratic forms of government were not acceptable; a superior must exercise personal authority and not merely act as an executor."[13]

### A Feminist Critique

While questions of hierarchical and personal authority were bantered about in religious congregations, a similar battle for the rights and welfare of women occupied the secular scene. "The feminist ideologies emerging with increased intensity in the 1960s . . . had considerable influence on both why and how sisters undertook their governmental renewal."[14] As did their secular sisters, women religious began to exercise a "hermeneutics of suspicion" when confronted by structures and systems that denied them access for full thriving. Schneiders defined feminism as "a comprehensive ideology which is rooted in women's experience of sexual oppression, engages in a critique of patriarchy as an essentially dysfunctional system, embraces an alternative vision for humanity and the earth, and actively seeks to bring this vision to realization."[15]

In light of the secular and religious changes of the decades after Vatican II, many women religious found feminism as the most appropriate lens through which to view their religious lives. With a renewed vision, many recognized that they had professed, worshipped, and loved a church that is "the most relentlessly patriarchal institution in the Western world" and that "they have been and

---

12. Kenneth A. Briggs, *Double Crossed: Uncovering the Catholic Church's Betrayal of American Nuns* (New York: Doubleday, 2006), xii.

13. O'Brien and Schaumber, "Conclusion," 194–95.

14. Gervais, *Beyond the Altar*, 161.

15. Sandra Schneiders, *Beyond Patching: Faith and Feminism in the Catholic Church* (Mahwah, NJ: Paulist Press, 1990), 164.

continue to be systemically oppressed in their own Church."[16] This realization inspired some, stymied others, and enraged most.

> In regard to the institutional church all women who are both Catholic and feminist desire passionately the conversion of the institution from the sin of sexism and . . . this requires a full and final repudiation of patriarchy. . . . The work of feminist Catholic theologians, ministers, and parents toward this end is carried on in the firm hope that one can use the master's tools to dismantle the master's house and that from the debris of the house of ecclesiastical patriarchy we will be able to construct the home of equal discipleship within which the reign of God can be realized.[17]

For those who remain within the church, their creative efforts have led to alternative liturgies, advocating for women, and challenges to church authority with the hope of creating conciliatory conversations. It was precisely this "feminist spirit" that Cardinal Rodé found suspicious. But not all sisters responded to the changes of Vatican II and feminist perspectives with enthusiasm. Some seek "to revisit the vision of religious life, rooted in the rich tradition of the church and the further unfolding of ecclesiology," depending "upon the guidance of the Magisterium to rediscover the uniqueness of religious consecration."[18]

### In the Midst of a Spiritual Awakening

The older cohort in the survey experienced the effects of Vatican II on religious life and developing ecclesiology and the rise of feminism and liberationist approaches in both theology and praxis. According to Strauss and Howe, the most recent "social awakening" occurred between 1967 and 1980,[19] precisely when the majority of this age cohort were making profession and entering into ministry and community life. Spiritual awakenings are described as "periods

---

16. Sandra Schneiders, *Buying the Field: Catholic Religious Life in Mission to the World* (New York: Paulist Press, 2013), 564.

17. Schneiders, *Beyond Patching*, 108.

18. O'Brien and Schaumber, "Conclusion," 209.

19. William Strauss and Neil Howe, *Generations: The History of America's Future, 1584 to 2069* (New York: HarperCollins, 1991), 78.

of culture revitalization that begin in a general crisis of beliefs and values and extend over a period of a generation or so, during which time a profound reorientation in beliefs and values takes place."[20] More than any of the other age cohorts, the sisters 65 plus have experienced the effects of this spiritual awakening, which reoriented not only their religious lives but their spirituality as well.

## Catholicism in the Aftermath: Post-Vatican II Sisters

There is no denying that American Catholicism at the end of the twentieth century is a church marked by diversity and difference. Catholics differ with one another about authority, abortion, issues of sex and gender, social and ethical concerns, and even spirituality. They differ with the Vatican on the same issues and the more central issues of identity and control: who is the church and who should be making the rules? Fifty years ago these were not questions. Catholics thought of the church as the hierarchy and ceded virtually all authority to administer the church to the pope, bishops, and priests, in that order. The laity were the footsoldiers in the army of Christ."[21]

The documents of Vatican II had ushered in a new era for the church. Many Catholics had enthusiastically embraced opening up the church to the modern world. The *Baltimore Catechism* was out, but nothing had yet replaced it. An entire generation of young Catholics only knew guitar Masses, home-made communion bread, and felt banners. Lots of felt banners. The formally familiar Catholic identity rooted in symbols, rituals, habits, and horarium was gone. What it meant to be Catholic was up for grabs. Church historian Chester Gillis described the setting:

Catholics protested against the Catholic "ghetto" of the 1940s and '50s and longed to be assimilated into the larger American culture. Since the 1960s they have been assimilated—to the point that many are now virtually indistinguishable from others in the society. A

20. William McLoughlin, *Revivals, Awakenings, and Reform: An Essay on Religion and Social Change in America, 1607–1977* (Chicago: University of Chicago Press, 1978), xiii.

21. Chester Gillis, *Roman Catholicism in America* (New York: Columbia University Press, 1999), 5.

simultaneous consequence of this successful assimilation is the loss of group identity, lack of a common vision, detachment from specific marks of identification, and appropriation of practices and values esteemed by the common culture, whether or not they adhere to Catholic principles.[22]

## The Church of Pope John Paul II

And then in 1978 a cardinal from Poland, Karol Józef Wojtyła, became pope. Almost immediately, the church's leader traversed the globe visiting the faithful where they lived. Pope John Paul II made over a hundred trips during his papacy, improving ecumenical and interreligious relationships and giving a public face to the faith. Returning to Poland as Pope, his efforts helped topple communism.

Suddenly, being Catholic was a thing. A public thing. A globally-respected thing. And young people weren't simply to be seen and not heard. In 1985, Pope John Paul II instituted World Youth Day and "earned the confidence of youth because he took them seriously. They sensed that he understood their concerns. He challenged them to give their lives to Christ. He appealed to their high ideals, inviting them to take a lead in the New Evangelization."[23]

Pope John Paul II, having been present at Vatican II, brought to his role a different interpretation of the Council. As George Weigel notes, in many respects Pope John Paul II stood with Pope John XXIII as "bookends of the Council."

> Over the course of a twenty-six-and-a-half-year pontificate, and with the aid of Joseph Ratzinger (another Vatican II veteran who would become John XXIII's fourth successor), John Paul II gave the Church the keys to an authoritative interpretation of Vatican II.[24]

The period of experimentation was closed, and under the direction of Cardinal Ratzinger whom the Pope appointed as head of the Con-

22. Gillis, *Roman Catholicism in America*, 278.

23. Bert Ghezzi, *Saints at Heart: How Fault-Filled, Problem-Prone, Imperfect People like Us Can Be Holy* (Chicago: Loyola Press, 2007), 102.

24. George Weigel, "John XXIII and John Paul II: Canonizing the Bookends," *First Things* (April 23, 2014), https://www.firstthings.com/web-exclusives/2014/04/john-xxiii-and-john-paul-ii.

gregation of the Doctrine of the Faith, a very different church began to take shape. The guitar masses were definitely on their last legs.

> As the post-Vatican II generation came into being, American society entered a period of political conservatism, witnessing the end of the Cold War [and] clearly divided along liberal/conservative lines. The hierarchy was trying to restore order in what it perceived as a chaotic Church . . . The post-Vatican II generation extended the previous generation's uncertainties about the centrality of being Catholic, became increasingly willing to disagree with the Church on what some viewed as optional Church teachings, and emphasized the similarities—not the differences—between Protestants and Catholics.[25]

The hierarchy moved to shore up what it perceived as dissolving foundations. The sacred liturgy was renewed (or returned), the Code of Canon Law revised, and finally the publication of the *New Catechism of the Catholic Church* assured that future generations of Catholics would know the faith. As proponents for the changes commented, "The age of Aquarius has ended!"

The experience of the sacraments, liturgy, and essentials of the faith under Pope John Paul II became rooted in a different interpretation of the Council, one that saw the centrality of the magisterium restored. Pope John Paul II also turned his attention to women religious. In his apostolic exhortation *Vita Consecrata* (1996) he reiterated the distinctiveness of religious life and called for a return to visible signs of profession, particularly the habit. Institutional convents were closing; sisters were leaving traditional educational ministry; and fewer women were entering. Though the diminishment results from a host of sociological and theological reasons, Rome focused on dress as an important identity marker.

> Such boundary markers are essential for the very existence of all human organizations and the preservation of their missions. Posing questions about boundary maintenance is sometimes seen as "conservative," but in reality, such questions are absolutely necessary in order to clarify an organization's reason for existence and thus its institutional vitality.[26]

---

25. D'Antonio et al., *American Catholics Today*, 18–19.
26. Johnson, Wittberg, and Gautier, *New Generations of Catholic Sisters*, 51.

## A Disorienting Flux

What we called God was also up for grabs. Not long after I had entered in the early 1990s, the vocation director invited those of us in initial formation to assist at a vocation retreat. During the opening prayer, the director called upon God who is Source of All Being, and the Word of Life, and the vivifying Spirit to be present. I had no trouble recognizing the alternative names for the Trinity. But later than evening two participants suddenly left the retreat. They explained to the vocation director that they didn't want to be part of this "New Age" thing where Jesus wasn't even mentioned. For many post-Vatican II Catholics the tightrope of what is or isn't Catholic continues to be difficult to traverse. As the authors of *New Generations of Catholic Sisters* recognized:

> The post-Vatican II generation's experience of the Church was often of an institution in constant and *disorienting* flux, unable to articulate anything worth believing in. Most remain relatively uninformed about religious history and Church teachings, preferring an eclectic, do-it-yourself spirituality.[27]

Post-Vatican II women who entered religious communities during these times were often the product of little catechesis, but great enthusiasm. Their spirituality evidenced the mixed experience of church and society that they had encountered.

## Not Your Parents' Church

Those who entered after the dust had settled following Vatican II grew up in a radically different church than their parents. The spirit of change had swept away the statues, opened the lectern to the laity, and re-envisioned the church as the people of God. Outside, the Catholic subculture began to fade as the once ghettoed Catholics now moved firmly into the upper middle class. Late Baby Boomers and early Generation X Catholics stood on the shifting sands of what once had been a mighty foundation. Some found the clarion call of Pope John Paul II a welcomed beacon in the fog, while oth-

---

27. Johnson, Wittberg, and Gautier, 64.

ers reacted to what seemed a heavy-handed return to the "good old days." As Mary Jo Weaver commented:

> How did American Catholics get to the point where they needed adjectives to describe themselves? Why is it no longer enough, as it was in 1955, for someone to say that he or she is Catholic? Why do we now, in 1995, meet Catholics who are "recovering," "communal," "cradle," "practicing," "Tridentine," "conciliar," "American," "disgruntled," "liberal," or "conservative"?[28]

The sisters in this middle cohort represent the diversity of a church between poles and a Catholicism of many names.

## A Church in Need of Mercy: Millennial Sisters

A most amazing thing happened on March 13, 2013. Jorge Mario Bergoglio, the archbishop of Buenos Aires, became Pope Francis. According to *America Magazine*, Cardinal Bergoglio accepted his election to the papacy with the words: "I am a sinner, but I trust in the infinite mercy and patience of our Lord Jesus Christ."[29] Not surprisingly, two years later, Francis declared an extraordinary Jubilee Year of Mercy and explained his choice of the theme:

> We need constantly to contemplate the mystery of mercy. It is a wellspring of joy, serenity, and peace. Our salvation depends on it. Mercy: the word reveals the very mystery of the Most Holy Trinity. Mercy: the ultimate and supreme act by which God comes to meet us. Mercy: the fundamental law that dwells in the heart of every person who looks sincerely into the eyes of his brothers and sisters on the path of life. Mercy: the bridge that connects God and [hu]man, opening our hearts to the hope of being loved forever despite our sinfulness.[30]

28. Mary Jo Weaver, "Who Are Conversative Catholics?," in *Being Right: Conversative Catholics in America*, ed. Mary Jo Weaver and R. Scott Appleby (Bloomington, IN: Indiana University Press, 1995), xi.

29. Stephen Bullivant, "'I Am a Sinner': The Deep Humility of Pope Francis," *America* (September 25, 2013), https://www.americamagazine.org/faith/2013/09/25/i-am-sinner-deep-humility-pope-francis.

30. Pope Francis, Bull of Indiction of the Extraordinary Jubilee of Mercy (*Misericordiae Vultus*), 21.

## A Church in Crisis

After the shattering news of the widespread clergy abuse, and what many named as Pope Benedict's and others failure to respond quickly and adequately, the church was indeed in need of mercy.

> In 2002–2003, [Catholics experienced] what some consider the most traumatic episode in U.S. Catholic history—the sexual abuse scandal. As the new generation of Millennial Catholics came of age, the scandal seemed to raise new questions about the importance of being Catholic, the substance of being Catholic, and the boundaries between Catholicism and other faiths.[31]

More than 11,000 cases of clergy sexual abuse were reported by the John Jay College Research Team, tasked by the US Conference of Catholic Bishops to investigate the scope and extent of the abuse.[32] "By 2012, in the United States alone, the U.S. Conference of Catholic Bishops acknowledged that 16,787 people had come forward with 'credible allegations' of abuse by priests when they were children."[33] In 2018, the Pennsylvania attorney general released the grand jury report documenting the abuse of more than 1,000 victims by more than 300 priests in its six dioceses. The reports of coverups, transfers of pedophile priests, and payouts stretching over decades further eroded confidence in the church's leadership and tarnished the church's moral credibility.

Not often attuned to church politics, my mother had heard the media reports of wide-spread clergy abuse which prompted her to ask warily, "Father didn't touch you when you were an altar server, did he?" How many parents feared asking their now adult children that very question? Having survived the tumult of Vatican II and the

---

31. D'Antonio et al., *American Catholics Today*, 19.

32. John Jay College Research Team, "The Causes and Context of Sexual Abuse of Minors by Catholic Priests in the United States, 1950–2010" (Washington, DC: USCCB, 2011), https://web.archive.org/web/20110601065536/http://www.usccb.org/mr/causes-and-context-of-sexual-abuse-of-minors-by-catholic-priests-in-the-united-states-1950-2010.pdf. The report also noted that nearly 4,400 Catholic clergy had been plausibly accused of sexual abuse of youths between 1950 and 2002.

33. Mayo Moran, "Cardinal Sins: How the Catholic Church Sexual Abuse Crisis Changed Private Law," *The Georgetown Journal of Gender and Law* 21 (2019): 102.

"Right-sizing" of the church under Pope John Paul II, US Catholics were again reminded how fragile and how human the institution really was.

For those entering religious congregations recently, the crisis has a decidedly chilling effect. In the 2020 CARA report on recent vocations, superiors reported of their newer members that "they are very idealistic and fervent, so the clergy sexual abuse scandal is difficult for them."[34] Part of that difficulty is the concern that the sexual scandal and its aftermath prevent them from responding to the mission of their institute. In the CARA study, new members reported that "the sexual abuse scandals consume too much time of our provincial leadership,"[35] and they are focused on maintenance and not mission.

## A Shifting Religious Landscape

Perhaps because the majority of reported abuse occurred before they were born, for most millennial Catholics clergy abuse is just one of many crises of faith. "The religious landscape of the country has indeed shifted considerably for young Catholics, a large percentage of whom resemble other adults in saying that they no longer belong to a particular religion."[36] While fewer Millennials overall practice or identify with their Catholic faith, Christian Smith did identify two hopeful categories: engaged Catholics and devout Catholics. "Engaged emerging adult Catholics enjoy their faith and are more or less engaged with and in the Church. They view their Catholic identity as important."[37] They may or may not regularly attend Mass and may or may not ascribe to all church teachings and doctrines. Many engaged millennial Catholics follow up their college years of social action and campus ministry with a year of volunteer commitment.

34. Mary L. Gautier and Thu T. Do, "Recent Vocations to Religious Life: A Report for the National Religious Vocation Conference" (Washington, DC: Center for Applied Research in the Apostolate, March 2020), 49.

35. Gautier and Do, "Recent Vocations to Religious Life," 137.

36. Johnson, Wittberg, and Gautier, *New Generations of Catholic Sisters*, 67.

37. Christian Smith et al., *Young Catholic America: Emerging Adults In, Out Of, and Gone from the Church* (New York: Oxford University Press, 2014), 110.

In this age of information, mine is a generation that bears an immense weight of responsibility . . . We have been bombarded by so much information, so fast, and at such an early age that none of us is blind. No one can claim to not be responsible or not know that injustice is wreaked in the world at every second. And so this generation seeks a kind of atonement—with some courageous enough to allow a bigger vision to reshape their lives . . . They seek to work hard and well, to effect change, to do good. Some do it for the sake of humanity, some for the sake of following Jesus. To be a Jesuit Volunteer, to spend one's first independent year in a simple community while living a life of service, is to make that desire part of our being for the rest of our lives.[38]

Of the new members surveyed in the CARA report on recent vocations, 12 percent reported that they had participated in a volunteer program like the Jesuit Volunteer Corp. Additionally, "among those who were engaged in ministry, most (57 percent) served in a volunteer capacity" before entering.[39]

### What Does It Mean to Be "Catholic"?

Those labeled "devout" by Smith are a growing movement of Millennials whose Catholicism "is devoted to the pope and follows strict interpretations of Catholic teachings; at the same time they are well-educated and savvy in U.S. popular culture."[40] A somewhat surprising—and some Vatican II sisters would say disturbing—development among young Catholics who still practice their faith is their return to pious practices like adoration.

These young adults are not opposed to contemporary American culture, nor do they reject the changes of the Second Vatican Council. Instead they stitch together a traditional interpretation of Catholic practices with millennial-American cultural norms and a search for authenticity in order to enact a contemporary Catholic identity."[41]

38. Gus Hardy, "Belonging, Missioning, and Being Present: A Short Digression on Life as Jesuit Volunteer," in *Young Adult American Catholics: Explaining Vocation in Their Own Words*, ed. Maureen K. Day (New York: Paulist Press, 2018).

39. Gautier and Do, "Recent Vocations to Religious Life," 76.

40. Katherine Dugan, "#Adoration: Holy Hour Devotions and Millennial Twenty-First Century Catholic Identity," *U.S. Catholic Historian* 36 (Winter 2018): 104.

41. Dugan, "#Adoration," 104–5.

Since they are the offspring of Vatican II grandparents and Post-Vatican II parents, they "have had little or no experience of traditional Catholic practices and catechesis that had formed the previous generations. Although they are more trusting of the Church than either the post-Vatican II or the Vatican II generations, they are also the least knowledgeable about Catholicism."[42] Their retrieval of past rituals is not a wistful nostalgia for the more traditional practices, since they never experienced them. Rather, it is an attempt to recreate for a new generation an identity that is expressly Catholic.

> When "devout" Catholic millennials sit before a consecrated host, they intentionally develop an understanding of self-identity when they say, "I am Catholic." They simultaneously knit themselves into a history of Catholic sacramental life and rely on those devotions to promote a Catholic identity that feels to them more authentic, more real than other aspects of their daily lives. Praying a Holy Hour connects these young adults to their Catholic heritage while also giving them a language of Catholic exceptionalism in the twenty-first century.[43]

While to their Vatican II grandparents (and religious sisters) these practices may be threatening or a cause for alarm, this generation is attempting to do what every cohort that proceeded them has done. They are asking what it means to be Catholic and to be faithful in this church for this generation and in this day.

More so than the previous age cohort, these sisters show an integration of various theological strands: feminism, evolutionary consciousness, and trinitarian. Indeed, Dugan is correct when she acknowledges:

> The pontificate of John Paul II, the long reverberations of Vatican II, along with a general trend of more Catholics moving into the American middle class, populate these millennials' religious identities with a different set of characteristics. Their Catholic imaginations write in hashtags and Snapchats about the Holy Hour. With a careful combination of these multiple sources, millennials are recrafting what it means to be Catholic.[44]

---

42. Johnson, Wittberg, and Gautier, *New Generations of Catholic Sisters*, 64.
43. Dugan, "#Adoration," 107.
44. Dugan, 122–23.

# Conclusion

Timing is everything. All three of our age cohorts are comprised of members of two different generations. The 65 plus cohort has sisters from the Silent and early Baby Boom generation. The cohort between 45 and 64 years of age are later Baby Boomers and members of Generation X. Sisters in the cohort between 25 and 44 are late Generation X and Millennials. Their social identity may have been formed by their generational cohort's formative experiences, but their religious and spiritual identity—in part—is a reflection of the church in which they were raised and later made profession.

## *You Had to Be There*

I can only imagine the excitement—coupled with trepidation—that many religious felt after the Vatican II Council, only to arrive at their golden jubilees still awaiting that promised breath of fresh air. But there are also those sisters for whom the half century since Vatican II has been a time of wandering in the desert, awaiting the church to come to its senses and return to its earlier, better self. This pall of disappointment may not cover everyone, but the numbers can be great enough to cast a shadow overall.

A sister was retelling an experience she had had in parish ministry, and when I asked a question for clarification, she responded with "You're not honoring my anger." It wasn't a lack of honor on my part, but an utter lack of understanding. We who only know Vatican II from a history book have no idea what the church and religious life were like prior to its gathering. Nor do we know the excitement and potential folks felt in its wake. We simply look around at our religious communities and wonder, "Why's everyone so angry? What'd I miss?" And occasionally when members of younger cohorts fail to respond with the same heightened level of outrage over yet another hierarchical choke hold, we are chastised.

Another sister said to me once in response to some papal announcement, "You should be angry about this." Perhaps I would be if I shared the same context or the same sense of disappointment.

> Any two generations following one another always fight different opponents, both within and without. While the older people may

still be fighting one battle, in such a fashion that all their feelings and efforts and even their concepts and categories of thought are determined by that adversary, for the younger people, this adversary may be simply non-existent: their primary orientation is an entirely different one.[45]

And that, I think, is one of the chief dilemmas for newer members. Older professed presume we share the same context—whether historical, social, cultural or even spiritual—as they do.

The intent of this chapter has been to present a historical review of developments in the church that have been experienced differently by the various age cohorts. Perhaps if we recognize that our orienting ecclesiology—like every other aspect of our lives—is contextual and that our personal views of religious life, spirituality, and what it means to be a faithful Catholic are rooted in a particular place and time, then we might be better able to respect our differences, be open to new ways of theologizing, and be more appreciative of the gift of our diversity. In so doing, we are more ready and able to move into our chapter of affairs.

45. Karl Mannheim, "The Problem of Generations," in *Essays on the Sociology of Knowledge* (New York: Oxford University Press, 1952), 298–99.

# Section Two

## Chapter of Affairs
### Responding to the Signs of the Times

The intent of the chapter of faults was to help maintain the well-being of the community, a community made of humans who on occasion are not at our best. Likely, as it was actually practiced, the chapter of faults might not have lived up to the ideal. In our work here, we think of the chapter of faults as the opportunity to "clear the air" so to speak, so as to situate our conversation on the findings of science, emerging theology, and religious life first in light of the results of the survey, then within the wider context of generations, and finally within our various experiences of church. Having explored the differences in historical, social, and ecclesial settings, we are better able to pursue the task at hand.

Within the parlance of religious life, we now enter the chapter of affairs. According to Canon 631, general chapter "is to be composed in such a way that, representing the entire institute, it becomes a true sign of its unity in charity." And as many congregations experience it, our chapters are divided in a chapter of affairs and a chapter of elections, the former attends to the renewal of the life and mission of the congregation; the latter elects the superior and council to lead the congregation in the fulfillment of its chapter enactments.

For most congregations, the chapter of affairs is actually the culmination of a preceding process of prayer, study, and discernment among all members. What is presented on the chapter floor is ordinarily not a surprise, but, rather, what has been carefully and prayerfully discussed at the local and regional levels. The question at issue is often how might this proposal facilitate our life and mission? How does it respond to the signs of the times, meet the needs of the underserved, and bring about the reign of God? It is weighty stuff we discuss at chapter.

And so, it seems fitting to think of our deliberations about the New Cosmology, emerging theology, and religious life as worthy content for our chapter of affairs. In the final section of this book, we begin a chapter of elections at which time we'll explore how—if we choose to frame our vowed life in new categories—the integration of scientific discovery and theology might provide a hermeneutical lens to view the future of religious life.

## Chapter Proposal: Investigating the New Trinity

Many Catholic sisters, among others, have found that some of the discoveries of science have the capacity to revitalize their spirituality. In some respects, a new trinity stands alongside the traditional one, sometimes in tension and sometimes in reflection. Discoveries about the origins and ends of the universe provoke questions about the work of the Creator. Quantum mechanics examines the movement of energy among particles and waves, not unlike the biblical portrait of the Holy Spirit with its ever present, animating force. Evolution argues for the slow, ordered development of life as it moves toward greater complexity and consciousness. Singularities are erupting along the continuum of evolution, unique one-off events not explainable by what proceeded. The incarnation of Jesus, God in human flesh, stands as one such singularity. The religious Trinity of Creator, Spirit, and Incarnate One are reflected or refracted in the scientific trinity of cosmology, quantum mechanics, and evolution to which we now turn.

### *The Process*

The scientist, precisely as a scientist, should not venture to tell the theologian how to engage in theology. On the other hand, the theologian, precisely as a theologian, cannot tell the scientist how to engage in science.[1]

As Zach Hayes realized, the work of the scientist and the work of the theologian are autonomous. But Pope John Paul II would add that both faith and reason are nonetheless important interlocutors, "because each without the other is impoverished and enfeebled. Deprived of what Revelation offers, reason has taken side-tracks which expose it to the danger of losing sight of its final goal. Deprived of reason, faith has stressed feeling and experience, and so runs the risk of no longer being a universal proposition."[2] What we need to undergird our faith is a theology that takes science seriously.

> Theology has been defined as an effort of faith to achieve understanding, as *fides quaerens intellectum*. As such, it must be in vital interchange today with science just as it always has been with philosophy and other forms of learning. Theology will have to call on the findings of science to one degree or another as it pursues its primary concern for the human person, the reaches of freedom, the possibilities of Christian community, the nature of belief and the intelligibility of nature and history. The vitality and significance of theology for humanity will in a profound way be reflected in its ability to incorporate these findings.[3]

Despite the excommunication of Galileo and other reactionary responses to emerging science throughout the church's history, for the most part, pontiffs, cardinals, and theologians today recognize that science is not anathema. And in fact, the more we engage thoughtfully with the findings of science, the better we are able to understand our faith in light of our world. Pope John Paul II

---

1. Zachary Hayes, "New Cosmology for a New Millennium," *New Theology Review* 12 (August 1999): 31.

2. Pope John Paul II, Encyclical On the Relationship Between Faith and Reason (*Fides et Ratio*), (September 14, 1998), 48, http://www.vatican.va/content/john-paul-ii /en/encyclicals/documents/hf_jp-ii_enc_14091998_fides-et-ratio.html.

3. Pope John Paul II, "Letter to the Reverend George V. Coyne SJ, Director of the Vatican Observatory" (June 1, 1988), http://www.vatican.va/content/john-paul-ii/en /letters/1988/documents/hf_jp-ii_let_19880601_padre-coyne.html.

recognizes that "Christians will inevitably assimilate the prevailing ideas about the world, and today these are deeply shaped by science. The only question is whether they will do this critically or unreflectively, with depth and nuance or with a shallowness that debases the Gospel and leaves us ashamed before history."[4]

To approach science through the lens of faith is no easy endeavor. We can hear echoes of Tertullian, "What has Athens to do with Jerusalem?" What might we lose in this encounter? John Haught posed the questions well.

> Is it possible that the universe has outgrown the biblical God who is said to be its creator? Can Christianity and its theological interpretations find a fresh foothold in the immense and mobile universe of contemporary science, or will science itself replace our inherited spiritualities altogether, as many now see happening?[5]

Fear not. This is not an "all or nothing" venture. We can engage the questions and remain deeply rooted in our faith. In fact, we may come to understand the implications of our faith more fully. Our next step is to determine how we will interact with science.

As Ian Barbour presents, various faithful people have attempted several different models of engagement between science and religion: conflict, independence, integration, and dialogue.[6] The conflict model is a competition in which there can be only one winner. One field or the other makes claims or assertions that properly belong to the other, and conflict occurs. There is only one legitimate view, and the other is simply wrong or mistaken. For example, biblical fundamentalists' literal interpretation of the Bible will conflict with a scientific theory of evolution.

An independent model leaves both fields to pursue their own separate agendas. "Science investigates the natural world to discover, control, and predict how things work. Religion articulates ultimate

---

4. Pope John Paul II, "Letter to the Reverend George V. Coyne SJ."

5. John F. Haught, *Christianity and Science: Toward a Theology of Nature* (Marknoll, NY: Orbis Books, 2007), xi.

6. Ian G. Barbour, *Religion in the Age of Science* (San Francisco: Harper & Row, 1990), 77–105.

meanings and a path of moral behavior befitting those meanings."[7] And never the twain shall meet. The integration model is nearly the opposite. Here "thinkers form a deep synthesis of scientific ideas with religious belief,"[8] akin to the work of Teilhard de Chardin.

Barbour's fourth model of dialogue recognizes and respects the differences between science and religion but allows for a meaningful conversation between the two. As Elizabeth Johnson notes, "Science informs theology's view of the very world it reflects on in light of God. Religion offers grounding reasons why the world which science investigates is such an orderly, beautiful, coherent totality, so very comprehensible."[9] In this book, we will adopt this model of dialogue as we ponder how scientific findings inform theological reflection in our lives as women religious.

In the following three chapters, we will respect the integrity of both scientific inquiry and theological reflection. The first section of each chapter highlights the scientific discoveries and subsequent theories as reported by scientists or science writers themselves. In the second part of each chapter, the rostrum will be given over to the theologians who endeavor to explain the significance of the scientific findings for our understanding of God as Creator, the Spirit as animator, and Christ as the evolutionary incarnation of the divine.

7. Elizabeth A. Johnson, *Ask the Beasts: Darwin and the God of Love* (London: Bloomsbury, 2014), 8.

8. Johnson, 10.

9. Johnson, 10.

# Chapter Four

# The Cosmos and Creation

Can you bind the chains of the Pleiades,
  or loose the cords of Orion?
Can you lead forth the Mazzaroth in their season,
  or can you guide the Bear with its children?
Do you know the ordinances of the heavens?
  Can you establish their rule on the earth?

—Job 38:31-33

## Introduction

Only recently in human history could one dare to answer God affirmatively, "yes, we do know the ordinances of the heavens." Such is not hubris but the result of an intersection of technology, science, and human insight. In 1610, Galileo published *Sidereus Nuncius (Starry Messenger)*, which described heretofore unknown aspects about the celestial bodies that he had seen through his optical telescope trained on the night skies. The moon was not smooth after all. Rings surrounded Saturn. And Jupiter had moons. He concluded that heavenly bodies did not revolve around the Earth. The Ptolemaic model of an earth-centered solar system would be disproven, and Copernicus' heliocentric model would triumph.

Today, telescopes attached to satellites are able to see several billion light years into the distance.[1] Launched in 1990, the Hubble Space Telescope was the first such orbiting eye. In addition to providing a

---

1. A light-year (the distance that light travels in one year) is $5.87 \times 10^{12}$ miles.

never-before glimpse into the far reaches of the universe, the Hubble telescope has enabled researchers to measure the universe's expansion rate and distances between galaxies.[2] When launched, the James Webb Space Telescope (JWST) will likely replace the Hubble when it is retired in 2021. With 18 hexagonal segments of mirrors, each 1.3 meters in diameter, the JWST will have the capacity to view visible and infrared light with the goal of gathering data on the formation of the first galaxies and their stars and planets.

Despite the increasing data and advancing technology, "Cosmology is still different from most other branches of science: one cannot experiment with the universe—it may be unique—and speculations about processes at very early and very late times depend upon theories of physics which may never be directly testable."[3] The theories proposed by observational astronomers and physicists are often translated into sound bites for the non-scientific community that uncritically assumes that if it's science, it's true. But as Overbye explains:

> It's a great story, the modern version of the history of the universe, and maybe it's even true. It is probably part of the human condition that cosmologists . . . always think they are knocking on eternity's door, that the final secret of the universe is in reach. It may also be part of the human condition that they are always wrong. Science, inching along by trial-and-error and by doubt, is a graveyard of final answers.[4]

Acknowledging that cosmological theories are mutable shouldn't be too startling for those willing to read a book on cosmology and evolution. Science, like life, like the universe, is in process. In this chapter, we'll discuss some of the theories that currently hold sway, recognizing that as more data is culled and clever minds assess that data, new theories of the origins, development, and potential demise of the universe will replace what we once thought were rock-solid.

---

2. "Cosmic Magnifying Glasses Yield Independent Measure of Universe's Expansion," NASA News Release (January 8, 2020), https://hubblesite.org/contents/news-releases/2020/news-2020-04.

3. Bernard Carr, "Cosmology and Religion," in *The Oxford Handbook of Religion and Science*, ed. Philip Clayton (Oxford: Oxford University Press, 2008), 140.

4. Dennis Overbye, *Lonely Hearts of the Cosmos: The Story of the Scientific Quest for the Secret of the Universe* (Boston: Back Bay Books, 1999), 3.

As Overbye notes, "It should probably come as no surprise that strife and controversy, as well as love and loyalty, characterize this story. Cosmologists rarely speak with one voice, no matter how seamless whatever version of cosmic history temporarily in vogue appears to be."[5] When old theories are disproven, we make room for the new. Perhaps we might even understand the awe and excitement of Galileo as he looked through his remarkable optical telescope and saw what had never been imagined. Only when our best theories fail, do we risk what lies beyond.

## The Ordinances of the Heavens

The late July sky over Knoxville spread out like a pin-holed navy blanket. My brother and I lay on lounge chairs staring into the heavens awaiting a light show that was a late summer meteor shower. Like silent fireworks, bits of cosmic rock and dust streaked across the clear sky. It was literally raining fire rocks over our heads, and we couldn't have been more pleased. "When you wish upon a star / Makes no difference who you are / Anything your heart desires will come to you," or so sang Jiminy Cricket to the disheartened Pinocchio. Streaking across the sky, the fallen stars could have granted a thousand wishes that night.

The night sky has always held wonder. To the ancients, the stars were heavenly beings worthy of worship, an action the Book of Deuteronomy warned against:

> And when you look up to the heavens and see the sun, the moon, and the stars, all the host of heaven, do not be led astray and bow down to them and serve them. (Deut 4:19)

Indeed, the magnitude of the heavens and their luminaries struck the observer with awe.

> When I look at your heavens, the work of your fingers, / the moon and the stars that you have established; / what are human beings that you are mindful of them, / mortals that you care for them? (Ps 8:3-4)

5. Overbye, 4.

It is with the same fear and a bit of trepidation that I attempt to summarize some of the theories regarding our universe, that vast starry blanket wrapped round us.

## The Big Bang

Whether your favorite is the book *A Wrinkle in Time* (Madeleine L'Engle, 1962), the movie *Back to the Future* (1985), or the television series *Doctor Who*, we are fascinated by the idea of time travel. But cosmologists don't just read about time travel, they witness it.

> Because light travels at a finite speed, when we look out in space, we look back in time. We see the sun as it was eight minutes ago, and we see nearby stars as they were five, ten, or a hundred years ago. It takes light approximately 2.5 million years to travel from the Andromeda galaxy to our eyes, so when we stare at our nearest major neighbor with a telescope, we observe Andromeda as it was back before the dawn of [the hu]man. The farther out we look, the farther back we look in time.[6]

This ability to look back in time via the Hubble Space Telescope among others allows astronomers and physicists to see into the universe's past. But before Hubble the Telescope there was Edwin Hubble the astronomer (1889–1953), whose study of redshift data in the 1920s led to a monumental discovery. As seen through a spectroscope, redshift refers to a spectrum of the spectral lines visible from the light waves of a star. The shorter lengths are blue and indicate an object is moving closer to the observer, while longer wave lengths are red and show an object moving away.[7]

> Hubble fell on what would be the prime fact of the twentieth century, the most amazing scientific discovery of all time—the first one that pointed beyond science altogether—the cipher that would haunt

---

6. David Spergel, "Cosmology Today," *Daedalus* 143 (2014): 125.

7. "As a scientific tool, the invention, or discovery, of spectroscopy in the nineteenth century rivaled the telescope itself . . . In spectroscopy, a prism or diffraction grating is used to 'unblend' the light and spread it out into its different wavelength components, the way the sun's light is spread into a rainbow by raindrops, so that the physicist or astronomer can discern which wavelengths are present and which are absent" (Overbye, *Lonely Hearts of the Cosmos*, 45).

. . . future generations of cosmologists and drive them to the sky clawing for patterns in the darkness between the galaxies, seeking the signatures of particles, forces, dimensions, and energies only a heartbeat from eternity, demanding from the blank crumpled night some explanation of the origin and fate of time itself.[8]

Coupled with the predictions from Einstein's general theory of relativity,[9] Hubble's measurement of redshift data indicated "that distant stars are moving away from us and moving faster in direct proportion to their distance. Thus, the data indicate an expanding universe."[10]

Hubble's investigation of redshifts overshadowed the theories of a then lesser-known Belgian astronomer, Fr. Georges Lemaître (1894–1966), who along with physicist Alexander Friedmann (1888–1925) could be called the founders of modern cosmology.[11] Friedmann studied Einstein's theory of general relativity and proposed that an expanding universe would explain why the universe, under Einstein's theory, was not collapsing. Some years later, Fr. Lemaître would come to the same conclusion.

> In hindsight, it is remarkable that a young postdoctoral researcher who was a virtual outsider in the ranks of professional astronomers, Georges Lemaître, formulated one of the greatest predictions of modern physics, that the universe should be expanding.[12]

Unlike some of the other astronomers of his day, Fr. Lemaître had no problem accepting that if the universe was expanding, there was

8. Overbye, 47.

9. Einstein's general theory of relativity proposed that empty space-time would be flat but add matter and energy and what was once flat now bent. "Under their influence, so-called straight lines would bend and even light beams would curve . . . In effect, space and matter manipulated each other" (Overbye, 90).

10. Hans Halvorson and Helge Kragh, "Cosmology and Theology," in *The Stanford Encyclopedia of Philosophy*, ed. Edward N. Zalta (Stanford, CA: Metaphysics Research Lab, Stanford University, 2019), https://plato.stanford.edu/archives/spr2019/entries/cosmology-theology.

11. Joseph Silk, *Horizons of Cosmology: Exploring Words Seen and Unseen* (West Conshohocken, PA: Templeton Press, 2009), 3.

12. Joseph Silk, *The Infinite Cosmos: Questions from the Frontiers of Cosmology* (Oxford: Oxford University Press, 2006), 107.

a point from which that expansion started. After all, it fit well with his own religious belief. In 1931, Fr. Lemaître proposed what many years later could be called the cold big bang theory, which began with the explosion of a "primeval atom."[13] Lemaître's proposal was not well-received at the time because astronomers and physicists preferred the steady state proposal then in vogue. In fact, the term "big bang" was first used to ridicule Lemaître.

> Seldom charitable towards his scientific adversaries, Fred Hoyle made fun of Lemaître by calling him "the big bang man." In fact he used for the first time the expression "big bang" in 1948, during a radio interview. The term, isolated from its pejorative context, became part of scientific parlance thanks to a Russian-born American physicist George Gamow, a former student of Alexander Friedmann. Hoyle therefore unwittingly played a major part in popularising a theory he did not believe in.[14]

Following Hubble and Lemaître, various cosmological models were proposed to predict the rate of expansion of the universe based on the data, with the Friedmann-Robertson-Walker (FRW) models considered the most accurate. FRW models could predict the shape of expansion going forward, but they could not measure back to a point of origin. If $t$ equals the time factor, then the universe "exists at all times after $t_0$, but not before or at time $t_0$. A space-time model with this feature is called singular, and the ideal point that is never reached is called a singularity."[15] The models thus concluded that if the universe began at a moment in time, there was a time when the universe did not exist. There was a beginning, a singularity, that set the expansion into motion.

In the 1940s, George Gamow (1904–1968), a physicist and astronomer, had proposed that singular moment occurred when a

---

13. Georges Lemaître, *The Primeval Atom: An Essay on Cosmogony* (New York: Van Nostrand, 1950), 78.

14. Jean-Pierre Luminet, "The Rise of Big Bang Models, from Myth to Theory and Observation," in *Proceedings: Antropogenesi, Dall'Energia al Fenomeno Umano*, ed. E. Magno A. Pavan and E. Magno (Portogruaro: Il Mulino Editore, 2008), 8.

15. Halvorson and Kragh, "Cosmology and Theology," section 2.

thermonuclear fireball exploded into a dense gas of protons, neutrons, electrons, and gamma radiation.[16] However, he wasn't able to demonstrate how those first atomic nuclei could form into heavier elements, a necessity for star formation. Gamow also predicted that cooled radiation from the hot big bang would still be evident in the universe. It would be two decades before others would prove Gamow's theory.

In 1964, two Bell Laboratory radio astronomers, Arno Penzias and Robert Wilson, detected cosmic background radiation while attempting to decipher the source of a constant hiss in their horn antenna. "Twenty-five years later, the COBE (Cosmic Background Explorer) satellite found that this nearly uniform microwave radiation had exactly the spectral properties predicted by the hot Big Bang model. This measurement of the cosmic background is one of the foundational observations for the hot Big Bang model."[17] Scientists confirm that the big bang is the most likely theory that explains the origins of the universe as we know it. And now we can hear it for ourselves. The static of the cosmic background radiation that occurs on your television is literally the echo of the universe's birth pangs. As Silk outlines, the predictions of the big bang theory have been scientifically proven:

> The recession of galaxies, the abundance of light elements in the universe, the existence of a cosmic background radiation (blackbody) that is uniform, and finally predicted rates of fluctuations in that same radiation. These four lines of evidence ought to be enough to quench even the most biased critics of what at first sight is a highly implausible theory.[18]

The acceptance of the hot big bang theory means that scientists generally hold that the universe is expanding, and that expansion began at a particular moment in time some 13.77 billion years ago. The next question becomes: does the universe have an end?

---

16. Overbye, *Lonely Hearts of the Cosmos*, 38.
17. Spergel, "Cosmology Today," 127.
18. Silk, *Horizons of Cosmology*, 19.

The likes of Einstein and Lemaître argued for a finite universe, while proponents of the steady-state model of the 1950s held that the universe was homogenous and infinite.

> Since the 1970s "physical eschatology" has emerged as a new sub-field of astrophysics and cosmology, pioneered by Freeman Dyson, Jamal Islam and others . . . The field deals primarily with the state of the universe in the remote future as based on extrapolations of cosmological models and the assumption that the presently known laws of physics will remain indefinitely valid.[19]

Two different scenarios describe the universe's final moments. In the first, the universe is open and will continue to expand until about $10^{100}$ years from now. As it expands it will eventually be composed of a thin plasma within a cold radiation. Another scenario predicts a big crunch in which the closed universe folds in on itself. The end isn't pretty no matter the scenario, as Russell presents (italics his):

- In 5 billion years, the sun will become a red giant, engulfing the orbits of Earth and Mars.

- In 40–50 billion years, star formation in our galaxy will have ended.

- In $10^{12}$ years, all massive stars will have become neutron stars or black holes.

- *If the universe is closed, then in $10^{12}$ years, the universe will have reached its maximum size and then will recollapse back to a singularity like the original hot big bang.*

- In $10^{31}$ years, protons and neutrons will decay into positrons, electrons, neutrinos, and photons.

- In $10^{34}$ years, dead planets, black dwarfs, and neutron stars will disappear, their mass completely converted into energy, leaving

19. Hans Halvorson and Helge Kragh, "Physical Cosmology," in *The Routledge Companion to Theism*, ed. Charles Taliaferro, Victoria S. Harrison, and Steward Goetz (New York: Routledge, 2003), 252.

only black holes, electron-positron plasma, and radiation. All carbon-based life forms will inevitably become extinct.

- *If the universe is open, it will continue to cool and expand forever. All of its early structure, from galaxies to living organisms to dust, will vanish forever without a trace.*[20]

These end-time scenarios are based on effects whose origin we can't see directly. Astronomer Vera Rubin (1928–2016) first proposed that there existed something else, something unseen but whose gravity was affecting the stars and galaxies and would have implications on their future.

Rubin's "calculations showed that galaxies must contain about ten times as much 'dark' mass as can be accounted for by the visible stars. In short, at least ninety percent of the mass in galaxies, and therefore in the observable universe, is invisible and unidentified."[21] This "dark" mass became known as "dark matter," and it had an attractive gravitational effect on celestial bodies. In 1998, an additional force, called "dark energy," was discovered. This "dark energy" had a repulsive effect, so that it was causing the stars and galaxies to accelerate away from each other. Imagine a cosmic-sized invisible "Pushmi-Pullyu," of Doctor Dolittle fame.

> Once upon a time cosmologists thought there might be enough dark matter in the universe for its gravity to stop the expansion of the cosmos and pull everything back together in a Big Crunch. Then astronomers discovered an even more exotic feature of the universe, now called dark energy, which is pushing the galaxies apart and speeding up the cosmic expansion. These discoveries have transformed cosmology still further, into a kind of Marvel Comics superstruggle between invisible, titanic forces. One, dark matter, pulls

---

20. Robert John Russell, "Cosmology and Eschatology," in *The Oxford Handbook of Eschatology*, ed. Jerry L. Walls (Oxford and New York: Oxford University Press, 2008), 566.

21. "Vera Rubin and Dark Matter," in *Cosmic Horizons: Astronomy at the Cutting Edge*, ed. Steven Soter and Neil deGrasse Tyson (New York: New Press, 2001), https://www.amnh.org/learn-teach/curriculum-collections/cosmic-horizons-book/vera-rubin-dark-matter.

everything together toward its final doom; the other, dark energy, pushes everything apart toward the ultimate dispersal, sometimes termed the Big Rip. The rest of us, the terrified populace looking up at this cosmic war, are bystanders, made of atoms, which are definitely a minority population of the universe. [22]

The big bang theory explains how the expanding universe emerged at a finite moment in time, but it also suggests that the universe has an end date, one thankfully that we will not be around to experience.

### But Wait . . .

Long before Lemaître, Hubble, and Gamow, there was Aristotle, who pictured a very different cosmology in which the universe was changeless and eternal. This steady-state theory has had various incarnations, the recent ones attempting to rival the big bang theory. Shortly after Gamow proposed the fiery big bang, other astronomers and physicists countered with the steady-state theory, arguing for the constant state of the universe with no beginning and no end. "According to the classical steady-state theory, the universe has expanded for an infinity of time and will continue to do so for ever; yet the average density of matter remains constant because matter, or rather matter-energy, is continually being created out of nothing."[23] In 1948, Fred Hoyle, Thomas Gold, and Hermann Bondi published their alternative to the hot big bang. The theory built on the "perfect cosmological principle," a proposal that the universe is spatially and temporally homogeneous. The classical steady-state theory lost scholarly support in the 1960s when it couldn't explain new discoveries like the cosmic microwave background.

Cosmologists agree that the hot big bang theory is "a very successful description of the evolution of the universe . . . from about one second after the big bang to the present. Nonetheless, the standard big bang theory has serious shortcomings."[24] In light of some

22. Dennis Overbye, "Vera Rubin Gets a Telescope of Her Own," *New York Times* (January 11, 2020), https://www.lsst.org/news/vera-rubin-gets-telescope-her-own.

23. Halvorson and Kragh, "Physical Cosmology," 246.

24. Alan H. Guth, "The Inflationary Universe," in *Cosmology: Historical, Literary, Philosophical, Religious, and Scientific Perspectives* (New York: Garland Publishing, 1993), 411.

of these "shortcomings," cosmological theorists have changed the direction of their research. These models don't begin by looking up through a telescope. Rather, they start by staring down into a microscope. The investigation of subatomic parts is the purview of quantum mechanics.

> Recent developments in quantum cosmology depict our universe as emerging from a prior superspace of universes that are multiply connected. Some are like ours while others are radically different. Other developments involve multiverse and brane cosmologies. Quantum cosmology is a highly speculative field, and its interpretation is complicated by the complex philosophical issues associated with quantum mechanics.[25]

In the field of quantum cosmology, loop quantum cosmology (LQC) may be an up-and-coming rival to the big bang. Using "an interplay of sophisticated analytical and numerical techniques," LQC argues for a non-singular cyclic model of the universe; thereby negating the need for a big bang.[26] According to scholars, it's too early to assume that the LQC has overturned the big bang theory. But, "there is a non-negligible probability that the big bang is not the beginning of the universe, and a fortiori, not the creation event."[27]

Another proposal is String theory.

> In this scenario, the absolute big bang disappears and is replaced by a saddle point in the dynamical evolution of spacetime curvature: before this point, curvature is increasing, and after this point, it is decreasing.[28]

Finally, and perhaps more controversially, the multiverse theory as its name implies proposes a huge number of other universes.

25. Robert John Russell, "Cosmology and Eschatology," in *The Oxford Handbook of Eschatology*, ed. Jerry L. Walls (Oxford: Oxford University Press, 2008), 566.

26. Ivan Agullo and Parampreet Sing, "Quantum Cosmology: A Brief Review," in *100 Years of General Relativity*, eds. A. Ashtekar and J. Pullin (Hackensack, NJ: World Scientific, 2017), 183.

27. Halvorson and Kragh, "Physical Cosmology," 248.

28. Halvorson and Kragh, 248.

Thus, our universe is not unique; it's simply home to us. "The theory of the multiverse has seductively great explanatory power (while it has almost no predictive power), which is a major reason why many physicists and cosmologists find it attractive. On the other hand, other physicists dismiss it as pseudoscience because it is practically untestable."[29]

Though the hot big bang theory is accepted among most cosmologists, as we learn more about the universe through observation and analysis, other more plausible theories may emerge. In other words, the big bang isn't the final answer to the origin, evolution, and demise of our universe. It is simply the best answer we currently have. As astronomer Allan Wirth of the Massachusetts Institute of Technology's Lincoln Laboratory well noted:

> We only see about 10 percent of the whole universe. Making decisions about its origins is like driving your car if you could only see out 10 percent of your windshield. Not a good idea.[30]

### The Stardust of Yesterday

When Hoagy Carmichael (1899–1981) wrote the music for "Stardust," in 1927, and Mitchell Parish added lyrics in 1929, Lemaître and Hubble were worlds away literally studying stardust. When Nat King Cole immortalized the song in his 1956 version, the United States and the Soviet Union had just separately announced their intentions to launch a satellite into space.

> . . . High up in the sky the little stars climb
> Always reminding me that we're apart . . .
> Love is now the stardust of yesterday.[31]

Now in the twenty-first century, we know stardust is not only some wistful metaphor of ephemeral love, it is literally what we're made of! David Ellyard says it rather poetically:

29. Halvorson and Kragh, 249.
30. Allan Wirth, email to Laurie Brink, July 19, 2019.
31. Hoagy Carmichael and Mitchell Parish, "Stardust" (New York: Mills Music, 1929).

In this way was made all the iron we now find in our blood, all the phosphorus and calcium that strengthens our bones, all the sodium and potassium that drives signals along our nerves. Atoms so formed are thrown off into space by aged stars in their death throes. Natural forces recycle them into new stars, into planets and plants and people. We are all made of stardust.[32]

The initial fiery big bang sent out a massive wave of radiation, but there was "a time before which there could be no atoms; a time before which there could be no stars; a time before which the complexities of biochemistry could not exist."[33] One second after the big bang, the universe is a 10-billion-degree oven baking neutrons, protons, electrons, anti-electrons, photons, and neutrinos.[34] As it cools, at about three minutes, these subatomic particles begin to combine, forming a plasma of photons, electrons, and light nuclei of hydrogen, helium, deuterium (isotope of hydrogen), and lithium. But the heavier elements necessary for life—carbon, nitrogen, oxygen, phosphorous, and silicon—will take billions of years to form. The big bang gave birth to the universe, but it would be the death of stars that bear life.

> When stars exhaust their fuel, they contract and explode. In the extreme conditions of these supernova explosions the biological elements are made. Every atom in our bodies is made of elements that have been through an exploding star. We are indeed simply stardust. But this stellar alchemy which converts primordial hydrogen and helium from the Big Bang into the building blocks of life takes a long time to complete—more than ten billion years of nuclear burning is required.[35]

From our vantage point to the edge of the observable universe is a distance of 46 billion light years. This universe contains two trillion

32. David Ellyard, *Sky Watch: A Guide to the Southern Skies* (Crows Nest, NSW: Australian Broadcast Corporation, 1988), 85.

33. John D. Barrow, "The Evolution of the Universe," *New Literary History* 22 (1991): 843.

34. *NASA Science: Share the Science* explains the formation of celestial bodies in the universe using non-scientific jargon. See https://science.nasa.gov/astrophysics.

35. Barrow, "The Evolution of the Universe," 845.

galaxies and each with a hundred billion stars. The numbers are staggering, but scientists propose that it takes such immense numbers and expanse to create the environment "to support just a single lonely outpost of life."[36] Our lives and all life on Earth are the result of the death of a star, many stars. Without their explosion, their death throes of nuclear immolation, the very carbon that is the basis of life could not exist.

Indeed, we could answer the query of the Psalmist:

> When I look at your heavens, the work of your fingers,
>     the moon and the stars that you have established;
> what are human beings that you are mindful of them,
>     mortals that you care for them? (Ps 8:3-4)

What we are is literally the stuff of the heavens.

## Science Seeking Understanding: Faith Reflecting on Science

Not a few astrophysicists, some of whom are at best agnostic, have said to me something to the effect of: "There is something beyond the science. Something that started all this. I just don't know what that is." For those of us who are believers, that something we call, "God." But before siding with one perspective or the other, let us acknowledge that neither science nor theology has to agree. "Some have said that science is attentive to the *how* of the natural world, while religion is concerned with the *why*."[37] The two are not so much at odds as they are on different playing fields. John Haught among others proposes that we think of the discoveries of the universe as part of "the long cosmic preamble to human history," which is "the story of everything that [has] taken place in the past, including what was going on in the universe before Homo sapiens arrive,"[38] something called "Big History." But that's just one part of

---

36. Barrow, 844.

37. Dianne Bergant, "'In the Image of God' but What Is the Image?," in *Forget Not God's Benefits (Ps 103:2): A Festschrift in Honor of Leslie J. Hoppe, OFM* (Washington, DC: Catholic Biblical Association, 2022), 11.

38. John F. Haught, *The New Cosmic Story: Inside Our Awakening Universe* (New Haven, CT: Yale University Press, 2017), 1.

the larger drama. He argues that we should turn our focus to the "inside story of the universe."[39]

> We cannot expect to understand well what is going on in cosmic history apart from a careful examination of what goes on in the interior striving of life that reaches the summit of its intensity in humanity's spiritual adventures.[40]

Religious experience is part of this inside story. Indeed, "science, precisely as science, can describe those things which it finds actually existing in the cosmos . . . but . . . it cannot talk about what might be the deepest meaning of existence."[41] That is the task of theologians "to create a road map of reality in which the descriptions and models of science can be brought into contact with a framework of religious meaning and values."[42]

So, the story of the cosmos is a both/and. It is a story of scientific discovery and emerging interiority. This emerging interior world consists "of sentience, intelligence, moral aspiration, and religious passion."[43] Broadly speaking, religion developed as "a highly symbolic search for something permanently trustworthy, something we can always rely on to give us the courage to conquer the anxiety that comes with being finite, striving, and mortal beings."[44] Throughout human history religion became the evolving story of the experience of Big History from the insiders' perspective.

When we turn to the inside story of the universe, we are faced with questions of deeper meaning and integration, in a word, questions about faith. What role does God play in the originating moment—variously called the big bang or the Primordial Flaring Forth—of this Big History? Though all language about God is inadequate, which metaphor best captures our theological thinking of how God continues to respond to creation? Scientific theories propose an end to the expanding universe in the far distant future.

39. Haught, 2.
40. Haught, 2.
41. Bergant, "In the Image of God."
42. Hayes, "New Cosmology for a New Millennium," 32.
43. Haught, *The New Cosmic Story*, 3.
44. Haught, 4.

How does the end of the cosmos relate to our Christian eschatology? In other words, what do the scientific discoveries about the origin, expanse, and demise of the universe add to our understanding of the divine? These are the questions proper to a theology that begins with the results of science and then asks, "what does this mean?" As it relates to the universe, the answer

> can be spelled out in three inter-related statements: first, it is the one God who creates the whole cosmos as one diverse but inter-related system; second, this same creator is present to every part of the cosmos sustaining and empowering it; third, this same God will bring the whole movement of evolving creation to its completion."[45]

In the following sections, we'll look through a theological lens at the origins of creation, the unfinished universe in which God continues to act, and the telos of the cosmos.

### Origins: Before the Big Bang

Scientists are in disagreement as to what, if anything, preceded $t_0$, the moment of the big bang, since neither theory nor mathematical formula have adequately described it. "The big-bang episode . . . offers no explanation of cosmic existence but only a description of the early formative development of the cosmos that exists."[46] Thus, cosmogenesis—the theory about the origins of the cosmos before $t_0$—remains a debated field. Some theologians might argue that *creatio ex nihilo* provides the best answer. "Creation *ex nihilo* . . . is fundamentally a metaphysical concept that offers a biblically based, theistic answer to the question of cosmogenesis: How does the universe come to have existence?"[47] But as Van Till presented, the big bang theory and *creatio ex nihilo* answer different questions.

> The big-bang model, with its idea of a singular and spectacular be-ginning may serve to reinforce the traditional concept of the finite

---

45. Denis Edwards, *Jesus and the Cosmos* (New York: Paulist Press, 1991), 24.

46. Howard J. Van Till et al., *Portraits of Creation: Biblical and Scientific Perspectives on the World's Formation* (Grand Rapids, MI: Eerdmans, 1990), 114.

47. Till et al., 114.

temporal duration of the created realm, but it should neither be identified with nor counted as compelling evidence for the doctrine of creation *ex nihilo*. Creation *ex nihilo* is a rich theological concept not merely about temporal beginnings but concerning the fundamental identity of the world and the source of its existence at all times.[48]

In essence, Van Till argued—and we would agree—God is bigger than the singular moment of the big bang. In fact, Augustine and others considered that "time" itself was a creation of God (*Confessions*, book 11, chapter 13). Thus, we can see resonances with our biblical account that "envisions God calling the Creation into existence in nascent form and directing its formation in the coherent manner described by the standard big-bang model of scientific cosmology."[49] And here, we are obliged to turn to our biblical narrative.

> In the beginning when God created the heavens and the earth, [2] the earth was a formless void and darkness covered the face of the deep, while a wind from God swept over the face of the waters. Then God said, "Let there be light"; and there was light. [4] And God saw that the light was good; and God separated the light from the darkness. (Gen 1:1-4)

The Book of Genesis opens with a chaotic canvas, a lone artist, and a desire to create. This poetic narrative credits the origin of the universe to the spoken word of God. The creative speech of God proceeds $t_0$ and sets in motion "the totality of cosmic phenomena."[50]

---

48. Till et al., 114. To the question of the creation event, Anne Clifford distinguishes creation from the big bang: ". . . the big bang does not refer to the ultimate beginning of time. The big bang theory provides a plausible account of the evolution of the universe from a fraction of a second after the initial singularity that set in process the expanding universe that we can observe. It does not account for an absolute beginning per se. The initial singularity could very well have been preceded by a contraction as part of an infinitely repeatable cycle of an oscillating universe" (Anne Clifford, "Creation," in *Systematic Theology, Roman Catholic Perspectives*, ed. Francis Schüssler Fiorenza and John P. Galvin (Minneapolis: Fortress Press, 2011), 201–54, here 230.

49. Till et al., *Portraits of Creation*, 114.

50. Nahum Sarna, *Genesis* (Philadelphia: Jewish Publication Society, 1989), 5.

The first epitaph given to God, "Creator," is drawn from this original speech act. "Creation" is a theological term that means that "natural world studied by science is being viewed through the lens of religious belief."[51] After the Creation, "maker of heaven and earth" became a common title for God in Scripture (Gen 14:19, 22; Exod 20:11, 31:17; 2 Kgs 19:15; Neh 9:6; Pss 115:15, 121:2; 124:8; 134:3; 146:6; Isa 37:16; Acts 4:24, 14:15; Rev 14:7, 18:1) and finds its way into the Nicene and Apostles' Creeds. For those old enough to remember, the *Baltimore Catechism* confirmed that "God made the world," and "God is the Creator of heaven and earth, and all things." Indeed, if God made the cosmos, then God can rightly be named as creator, the second most frequent term our survey respondents used for the First Person of the Trinity.

As Greenwood notes, "the vision of the cosmos in these first verses of Genesis is one in which the entirety of an uninhabitable earth is submerged in a dark abyss, one only God can make hospitable to life and productivity."[52] The first creation account in Genesis 1:1–2:3 presents God as the source of all being who then orders the cosmos into a three-tiered system, consistent with ancient Near Eastern cosmology. The heavens represent the first tier consisting of the upper realm—reserved for the deities and divine beings, and the lower—the habitation for birds, planets, stars. The middle tier is envisioned as a flat earth anchored on four pillars. At death, one was buried and remained in Sheol, the abode of the dead somewhere in this middle tier. The entire cosmos was surrounded by the waters, the third tier. The firmament held back the waters from the heavens. The seas below were the source of water on earth, but "were also the source of chaos . . . whose powers needed to be constrained."[53] This three-tiered system is evident in other biblical texts, especially the hymn of Wisdom in Proverbs 8:22-31.

---

51. Elizabeth A. Johnson, *Ask the Beasts: Darwin and the God of Love* (London: Bloomsbury, 2014), 4.

52. Kyle Greenwood, *Scripture and Cosmology: Reading the Bible Between the Ancient World and Modern Science* (Downers Grove, IL: IVP Press, 2015), 107.

53. Greenwood, 102.

The LORD created me at the beginning of his work,
>    the first of his acts of long ago.
Ages ago I was set up,
>    at the first, before the beginning of the earth.
When there were no depths I was brought forth,
>    when there were no springs abounding with water.
Before the mountains had been shaped,
>    before the hills, I was brought forth—
when he had not yet made earth and fields,
>    or the world's first bits of soil.
When he established the heavens, I was there,
>    when he drew a circle on the face of the deep,
when he made firm the skies above,
>    when he established the fountains of the deep,
when he assigned to the sea its limit,
>    so that the waters might not transgress his command,
when he marked out the foundations of the earth,
>    then I was beside him, like a master worker;
and I was daily his delight,
>    rejoicing before him always,
rejoicing in his inhabited world
>    and delighting in the human race.

In the beginning, Wisdom was "brought forth," and along with God was present for the creation of earth (vv. 23-26), the heavens (vv. 27-28), and the waters (vv. 28-29).

When the Jesuit paleologist Teilhard de Chardin reflected on Wisdom, whom he called "the eternal feminine," he wove together the biblical text and his knowledge of the universe's origins.

> In the beginning, I was no more than a mist, rising and falling: / I lay hidden beneath affinities that were as yet hardly conscious, / beneath a loose and tenuous polarity. / And yet I was already in existence. / In the stirring of the layers of the cosmic substance, whose / nascent folds contain the promise of worlds beyond number, the / first traces of my countenance could be read.
>
> Like a soul, still dormant but essential, I bestirred the original / mass, almost without form, which hastened into my field of / attraction; and I instilled even into the atoms, into the fathomless / depths

of the infinitesimal, a vague but obstinate yearning to / emerge from the solitude of their nothingness and to hold fast / to something outside themselves.[54]

Teilhard de Chardin understood "the spiritual power of matter as the feminine aspect of God's nature embedded in all of creation. [This] captures Teilhard's profound understanding of what is occurring in the cosmos."[55] For Teilhard, the answer to what animated the Primal Flaring Forth was this "eternal feminine . . . the cosmic unifying and spiritualizing force at work in creation."[56]

By God's hand and Wisdom's accompaniment, once the firmament and heavens, waters and earth are formed, living creatures are created. Genesis chapter 1 describes a hierarchy of creation in which human beings are the pinnacle: "So God created humankind in his image, / in the image of God he created them; / male and female he created them" (Gen 1:27). That the first human beings are commissioned to have "dominion" over the rest of the living creatures has over time prompted an anthropocentric reading and often a harmful abuse of the created world. But Dianne Bergant argues that "ancient peoples never doubted their connection with, even total dependence upon, elements of the natural world," so it is possible "that this anthropocentric point of view has been imposed by the biblical reader rather than implied by the biblical author."[57] Today, reading the biblical texts requires a more nuanced understanding not only of the historical context and poetic aspect of Scripture, but also of its history of interpretation. If we read both Creation narratives (Gen 1:1–2:3; 2:4-25) in a non-hierarchical manner, we see the formation of an integral community.

54. Teilhard de Chardin, *Writing in Time of War*, trans. René Hague (New York: Harper & Row, 1968), 192–93.

55. Kathleen Duffy, SSJ, "Sophia: Catalyst for Creative Union and Divine Love," in *From Teilhard to Omega: Co-Creating an Unfinished Universe* (Maryknoll, NY: Orbis Books, 2014), 26.

56. Duffy, 26.

57. Dianne Bergant, *A New Heaven, A New Earth: The Bible and Catholicity* (Marknoll, NY: Orbis Books, 2016), 3.

In this community of all creation each species has its own unique place. Every creature bears the "stamp of origin" of the creator, the one primordial ground of all being. Every type of creature, then, must be understood as reflecting something of the mystery of the creator. Humankind is part of a world of beings which are all related to one another as one community grounded in the life of God.[58]

Though approaching the origins of the universe through different lenses, both science and theology contribute to our understanding and appreciation of "the inside story of the universe."[59]

The big bang presents us with original unity. A moment of potential that has been unfolding for 13.77 billion years. The Bible imagines that unfolding as the desire of God to order and create and pronounces "indeed, it was very good" (Gen 1:31). Despite its antiquated ancient Near Eastern cosmology, the Bible got it right, it would seem. God is creator, maker of heaven and earth, and Wisdom is the accompanying spark of ignition. This biblical cosmology more or less continued to underlie the ancient writers' understanding of God's creative acts and the visible world known to them.

> Israel's recollection of God's creative act was an integral part of their worship. It reminded them that God was able to do all things, since he was the one who brought the cosmos into existence. It also reminded them that the God who had been faithful in the past would be faithful to them in the present and future.[60]

### The Unfinished Universe

With poetic license and the eyes of faith, we can see resonances between the biblical story of the universe's beginnings and the scientific one, but once we get to the encounter in the garden with Adam, Eve, and the serpent, we have left any semblance of the scientific and entered into the etiological. The origin of sin in Genesis chapter 3 sits firmly upon the static biblical cosmology. There was

---

58. Edwards, *Jesus and the Cosmos*, 24.
59. Haught, *The New Cosmic Story*, 2.
60. Greenwood, *Scripture and Cosmology*, 119.

paradise, perfection in the beginning, and then through human action, we lost it all.

> Then the LORD God said, "See, the man has become like one of us, knowing good and evil; and now, he might reach out his hand and take also from the tree of life, and eat, and live forever"—therefore the LORD God sent him forth from the garden of Eden, to till the ground from which he was taken (Gen 3:22-23).

In its context, the first eleven chapters of Genesis describe the primeval history of humanity. The story of Adam and Eve becomes known as "The Fall" in Christian theology, and "it is assumed that the human condition, subject to suffering and death, is due to the sin of Adam."[61] For the apostle Paul, the sin of Adam becomes the reason for Christ's passion. "Therefore, just as sin came into the world through one man, and death came through sin, and so death spread to all because all have sinned" (Rom 5:12). In the fourth century, Augustine's reflections on Genesis chapter 3 and the letters of Paul form the foundation for his doctrine of original sin. But if there was no original perfection, no completed paradisal creation, how do we envision the origin of sin? Haught answers:

> Original sin means that each of us is born into a still unfinished, imperfect universe where there already exist strong pressures—many of them inherited culturally over many generations—for us to acquiesce in an indifference to God's creative cosmic aim of maximising beauty.[62]

But an unfinished universe doesn't imply that there is no moral evil. Interpreting sin in light of evolution, Franciscan theologian Eric Doyle proposed that "original sin is the sinful condition of the human race; it is the turning away from God at the beginning of the human race (not necessarily the first human act) because it is a turning away from brother and sister which in turn brings a disunity

---

61. John J. Collins, *A Short Introduction to the Hebrew Bible*, 3rd ed. (Minneapolis: Fortress Press, 2018), 48.
62. John F. Haught, *God After Darwin: A Theology of Evolution*, 2nd ed. (New York: Routledge, 2018), 138.

into the order of grace and nature."[63] Likewise, Ryan among others recognizes that the concept of original sin includes more than simply indifference to God's creative plans.

> In creating an evolving world, it appears that God limits God's self in order to allow creation to be and to develop . . . God respects the free processes involved in the agency of finite creatures, which include the free decisions of human beings. This makes the history of cosmos and human history an adventure full of risks. It becomes a history that includes the pain, suffering, and loss within creation.[64]

As cosmologists and evolutionary biologists have confirmed, life hasn't reached completion or perfection. The universe is unfinished. And while paradise remains a theological construct, in reality, we are part of an evolving intergalactic ecosystem—full of risks.

Einstein's theories, Hubble's redshift observations, and a host of cosmological discoveries confirm that the universe is continually expanding and birthing new stars out of the remnants of old ones. If we choose to take the science seriously, then this emerging universe has implications for our faith. But many "ecclesiastical institutions and most religious education still cling at least tacitly and sometimes literally to ancient and medieval images of a fixed universe, primordial human innocence, a historical fall, and a creator who watches over the natural world from up above."[65]

To prod the institutional church toward more evolutionary thinking, Haught proposes four points to ponder in light of our living as faithful people in an unfinished universe: a moment of perfection like Eden didn't exist, focusing on otherworldly expectations can lead to indifference, cosmic pessimism is not so easily justified, and a new kind of hope still awaits.[66] First, about the garden of Eden,

63. Brenda Abbott, "Eric Doyle OFM: Blessed John Duns Scotus, Teilhard De Chardin and a Cosmos in Evolution," *Franciscan Studies* 75 (January 2017): 521.

64. Robin Ryan, *Jesus and Salvation: Soundings in the Christian Tradition and Contemporary Theology* (Collegeville, MN: Liturgical Press, 2015), 155.

65. John F. Haught, "Teilhard de Chardin: Theology for an Unfinished Universe," in *From Teilhard to Omega: Co-Creating an Unfinished Universe*, ed. Ilia Delio (Maryknoll, NY: Orbis Books, 2014), 9.

66. Haught, 11–13.

Haught points out that the science puts "an end to the idea that God's creation has at any time been perfect or paradisal."[67] This does not mean that God is not perfect, but that God's creation is in process, evolving, incomplete. Scientific cosmology contravenes biblical cosmology and debunks Genesis' claim that after the sixth day, "the heavens and the earth were finished" (Gen 2:1). "If the world is still emerging," Haught writes, "we need no longer think of Christ and his mission in exactly the same way as previous ages did."[68] The role of Jesus as the Christ within a new cosmology will be further discussed in chapter 6.

Second, most biblical and much theological thinking despairs of this world with its primal Fall and sinful acts. The goal becomes reaching the heavenly realm. As Paul encourages, "our citizenship is in heaven, and it is from there that we are expecting a Savior, the Lord Jesus Christ" (Phil 3:20). For Augustine, Christ "is by degrees withdrawing His servants from a world decaying and collapsing under these evils, in order to build with them an eternal and most glorious City" (*City of God*, book 2, chapter 18).[69] Even Pope Francis, who is committed to alleviating suffering in the here and now, still aims for the heavenly realm as envisioned in a biblical cosmology. In an address from his papal palace library, he urged, "Let us not forget this: the dwelling place that awaits us is Paradise. We are in transit here. We are made for Heaven, for eternal life, to live forever."[70] Haught argues that "shadows of a prescientific cosmology . . . still often restrain human expectation by channeling our aspirations toward a timeless spiritual heaven outside the physical universe."[71] Overly focusing on "the heavenly home" that awaits has excused many Christians from attending to the significant social, economic, and environmental sins surrounding us today.

67. Haught, 11.

68. Haught, 12.

69. Augustine, *City of God: Against the Pagans*, trans. R. W. Dyson (Cambridge: Cambridge University Press, 1998), 72.

70. Pope Francis, "Regina Caeli," Library of the Apostolic Palace (May 10, 2020), http://w2.vatican.va/content/francesco/en/angelus/2020/documents/papa-francesco_regina-coeli_20200510.html.

71. Haught, "Teilhard de Chardin," 12.

The assumption of an initially completed creation tends to limit the significance of ethical life to the acquiring of virtuous habits that enhance our moral character and worthiness to inherit eternal life, but it has little to do with building the world, a motivation that Vatican II understood to be essential to Christian ethical life.[72]

Third, though coming from a different place, scientists themselves can also suffer from a "Why bother?" attitude. Haught calls this a "cosmic pessimism . . . the belief that nature has no purpose and that whatever meaning exists in the world is our own human creation."[73] But an unfinished, evolving universe challenges that pessimistic attitude. One can hardly claim indifference to the cosmic drama being played out, since "none of us is in a secure position to declare with absolute certitude here and now that it makes no sense ultimately."[74]

Finally, the "cosmic drama of transformation" births a new sense of purpose. When we recognize that we are within this unfinished universe and that, we, ourselves, are still in the process of becoming, we catch sight of a new hope, a renewed sense of direction.

> Perfection, evolution helps us to see, lies in the eschatological future, not in the indefinite temporal past, nor in an eternal present immune to the travails of becoming . . . Whereas in a pre-evolutionary world the transient beauty and bliss we experience could easily be disheartening reminders of what could have been, in an evolving—and therefore unfinished—universe, they are joyful harbingers of new and unprecedented epochs of creation yet to come. Nature is essentially promise.[75]

The apostle Paul in his Letter to the Romans espouses something similar.

> We know that the whole creation has been groaning in labor pains until now; and not only the creation, but we ourselves, who have the first fruits of the Spirit . . . For in hope we were saved. Now

72. Haught, 20.
73. Haught, 12.
74. Haught, 12.
75. Haught, *God After Darwin*, 142.

hope that is seen is not hope. For who hopes for what is seen? But if we hope for what we do not see, we wait for it with patience. (Rom 8:22-24)

Evolutionary biology and cosmology show us that we haven't so much lost "paradise," as we have found a new, still unfolding path that invites participation. In fact, obliges participation!

Scientific cosmology now confirms the Pauline intuition that the lifting up of our hearts at the news of God's coming is remarkably continuous with the anticipatory drama we call the universe.[76]

We can't sit this one out. We have roles to play in this ongoing drama. As Denis Edwards announced, "The unfolding of the universe continues in the human person and in human community. It is manifest in growing global solidarity, in culture, and in human interaction with the rest of creation."[77]

### Questions of Eschatology

The world is coming to an end. On this, it would seem, science and Christian theology agree. Cosmologists propose either a slow cool down or a fiery implosion billions of years in the future. Christians await the Parousia, the second coming of Jesus, at which time we will experience the fullness of the reign of God. How might Christian expectations of the end times compare or contrast with emerging science?

First, Christian eschatology—the study of the eschaton or last days—is biblically-based, built on the portrayal that God is faithful (Deut 7:9). *Hesed* did and will continue to describe God's relationship with all of creation. As Brother John Barker, OFM, explains:

*Hesed* [is] to be grounded in God's fidelity and commitment to relationship. The word and the reality point to the absolute devotion, faithfulness, and commitment of God to those with whom God is in relationship. What God does when God does *hesed* is an expression

76. Haught, "Teilhard de Chardin," 21.
77. Edwards, *Jesus and the Cosmos*, 29.

of God's commitment and fidelity to the relationship . . . God wants a people who know what it means to be faithful, committed, and just to each other in the same way that God is faithful, committed, and just toward Israel.[78]

Thus, the people of God could trust that the Abrahamic, Mosaic, Davidic, and Prophetic promises would be fulfilled. Their delay was the result of human failure to live up to the covenant. As it would develop, "the oracles of restoration found throughout the prophetic writings came to be seen as descriptions, or at least intimations, of a definitive moment not in the immediate future but in some later time when God would bring about a complete change of circumstances not only for Israel but for the whole world."[79]

This Old Testament eschatology was not one single doctrine but rather a variety of views on how God would restore Israel.

> In all its forms, Jewish eschatology took as its starting point the conviction that the way the world is now is not the way God ultimately wants it to be. The divine project, so to speak, is not finished. The world is filled with injustice, greed, war and violence, and faithlessness. Jewish tradition held that such was not the will of God, and firm belief in divine justice led to the hope that one day God would intervene to set things right.[80]

The Book of Genesis may have declared creation complete (Gen 2:1), but the work of God was far from over. As the Bible presents it, God and God's creation is an act in process.

The New Testament authors, for the most part Jews themselves, would interpret the life, death, and resurrection of Jesus in light of Jewish messianic and apocalyptic eschatology. The good news of the reign of God was, indeed, at hand (Mark 1:15), present in the person of Jesus. Those baptized in his name were a new creation already in process, according to the apostle Paul. "So if anyone is

---

78. John Barker, OFM, email to author, July 4, 2018.

79. Barbara E. Bowe, *Biblical Foundations of Spirituality: Touching a Finger to the Flame* (Lanham, MD: Rowman & Littlefield, 2017), 127.

80. Bowe, *Biblical Foundations of Spirituality*, 128.

in Christ, there is a new creation: everything old has passed away; see, everything has become new!" (2 Cor 5:17). Through an apocalyptic lens, the visionary of Patmos sees the establishment of a new heavens and a new earth:

> And the one who was seated on the throne said, "See, I am making all things new." Also he said, "Write this, for these words are trustworthy and true." [6] Then he said to me, "It is done! I am the Alpha and the Omega, the beginning and the end." (Rev 21:5-6)

And foundational to Christian eschatology is the bodily resurrection of Jesus.

> Blessed be the God and Father of our Lord Jesus Christ! By his great mercy he has given us a new birth into a living hope through the resurrection of Jesus Christ from the dead. (1 Pet 1:3)

Indeed, the bodily resurrection of Jesus signaled the inbreaking of the reign of God and marks the foundational *kerygma* of the church.

> But in Christ has been raised from the dead, the first fruits of those who have died. For since death came through a human being, the resurrection of the dead has also come through a human being; for as all die in Adam, so all will be made alive in Christ. But each in his own order: Christ the first fruits, then at his coming those who belong to Christ. Then comes the end, when he hands over the kingdom to God the Father, after he has destroyed every ruler and every authority and power. (1 Cor 15:20-24)

For Christians, Jesus will return, judge the living and the dead, and then usher us into the fullness of the reign of God. "But about that day and hour no one knows, neither the angels of heaven, nor the Son, but only the Father" (Matt 24:36). The question becomes: How can we hold in tension what science proposes as cosmic eschatology and Christian hope in the resurrection?

The topic is rigorously discussed and debated among theologians. Some suggest cosmological eschatology and Christian eschatology cannot be reconciled. The promises of God for a new heaven and a new earth cannot be met within a closed universe that will collapse in on itself or an infinite universe that will freeze. Pessimistically, theologian Ted Peters comments, "Should the final future as forecasted by the combination of the big bang cosmology and the second law of thermodynamics come to pass . . . we would have proof that our faith has been in vain."[81]

From the perspective of science, some propose a physical eschatology that could resemble "eternal life." But it isn't pretty. Life would be "reduced to information processing and thus freed from its biological basis, then life can continue into the infinite future."[82] A step toward this might be what Ilia Delio describes as the "posthuman," who "is no longer the liberal subject of modernity—living from a will to power—but the person who now *lives from the splice*, that is, the interbiological space between biology and machine/device."[83]

From a perspective of dialogue, more promising is the work of John Polkinghorne who proposes that the new creation anticipated in Christianity will not emerge *ex nihilo* but *ex vetere* (from the old). What will become must be in continuity and yet in discontinuity with what existed previously, "just as the Lord's risen body bears the scars of the passion but is also transmuted and glorified."[84] The discontinuities, he argues, are properly the arena of theologians, but science has much to offer when considering the continuities.

> The nature and degree of the continuities, required by consistency if the eschatological world is to be truly a resurrected world, are things on which science may hope to comment to some degree, and even contribute some modest insight into the form of coherent possibility.[85]

81. Ted Peters, *God as Trinity: Relationality and Temporality in the Divine Life* (Louisville, KY: Westminster John Knox Press, 1993), 175–76.

82. Russell, "Cosmology and Eschatology," 568.

83. Ilia Delio, "Way of Posthuman Life Could Revitalize Religious Communities," *Global Sisters Report* (October 3, 2019), https://www.globalsistersreport.org/news/global-sisters-report/way-posthuman-life-could-revitalize-religious-communities.

84. John Polkinghorne, "Eschatology: Some Questions and Some Insights from Science," in *The End of the World and the Ends of God: Science and Theology on Eschatology*, ed. John Polkinghorne and Michael Welker (Harrisburg, PA: Trinity Press International, 2000), 29–30.

85. Polkinghorne, "Eschatology," 30.

For example, from theories of special relativity, quantum mechanics, and thermodynamics, we get a sense of the features of our universe, which we might expect to all be present in the new creation. We can anticipate "relationality and holism, energy and pattern (form), mathematics."[86]

Indeed, the discoveries and theories of scientists might contribute to our imagining aspects of the new creation, but what's the point if that new creation will likely disappear with the universe's demise? But will it? Russell asks. What if we see the laws of nature on which science builds as descriptive rather than prescriptive? If the former, then theologically we can argue that science is describing a nature that has resulted from God's continuing action. God, being God, is free to act in new and surprising ways in both human and cosmic history.

> Because of this, we can claim that the scientific predictions are *right but inapplicable* since God did act in a radically new way at Easter and will continue to act to bring about the new creation. In doing so, we are not in conflict with science but with a philosophical interpretation brought to science. In short, the future of the universe *would have been* what science predicts (i.e., freeze or fry) had God *not* acted at Easter and if God did not *continue* to act in the future.[87]

Classical theology describes God's relationship with creation as *creatio originalis*, *creatio continuo* and *creatio nova*. First, creation is brought into being by God, then it is sustained by God, and finally, it will come to glory by God's hand.

> The ever-creating God of life, source of endless possibilities, continues to draw the world to an unpredictable future, pervaded by a radical promise: at the ultimate end of time, the Creator and Sustainer of all will not abandon creation but will transform it in an unimaginable way in new communion with divine life. Being created means that living creatures are the bearers of a great and hopeful promise: "Behold, I make all things new."[88]

---

86. Russell, "Cosmology and Eschatology," 573.
87. Russell, 573–74.
88. Johnson, *Ask the Beasts*, 124.

## Conclusion

The current scientific consensus dates our universe at 13.77 billion years. From a hot big bang, cosmic dust blew forth in a gaseous cloud of potential. As the universe cooled amazing and remarkable things occurred. At about three minutes, the subatomic cosmic dust begins to combine, forming a plasma of photons, electrons, and light nuclei of hydrogen, helium, and lithium. Some 400 million years later, stars and galaxies begin to form. Today two trillion galaxies each with a hundred billion stars dot our night sky. But that's the matter we can see. Scientists estimate that 90 percent of the universe is dark matter that is invisible to us. Nine billion years after the big bang, the planet Earth forms. Nearly ten billion years after the big bang, life begins on Earth. We are late to this evolutionary party. We don't make an appearance until 300,000 years ago.

So we weren't there. In the beginning. And, barring some cosmic catastrophe, we won't be here at the universe's end. Like those who first stared up at the heavens, we ponder our reality, the meaning of life, and what small part we are to play. While astronomers and physicists look up, as women religious, we look beyond. It isn't enough to know the results of scientific inquiry, as interesting as it is. We, people of faith, are invited to search for meaning, for relationship divine and cosmic and personal.

> Borne up by the conviction that God is faithful, the community's understanding can then be predicated backward and forward beyond time, to where no experience can go. On the strength of the experience of grace here and now, the language of faith can claim: as the living God is now, so God was and will be. This way of interpreting faith assertions about the world's ultimate beginning and end makes clear that these are not claims to empirical information but articulations of deep trusting faith.[89]

Science proposes our cosmic origins and speculates on the universe's dramatic destruction, and while this all might seem a bit far afield for women religious, "The Christian community . . . gains nothing by closing its eyes to the results of scientific cosmology. One might

89. Johnson, 212.

even argue that an adequate Christian witness to a scientifically well-informed culture *demands* a thoughtful employment of these results."[90] If nothing else, astronomers and cosmologists have revealed to us the grand tableau that is God's creation—the intricacies, the singularities that spark leaps of development, the interconnection from the very beginning. It may sound a bit airy-fairy to say we are made of star-dust (I admit I once thought that), but to do so reminds us that we are part of something much bigger than ourselves. Part of something that lasts longer than our mere mortal lives. We are part of something incomprehensibly beautiful. Perhaps "Creator" isn't a big enough title for the magnitude of what our God has and continues to do in the universe. "In theology's conversations with contemporary science, it is more helpful to think of God as the infinitely generous ground of new possibilities for world-becoming."[91] It's a mouthful, but this "infinitely generous ground of new possibility" that we call God not only set in motion this evolving and expanding universe, but as we shall explore in the next chapter, has attended to the tiniest of detail.

90. Till et al., *Portraits of Creation*, 119.
91. Haught, *God After Darwin*, 119.

# Chapter Five

# The Quantum World of the Spirit

## Introduction

Two novices attending a conference stood staring out the wide window overlooking the Wisconsin cornfields. The sister from the Bronx said, "I've never seen houses so far apart." The sister from Montana replied, "I've never seen houses so close together." We orient ourselves in space and time. Our geography shapes our sense of self and identity. But when it comes to the universe all bets are off. The observable universe is approximately 93 billion light years in diameter. One light year is 5.9 trillion miles. An astronomical unit (AU) is the distance from the Earth to the Sun: on average 93 million miles. One light year equals 63,241 AUs or 31,620 round trips from the Earth to the Sun. The numbers are mind-boggling, even mind-numbing. With the discovery that the universe is expanding, those numbers are increasing. Our novices can now say, "We've never seen stars so far apart . . . and getting farther."

When we turn to the topic of quantum mechanics (which attends to the laws governing subatomic particles), it's almost as if we are falling down Alice's rabbit hole. What had been inconceivable distance is now unimaginable smallness. Quantum refers to a unit of energy, charge, or momentum, and describes particles at the subatomic level. In the study of the cosmos, quantum mechanics offers interesting insights about the fraction of a second after the Big Bang.

## The Quantum World of Weirdness

The hot big bang theory explains much of what we know about the observable universe with the exception of three key problems: the horizon problem (how do we account for the striking uniformity of the universe when some regions were never in contact with each other?), the flatness problem (we would expect curvature in our universe but instead it seems to have emerged flat), and the density fluctuation problem (the large scale structures like galaxies seem to have emerged from small fluctuations or lumps whose origin is not explained by the big bang). The answer may lie in quantum cosmology where quantum mechanics meets the universe. Since the 1980s some cosmologists have turned from the macroscopic of space to the microscopic of matter in order to answer questions about the initial conditions that gave rise to our universe today.

Let's begin with what we think we know. Prior to the big bang, there was an exceedingly dense, exceedingly tiny bundle of subatomic material under extraordinary pressure. And then it exploded. We know that cosmic background radiation blanketed space a few hundred thousand years after the big bang. The oldest galaxy yet to be discovered, GN-z11 in the Ursa Major constellation, began forming 400 million years after the big bang. But what of the first moments after that explosive singularity? Enter quantum theory, which "was originally developed in an attempt to account for the phenomena whose description appeared to lie beyond the scope of classical mechanics."[1]

This field built upon the work of many, including Niels Bohr (1885–1962), Erwin Schrödinger (1887–1961) and Werner Heisenberg (1901–1976) whose insights we will discuss below. But it was Max Planck (1858–1947) who noted that the energy of molecules moved in discrete "quantized" units. Quantum theory "took its name from the initial simple but puzzling observation that atoms absorbed and emitted energy only in certain discrete amounts called *quanta* after the Latin *quantus* for 'how much?' "[2]

---

1. Jonathan F. Halliwell, "Quantum Cosmology and the Creation of the Universe," in *Cosmology: Historical, Literary, Philosophical, Religious, and Scientific Perspectives*, ed. Norriss S. Hetherington (New York: Garland Publishing, 1993), 483.

2. Dennis Overbye, *Lonely Hearts of the Cosmos: The Story of the Scientific Quest for the Secret of the Universe* (Boston: Back Bay Books, 1999), 109.

During the early twentieth century, physicists explored the quantum world, while observational cosmologists like Hubble were looking much further afield. It would not be until the 1980s that quantum mechanics and cosmology would become strange bedfellows.

> Particle physics and cosmology had been moving closer and closer ever since Gamow had tried to use nuclear reactions to explain the big bang. Astrophysicists had learned to explicate the cosmos in terms of successively smaller and stranger objects. Atoms, microwave photons, quarks and neutrinos all had their moment on center stage as the theorists worked their way back in time closer and closer to the beginning.[3]

Rolling back the clock to the fraction of a second immediately following the big bang, Alan Guth brought his studies of physics to the problem of the initial conditions of the universe. Guth discovered that the horizon, flatness, and lumpiness of the universe could be explained by a rapid inflation that occurred prior to $10^{-32}$ seconds after the big bang. "Inflation is . . . an incredibly brief glitch tacked onto the beginning of the hot big bang model, but during this time—a blink of an eye even on the subatomic scale—a whole host of cosmological problems are swept under the carpet."[4] And as some might add, a very lumpy carpet indeed.

Quantum mechanics deals with the probability for phenomena on the scale of atoms and molecules and not the development of the massive structures of the universe. And yet, "inflationary cosmology implies that for a short period the scales of distance increased very rapidly with time. Thus, the quantum effects that occurred on very small particle-physics-length scales were later stretched to the scales of galaxies and clusters of galaxies by the process of inflation."[5] Guth's inflationary universe is literally the parable of the mustard seed writ large. Very large.

---

3. Overbye, 247.

4. Halliwell, "Quantum Cosmology," 479.

5. Alan H. Guth, "The Inflationary Universe," in *Cosmology: Historical, Literary, Philosophical, Religious, and Scientific Perspectives* (New York: Garland Publishing, 1993), 440.

### *What's the Matter?*

Artists seem to intuit what quantum physicists and others have taken a long time to discover. Life is made up of parts—lots of them—wonderfully exemplified by nineteenth-century pointillists such as Seurat. Stand too close to "A Sunday on La Grande Jatte" at the Chicago Art Institute, and all you see are collections of dots. But take several steps back from the six-by-ten-foot canvas, and you are transported back to a sunny day in a Parisian park. When first exhibited in 1886, the painting received heavy criticism, being called "bedlam," "scandal," "hilarity," "mathematical," and even "robotic."

The fifth-century Greek philosophers Leucippus and Democritus could empathize with Seurat. Their theory was that matter was composed of voids of space and "uncuttable" particles they called atoms (from the Greek *atomos* = *a* [not] + *tomos* [cut]). They were met with criticism from Aristotle and others who argued that matter was made up of the four elements of air, water, fire, and earth. Not until the nineteenth century did Leucippus and Democritus' theories receive a fuller hearing when John Dalton (1766–1844) adopted their atomic model. What followed was a succession of discoveries that confirmed and built upon Leucippus and Democritus. J. J. Thomson (1856–1940) discovered the electron. Ernest Rutherford (1871–1937) proposed that the atom possessed a nucleus with electrons orbiting it like miniature solar system, and Niels Bohr built on Rutherford's model.

More recently, quantum physicists have confirmed that matter is a complex world of smaller elements with a variety of charges. Atoms are composed of electrons occupying orbits around nuclei of protons and neutrons. Protons and neutrons are themselves composed of two kinds of objects known as quarks, oddly called the "up" quark and the "down" quark. Photons are the particles that along with waves make up light. Cosmic background radiation is comprised of very low-energy photons emitted after the big bang. "While not a major contributor to the total energy of the universe, the number of photons in this background is a billion times greater than the number of atoms in all the galaxies."[6]

---

6. Victor J. Stenger, *Quantum Gods: Creation, Chaos, and the Search for Cosmic Consciousness* (Amherst, NY: Prometheus Books, 2009), 79.

As the building blocks of protons and neutrons, quarks have interesting properties. Part of the theory of how quarks interact, known as quantum chromodynamics (QCD), proposes that quarks come in specific colors: red, green, or blue. These colorful quarks are drawn to each other, and the farther apart they are, the stronger their attraction. This force between quarks became known as gluons. "So the proton became a busy place. Inside were three pointlike quarks arrayed like the colors of the rainbow, dancing amid a hail of gluons like third graders in a snowball fight."[7]

In this subatomic snowball fight, elementary particles line up on either "Team Boson" or "Team Fermion." Bosons (i.e., photons, gluons) carry weak, strong, or electromagnetic forces. Fermions, on the other hand, are the particles that make up matter.

> The bosons are gregarious; they have a high quantum probability of all being in the same state. This lockstep phenomenon underlies the workings of the laser, behavior that is impossible to understand with classical concepts of probability. The fermions are just the opposite. The quantum probability of them being in the same state is exactly zero . . . Remarkably enough, quantum science revealed that the universe is extraordinarily simple: It is composed of fermions exchanging bosons. Other than natural law, that's all there is in the new physics. The fermions can be considered the bits of matter (electrons, quarks), and the bosons are the glue that keeps them together (photons, gluons). All the apparent complexity of the universe is just this one process happening very rapidly and in truly huge numbers.[8]

The matter of the universe of which we are familiar is made up of these elementary particles interacting with each other. Like the dots of Seurat's painting, these are a thing of beauty, combining to become the stuff of stars and the source of life on earth.

### Both/And: Waves and Particles

Quantum mechanics is weird. What something is depends on how that something is measured. Or more accurately, something

---

7. Overbye, *Lonely Hearts of the Cosmos*, 223.
8. Richard Llewellyn Lewis, "Inside the Quantum Atom Revolution," *World & I* 21, no. 5 (May 2006): 8.

exists *if* it is measured. Particles can be assessed for their position; waves for their wavelength. But the grand discovery was that an electron can be both a particle and a wave, simultaneously members of a "third category that shares some properties of waves (a characteristic frequency and wavelength, some spread over space) and some properties of particles (they're generally countable and can be localized to some degree)."[9] Louis de Broglie (1892–1987) was the first to recognize the extent of the wave-particle duality:

> The fact that, following Einstein's introduction of photons in light waves, one knew that light contains particles which are concentrations of energy incorporated into the wave, suggests that all particles, like the electron, must be transported by a wave into which it is incorporated . . . My essential idea was to extend to all particles the coexistence of waves and particles.[10]

While these quantum theories reflect the state of subatomic particles, Stenger suggests that "all material bodies, whether photons, electrons, protons, rocks, planets, or you and I, have both particle-like and wavelike properties."[11] Our weight and mass assure us of our particle nature, but we don't recognize our innate "waviness" because our size diminishes the effect.

This both/and of existence is further complicated because at the quantum level you can't predict an outcome of a problem, only the probability of the outcome.

In the late 1920s, Danish physicist Niels Bohr and his student Werner Heisenberg proposed that quantum particles can exist in multiple overlapping states, (i.e., a particle and a wave at the same moment) until they are observed at which time one or the other state collapses depending on what is being measured. Bohr's theo-

---

9. Chad Orzel, "Six Things Everyone Should Know About Quantum Physics," *Forbes* (July 8, 2015), https://www.forbes.com/sites/chadorzel/2015/07/08/six-things-everyone-should-know-about-quantum-physics/#6cafb1cd7d46.

10. Cited by Ibrahima Sakho, *Introduction to Quantum Mechanics. 1, Thermal Radiation and Experimental Facts Regarding the Quantization of Matter* (Hoboken, NJ: Wiley, 2019), 218.

11. Stenger, *Quantum Gods*, 117.

ries became known as Copenhagen interpretation.[12] For his part, Heisenberg developed a mathematical formula, known as the uncertainty principle, that showed that you can't measure both the wavelike and particlelike aspects of an electron at the same time. "The more precisely you knew one trait of a particle like an electron—say, its position—the less precisely you could know something else, like its momentum."[13]

In light of the uncertainty principle, Lewis proposes that at the quantum level even the most elementary of particles has what appears to be free will.

> In quantum science, natural law does not "force" matter to do anything, rather it generates the quantum probability of what matter will do. Somewhat unexpectedly, it has been proved beyond doubt that, within this weighted history, even simple things like electrons have freedom of choice—nothing determines what they actually do (within the confines of the quantum probability).[14]

Curiouser and curiouser!

## Entanglement: Spooky Action at a Distance

By a serious miscalculation on my part, I signed up for the wrong science elective in college. I thought Phys 250: Fundamentals of Physics would be easy. Don't let the word "fundamental" fool you. In my brief but tortured experience, I learned that physics isn't so much science as it is math. Complicated strings of equations with numbers and letters juxtaposed over and under long and short lines. But sometimes those football field-sized equations produce something akin to beauty. A symmetry. An insight. An answer to a question we didn't know we had. And sometimes those insights

---

12. "Today the Copenhagen interpretation is mostly regarded as synonymous with indeterminism, Bohr's correspondence principle, Born's statistical interpretation of the wave function, and Bohr's complementarity interpretation of certain atomic phenomena" (Jan Faye, "Copenhagen Interpretation of Quantum Mechanics," *Stanford Encyclopedia of Philosophy* [Winter 2019 Edition], https://plato.stanford.edu/archives /win2019/entries/qm-copenhagen).

13. Overbye, *Lonely Hearts of the Cosmos*, 108.

14. Lewis, "Inside the Quantum Atom Revolution," 18.

come from a cat. A cat that may or may not be dead. (If you're a cat lover, skip this part.)

One of the more notable thought experiments in response to the uncertainty principle has to do with the life or death of an imaginary cat (no cats were harmed in the making of this experiment). But before the cat comes the paradox that produced the need for the living and or dead hypothetical cat. In response to the Copenhagen interpretation, Albert Einstein (1879–1955), Boris Podolsky (1896–1966), and Nathan Rosen (1909–1995) wrote a paper, later known as the EPR paper, in which they argued that probability at the quantum level was an incomplete theory. Something else must be at work that hadn't been discovered.

> In a complete theory there is an element corresponding to each element of reality. A sufficient condition for the reality of a physical quantity is the possibility of predicting it with certainty, without disturbing the system.[15]

Einstein was none too happy with probability rather than precision. In a letter to Max Born (1882–1970) in 1926, he famously said, "Quantum theory yields much, but it hardly brings us close to the Old One's secrets. I, in any case, am convinced He does not play dice with the universe." And here comes the cat.

In correspondence with Einstein, Schrödinger, too, found the idea advocated by the Copenhagen interpretation incomplete. He proposed a thought experiment as an illustration. First, you put a cat in a locked steel box along with a vial of poison and a Geiger counter in which is set a tiny amount of radioactive material. If a radioactive atom decays, then the Geiger counter causes a release of the poison. The cat dies. But if the atom does not decay, the cat lives. According to the Copenhagen interpretation, as long as the box is shut the cat is both dead and alive, since only observation confirms the state of said cat. Schrödinger argued that what happened in the microsphere did not necessary translate into the macroworld. "It

---

15. Albert Einstein, Boris Podolsky, and Nathan Rosen, "Can Quantum-Mechanical Description of Physical Reality Be Considered Complete?," *Physical Review* 47 (May 15, 1935): 777.

is typical of these cases that an indeterminacy originally restricted to the atomic domain becomes transformed into macroscope indeterminacy, which can then be resolved by direct observation."[16]

> Schrödinger's point was not simply that quantum rules lead to apparent nonsense when applied at the everyday scale—you don't need a cat for that. Rather, he wanted to find an extreme demonstration of how deferring any assignment of a definite state (alive or dead) until measurement has been made (by opening the box to look) could lead to implications that seem not only odd but logically forbidden.[17]

Though the EPR paper wasn't able to establish a "complete description of physical reality," it did unintentionally introduce another interesting paradoxical quantum characteristic: the concept of non-locality. Einstein called this "spooky action at a distance," and in the same paper that introduced live/dead cats, Schrödinger would term it "entanglement."

> When two systems, of which we know the states by their respective representatives, enter into temporary physical interaction due to known forces between them, and when after a time of mutual influence the systems separate again, then they can no longer be described in the same way as before, viz. by endowing each of them with a representative of its own. I would not call that one but rather the characteristic trait of quantum mechanics, the one that enforces its entire departure from classical lines of thought. By the interaction the two representatives [the quantum states] have become entangled.[18]

Entanglement of quantum states of particles means that a measurement of one particle affects the state of the entangled particle, even

16. John D. Trimmer, "The Present Situation in Quantum Mechanics: A Translation of Schrödinger's 'Cat Paradox,' " *Proceedings of the American Philosophical Society* 124 (1980): 328.

17. Philip Ball, "Real-Life Schrödinger's Cats Probe the Boundary of the Quantum World," *Quanta Magazine* (June 25, 2018), https://www.quantamagazine.org/real-life -schrodingers-cats-probe-the-boundary-of-the-quantum-world-20180625.

18. Erwin Schrödinger, "Discussion of Probability Relations Between Separated Systems," *Proceedings of the Cambridge Philosophical Society* 31 (1935): 555.

at a distance. "At first glance, this implies that information would have to travel faster than the speed of light, which is forbidden by special relativity."[19]

Einstein's insight on nonlocality has been variously tested, beginning with John Bell's theorem in 1964, Alain Aspect and his collaborators' experiments in 1982, and more recently the research of Nicolas Gisin and others. The entanglement of photons has been measured over 1,200 kilometers. But nonlocality is a fickle thing, sometimes ending in "entanglement sudden death."

> No one knows how to describe the separation between the bizarre quantum world where entanglement exists and the everyday world where nature appears to operate via easy-to-spot causes and effects. Creating entanglement on a larger scale may help clarify this mysterious division.[20]

To that end, researchers are exploring the implications of quantum nonlocality for communications and quantum computing, ushering in what some are calling the second quantum revolution.

Quantum mechanics has helped to answer the questions about the observable universe we see today but not without resistance. Early twentieth-century physicists scratched their heads at the idea of something other than classical physics to explain the universe. Cause and effect could be seen, tested, and measured. But quantum mechanics argued for a different, deeper organization at the heart of reality. Light was both a particle and a wave. And at the quantum level, you couldn't determine both the position and the momentum of a particle. You could only count on a probability of location. Arguing against these ideas, Einstein and Schrödinger among others unwittingly discovered even weirder aspects of quantum mechanics: photons could be entangled so that the measurement of one determined the measurement of the other . . . at a distance! Perhaps the

19. Tu Zhoudunming, Dmitri E. Kharzeev, and Thomas Ullrich, "Einstein-Podolsky-Rosen Paradox and Quantum Entanglement at Subnucleonic Scales," *Physical Review Letters* 124 (February 14, 2020), https://link.aps.org/doi/10.1103/PhysRevLett.124.062001.

20. Laura Sanders, "Everyday Entanglement: Physicists Take Quantum Weirdness Out of the Lab," *Science News* 178 (November 20, 2010), 30.

take-away from this mini course on physics is "that at the heart of existence is a mystery, a mystery that ultimately cannot be solved so much as savored."[21]

## Divine Entanglement: The Fellowship of the Holy Spirit

We can see the results of the strange workings of the quantum world, but its failure to adhere to Newtonian physics means cause and effect has gone out the window. The enigmatic attractions and repulsions of fermions and bosons, the effect of subatomic particles on each other at a distance, and the dismissal of predictability in favor of probability—these all sound more like science fiction than science fact. In some respects, this invisible realm (at least to casual observers) is a bit like a scientific version of *Horton Hears a Who!*, the beloved Dr. Seuss book in which the big-eared elephant detects the plaintive calls of the residents of a tiny world. But in this case, it's a world in which a hypothetical cat in an imaginary box may or may not be dead.

The sheer perplexity of the quantum world means most of us non-physics geeks are left scratching our heads. Indeed, when it comes to quantum mechanics, we might well echo the apostle Paul, "Listen, I will tell you a mystery!" (1 Cor 15:51). Might this quantum mystery offer some insights into our Divine mystery? More specifically, how might knowledge of the quantum world enhance the portrait of another invisible yet highly effective entity, which we know as the Holy Spirit? In the following sections, we begin first by describing our understanding of the Holy Spirit as presented in the survey results, before turning to the biblical portrait of the activities of the divine Spirit. Finally, we'll explore the metaphorical nexus between the properties of quantum mechanics and the relationality of the Trinity.

### Our Experience of the Holy Spirit

"It is in the nature of human existence itself to sense (whether consciously or unconsciously) that there is something beyond ourselves, some ultimate reality, some mysterious presence that is responsible

---

21. Overbye, *Lonely Hearts of the Cosmos*, 420.

for and animates all of life."[22] The Holy Spirit is the force that beckons, cajoles, and inspires toward that ultimate reality. For Christians, the spirit is an active, animating member of the Trinity, and spirituality comes to define how we actively live our lives guided by that same spirit. Such a spirituality is multi-faceted, viewed as "the Spirit at work in persons (1) within a culture, (2) in relation to a tradition, (3) in memory of Jesus Christ, (4) in the light of contemporary events, hopes, sufferings and promises, (5) in efforts to combine elements of action and contemplation, (6) with respect to charism and community, (7) as expressed and authenticated in praxis."[23]

At various times, different elements of this complex are more apparent to us than others. As I write this chapter, the world is enduring the COVID-19 virus pandemic, and in the United States we are finally acknowledging the disease of racism. Men and women of faith and integrity are attempting to respond to these twin pandemics. Some of the more than one hundred survey responses to the question, "How do you envision the role of the Holy Spirit?" evidence a deep awareness of the pains and sufferings of our world and the power of the spirit to tend and heal. As one sister wrote, "The Holy Spirit is the person of the Trinity here on Earth at this time in history." Another agreed, "The role of the Spirit is to be God-with-us at this time in salvific history to remind, enliven, enlighten, surprise, comfort, and impel us to action on behalf of the Reign of God."

There are many activities of the spirit, but frequently in our survey responses, sisters named "energy" as its primary aspect. "The Holy Spirit is the divine energy that connects everyone and everything," while it is also "the spark—carrier and transmitter of Holy Mystery, energy, love," "animating force, primordial fire, within all life," "Holy wind that carries love energy to all," "Dynamism. Action. Movement," and "the love allurement present in all, positive energy."

---

22. Barbara E. Bowe, *Biblical Foundations of Spirituality: Touching a Finger to the Flame* (Lanham, MD: Rowman & Littlefield, 2017), 11.

23. Michael Downey, "Current Trends Understanding Christian Spirituality: Dress Rehearsal for a Method," *Spirituality Today* 43 (1991): 278–79.

In the Johannine sense, the spirit works as an advocate, "that un-seen force of love that helps us to understand God's will, that speaks to our heart, that guides us, accompanies us, and gives us what we need to become the person God created us to be," responded one sister. The spirit is both inspiration and relationship, and "flows in my experiences and helps to guide my actions."

Others wrote of the relationship within the Trinity. The Holy Spirit is "inspiring and invigorating Creation from within, par-ticularly animating humans to carry on Christ's mission of saving love," and "is the love between God and Christ and the being which animates all of life." Another sister brought in the importance of the sacrament of baptism in her description.

> He proceeds from the Father and the Son and is poured upon us through the Sacrament of Baptism, but as the Ruah is present in our world. Is the loving breath of the Father and the Son.

The Holy Spirit is named, "guide and companion, Sophia swells within us all and guides us on our journey. The Holy Spirit advocates for us and gifts with the wisdom we need." Another described the Holy Spirit as the "relationship between Creator and Jesus . . . , this is where my faith surfaces." The "Spirit prompts, nudges and invites. Spirit connects me, in the here and now, with my beloved and all of existence (nature, cosmos, etc.)."

And sometimes only metaphor can best describe our experience of the spirit. "The Holy Spirit is the background music of our lives. In this case the background music is written before the action. It is our job to listen and act upon this inspiration." Another respondent said, the Holy Spirit could be envisioned, "as a wave, a gentle breeze making her presence known and relaying intuition, messages, words, notions." Indeed, the scriptural portrait of the Holy Spirit to which we now turn shows that from the beginning, the third person of the Trinity has been active and ever-present.

### The Biblical Portrait of the Holy Spirit

Over time the black leather binding had cracked. The gold trimmed pages were onion-thin and almost translucent. The inside cover outlined a tree, on which my mother had carefully written our family members. As a child I hadn't noticed the significance, but the adding of our names into the book of the Bible made our family a part of the larger family of faith depicted in its pages. Fast forward to my adulthood and a paperback New American Bible with a colored cover of the Sea of Galilee. Here was a book meant to be read. I carried this Bible throughout my first sojourn through the Middle East. I distinctly remember sitting on the shores of the Sea of Galilee, reading about the Beatitudes and feeling as if the book in my hand allowed me to transcend time. It was a portal to the past, a compass that pointed me toward God, and an introduction to myriad men and women who had walked this way before me. The author of 2 Timothy said it rather succinctly. "All scripture is inspired by God and is useful for teaching, for reproof, for correction, and for training in righteousness" (2 Tim 3:16). Here among its many books, written over thousands of years, our portrait of the Spirit is more a mosaic than a photograph. In what follows, I will highlight some aspects of the biblical presentation of the Spirit that we will bring to our dialogue with the quantum world.

Our first problem is one of language, or rather the limitation of English. The word translated as "spirit" in the Bible is *ruaḥ* in the Hebrew and *pneuma* in the Greek, both of which can be rendered "Spirit," "breath," or "wind." In some passages, only the context provides the clue as to how the word should be translated. Another difficulty is determining if the word refers to God's Spirit or the spirit that resides in the individual. For example, in 2 Corinthians 6:6, Paul writes that he has commended himself to the Corinthians through "holiness of spirit." Is he referring to the breath of God given to all humans (Gen 2:7) or to a particular manifestation of the spirit especially given to Paul? Pushing aside the not inconsiderable questions of meaning, translation, and context, we will only focus on some of the activities of the Spirit of God: giving life, anointing for leadership, inspiring for prophecy, signaling conversion-initiation, and gifting charismatic activities.

The second creation narrative in Genesis chapter 2 situates the human as the first of the living creatures. Crafted from the stuff of the earth (*adamah*), the earth creature (*adam*) is brought to life by the breath/wind/spirit of God (Gen 2:7). Without this breath, all creatures meet their end.

> When you hide your face, they are dismayed;
> when you take away their breath, they die
> and return to their dust.
> When you send forth your spirit, they are created;
> and you renew the face of the ground. (Ps 104:29-30)

In Ezekiel's vision of dry bones, God commands "O breath, and breathe upon these slain, that they may live" (Ezek 37:9). Likewise, the New Testament also recognizes the Spirit's role in sustaining life. In the Gospel of John, we read, "It is the spirit that gives life" (John 6:63). And the most dramatic example occurs on the cross: "When Jesus had received the wine, he said, 'It is finished.' Then he bowed his head and gave up his spirit" (John 19:30).

In the Johannine sensibility, the Spirit of God that breathed life into the first human is replicated by the breath of Jesus who breathes his Spirit into his disciples, thus bringing to life the beloved community.

> Jesus said to them again, "Peace be with you. As the Father has sent me, so I send you." When he had said this, he breathed on them and said to them, "Receive the Holy Spirit. If you forgive the sins of any, they are forgiven them; if you retain the sins of any, they are retained" (John 20:21-23).

Not only does the Spirit of God quicken life, it also raises up and empowers leaders from among the people. The prophet Samuel "anointed [David] in the presence of his brothers; and the spirit of the LORD came mightily upon David from that day forward" (1 Sam 16:13). Centuries later, Isaiah of Jerusalem prophesied that a new Davidic leader would arise who himself would also possess the spirit.

> A shoot shall come out from the stump of Jesse, / and a branch shall grow out of his roots. / The spirit of the LORD shall rest on him, / the spirit of wisdom and understanding, / the spirit of counsel and might, / the spirit of knowledge and the fear of the LORD. (Isa 11:1-2)

But the Spirit that descends upon the favored one can be taken away. Poor Saul, once anointed by Samuel as king (1 Sam 15:1), finds his favored position is lost. "Now the spirit of the LORD departed from Saul, and an evil spirit from the LORD tormented him" (1 Sam 16:14).

For Israel's prophets, the Spirit of God empowered one to speak in God's name as we hear in Micah:

> But as for me, I am filled with power,
>   with the spirit of the LORD,
>   and with justice and might,
> to declare to Jacob his transgression
>   and to Israel his sin. (Mic 3:8)

But this spirit was episodic, "Then the spirit of the LORD fell upon me, and he said to me, 'Say, Thus says the LORD : This is what you think, O house of Israel'" (Ezek 11:5). Prophetic eschatology anticipated the Day of the Lord when God would "pour out my spirit on all flesh; / your sons and your daughters shall prophesy, / your old men shall dream dreams, / and your young men shall see visions" (Joel 2:28).

The apostle Peter will cite this text to explain the Pentecost event to those gathered outside the upper room (Acts 2:16-21). To this same crowd, Peter will invite their participation in this new spirit-filled movement. "Repent, and be baptized every one of you in the name of Jesus Christ so that your sins may be forgiven; and you will receive the gift of the Holy Spirit" (Acts 2:38). Though most often baptism precedes the Spirit, not so in the case of Cornelius the Centurion:

> Then Peter said, "Can anyone withhold the water for baptizing these people who have received the Holy Spirit just as we have?" (Acts 10:47)

The Spirit, according to the apostle Paul, becomes the down payment of the reign of God to come. "[W]e ourselves, who have the first fruits of the Spirit, groan inwardly while we wait for adoption, the redemption of our bodies" (Rom 8:23). This Spirit bestows gifts upon the believers for the upbuilding of the community.

> To each is given the manifestation of the Spirit for the common good.
> To one is given through the Spirit the utterance of wisdom, and to
> another the utterance of knowledge according to the same Spirit, to
> another faith by the same Spirit, to another gifts of healing by the
> one Spirit, to another the working of miracles, to another prophecy,
> to another the discernment of spirits, to another various kinds of
> tongues, to another the interpretation of tongues. All these are acti-
> vated by one and the same Spirit, who allots to each one individually
> just as the Spirit chooses. (1 Cor 12:7-11)

The Bible describes the multiple roles of the Spirit of God, in
which it initiates life, anoints leaders, inspires prophetic oracles, sig-
nifies the moment of conversion/initiation, and provides charismatic
gifts to build up the Christian community. As the Bible presents it,
the Spirit is the vivifying presence of God in creation. The question
becomes: What do the insights from quantum mechanics add to our
understanding of the Holy Spirit?

### Quantum Implications and the Actions of the Spirit

In what must have been a most confounding conversation for
poor Nicodemus, Jesus tells the Pharisee, "The wind blows where it
chooses, and you hear the sound of it, but you do not know where
it comes from or where it goes. So it is with everyone who is born
of the Spirit" (John 3:8). Again, the English translation misses the
evangelist's underlying theological comment. The word for both
"wind," and "spirit" is *pneuma*. Though we recognize the presence
of the Spirit/wind, its origin and direction remain a mystery. Might
some of the emerging theories about the quantum world shed light
on that mystery? The deep unity, probability, and nonlocality of the
subatomic elements may have particular relevance for our understanding of the Holy Spirit. But in order to make some comparisons,
a word about method.

In the chapter of affairs introduction, we discussed the various
models for the engagement of science and religion, choosing the
model of dialogue as our way forward. In dialogue both entities
maintain their own boundaries, operating principles, and methodology. Only by respecting the particularity of each can we enter into a
mutual conversation. But how might two very different projects find
a common language? The comparative mode of complementarity

provides a way in which quantum theory and theological concepts can be in the same room. As a means to explore mutually contrasting concepts, Honner described four different types of complementarity: weak, strong, circular, and parallel. For our purpose we are most interested in the latter two.

> When both elements of the conjugate pair originate from the same domain—for example, both "wave" and "particle" originate from the domain of classical physics—then they are said to be in parallel complementarity. On the other hand, if the terms derive from different domains—as do divine revelation and human history— then they are in circular complementarity. Consider Bohr's claim that classical and quantum physics are complementary: one theory presumes that nature is continuous and causal, while the other assumes a radical discontinuity in nature; and while quantum theory provides a more general point of view than does classical physics, it is dependent on classical, everyday concepts for its terminology and unambiguous frames of reference.[24]

We can make analogous comparisons between a theological concept, like the Holy Spirit, and a scientific theory, like those emerging from quantum physics. But those comparisons are descriptive not prescriptive. For example:

> Quantum physics suggests a fundamental discontinuity in nature so that, at a subatomic level, there is a limit to our ability to provide everyday, causal descriptions of what is happening; in other words, we have to take concepts from "this side" of that boundary and apply them to our mediated experiences of the subquantum realm; but this entails a paradox, for we are using terms from a less adequate theory (classical physics) in order to develop a more general theory (quantum physics). The puzzle is not unlike that involved in the use of analogical language about God, but it also raises the parallel paradox that, though the world is dependent on God, we can only find God by first living in the world.

---

24. John Honner, SJ, "Unity-in-Difference: Karl Rahner and Niels Bohr," *Theological Studies* 46 (1985): 482–83.

In essence, we are comparing apples to oranges, but we have no other recourse. But this isn't new to us. We are familiar with the analogous nature of our language about God whom we describe as "like and not like." Similarly, in order to talk about the quantum world, we are obliged to use terms from the world we know, even though those terms are inadequate to fully describe the quantum realm. As Simmons noted:

> It would seem that in relation to both the ultimate character of physical reality in physics and the nature of God in theology, human comprehension is driven to analogy and metaphor. The appropriation of metaphorical concepts in quantum mechanics for use in constructive theology, then, is not only appropriate but may indeed build on their use in physics itself.[25]

As we ponder the complementarity between the quantum world and the Spirit of God, we keep in mind that both derive from very different domains, so any comparison is suggestive and analogical.

### Observation and Intercession

In the quantum world, observation appears to affect the state of subatomic particles, so until it is observed, a photon or electron inhabits a state of both/and, being a wave and a particle.

> The Double Slit experiment shows that a single photon, given a choice of alternative slits on its passage to a screen, passes through both slits (and causes a wave interference pattern on the screen to prove it). But if an "observer" uses a photon detector to watch, or . . . to record the event, the photon then uses one slit only (as if it were merely a particle, not a wave) and the interference pattern disappears.[26]

Belben pondered if the effect of the Spirit and our efforts in intercessory prayer might work in a similar manner as the observation

25. Ernest L. Simmons, *The Entangled Trinity: Quantum Physics and Theology* (Minneapolis: Fortress Press, 2014), 140.

26. Tim Belben, "Quantum Creation? Cosmologists Are Coming Up with Some Strange Theories about the Origin of the Universe. Can Christian Theology Keep Pace?," *Modern Believing* 51, no. 2 (2010): 53n1.

of subatomic particles. When we observe a quantum object, we are "fixing" it to a particular state (wave or particle) for the purpose of our measurement. Something similar happens with petitionary prayer in which we ask for a change or alteration to occur. As Belben explained, according to Thomas Aquinas (1225–1274), the First Person of the Trinity is essence, infinite being, and infinite good. The Second Person of the Trinity is the self-knowledge or self-expression of God and has equal reality. Finally, the Third Person of the Trinity is God's will, which is love, "the will to give himself (his greatest gift) to his Word, who (as God the Son) offers it back. There is no sequence of action in this, it just is, but to us this 'Will to give infinite goodness' is infinite Love, the completeness of God, the 'person of the Spirit.' "[27] If the Holy Spirit is thought of as God's love, then perhaps by means of intercessory prayer, our prayer invites that love in a particular way.

> We need actually to believe (or trust) that the detail of human life will be changed by our prayer, or that the prayer will uncover what is already willed. It is hardly sensible for us to seek to change God's Will, whatever the Old Testament implies about God changing his mind. But if it is his Will, as Creator, to leave something of the probability of our existence undetermined and subject to human freewill, intercession can have a logical basis.[28]

This suggests that our prayer, in accord with the Spirit, can affect outcomes. According to Belben, "The notion is analogous to the scientific hypothesis that observation of a quantum state changes what happens, in the sense that the act of observation in some way determines the probability of what, measured in space-time, has already happened."[29]

In some respects, Scripture says something similar. The Spirit intercedes on our behalf as the apostle Paul writes in Romans:

> Likewise the Spirit helps us in our weakness; for we do not know how to pray as we ought, but that very Spirit intercedes with sighs

27. Belben, 50.
28. Belben, 52.
29. Belben, 52.

too deep for words. And God, who searches the heart, knows what is the mind of the Spirit, because the Spirit intercedes for the saints according to the will of God. (Rom 8:26-27)

Jesus himself encouraged us to ask and we will receive (Matt 7:7). If intercession wasn't possible, if the laws of nature precluded any interruption at the human level, then Jesus' commendation would be pointless. "So I tell you, whatever you ask for in prayer, believe that you have received it, and it will be yours" (Mark 11:24). Paul advises the Philippians community to do likewise. "Do not worry about anything, but in everything by prayer and supplication with thanksgiving let your requests be made known to God" (Phil 4:6).

## Entangled Trinity

In the quantum world, we are told that there exists a foundational oneness. "Physics has revealed a unity to the universe which makes it clear that everything is connected in a way which would have seemed inconceivable a few decades ago."[30] As quantum theories state, "the electrons in atoms are not tiny particles, little balls of matter, but are standing waves, wave functions, numerical patterns, or mathematical forms . . . In this way we find numerical relations at the foundation of reality—nonmaterial principles on which the order of the world is based."[31] This deep unity finds a divine counterpart in the perichoresis of the Trinity, to use a description from the Cappadocian Fathers. The Trinity is in a dance of relationship and unity. The interaction of fermions exchanging bosons rapidly and in great numbers, waves/particle duality, and entanglement that form quantum unity similarly reflect communion and interdependence of the Trinity. Both at the divine and quantum level, this deep unity cannot be explained by cause and effect.

Entanglement or nonlocality refers to the quantum phenomenon whereby electrons or photons appear connected even at distance.[32]

30. Bernard Carr, "Cosmology and Religion," in *The Oxford Handbook of Religion and Science*, ed. Philip Clayton (Oxford: Oxford University Press, 2008), 144.

31. Lothar Schäfer, "Quantum Reality and the Consciousness of the Universe," *Zygon: Journal of Religion & Science* 41 (2006): 507.

32. John Polkinghorne, *Quantum Theory: A Very Short Introduction* (Oxford: Oxford University Press, 2002), 79.

Entanglement is simply another way of addressing the fact that physical reality is interconnected at the deepest levels we currently know and that there is a superposition of states that is complementary (Bohr) rather than contradictory, as in classical (Newtonian) physics.[33]

Some theologians are drawing from the quantum reality of entanglement a new (or renewed) way to view the community of the Trinity.

The ability of electrons or photons to "act" on each other at a distance is nonlocational relationality. "Once a pair of particles or a divided single particle is entangled, they remain connected no matter where in the physical universe they travel."[34] Holism refers to the parts that are derived from the whole and is central to the concept of emergence. Simmons refers to the relationship between nonlocality and holism as "truly togetherness-in-separation."[35] These insights from the quantum realm by analogy help us understand a bit about the workings of the Trinity.

> If the divine is entangled, that is, interrelated and interdependent with multiple potentials such as a wave function, then the same entangled divine reality can be experienced as incarnation, not just origination . . . Finally, the community also experienced, within the community itself, the sustaining spirit, the "Comforter," the "creative Spirit," as the ongoing presence of the divine within the midst of the community.[36]

Thus, Simmons argues for a "panentheistic" understanding of the Trinity, drawing on Edwards:

1. Panentheism is understood in Trinitarian terms—in this form of panentheism, the universe is understood as being created from within the shared life of the Trinity.

2. It understands God as wholly other to creatures and, precisely as such, as radically interior to them. Divine transcendence and immanence are not polar opposites but presuppose each other.

---

33. Simmons, *The Entangled Trinity*, 146.
34. Simmons, 148.
35. Simmons, 148.
36. Simmons, 152–53.

3. The spatial image is of all-things-in-God and God in all things—though God transcends the world, so God is not literally some kind of container.

4. God is understood as a creator who enables creatures to have their own proper autonomy and integrity. There is an infinite difference between God's *creatio continua* (primary causality) and all the interacting connections and causal relationships between creatures (secondary causality).

5. It sees creation as a free act of divine self-limitation. Love involves free self-limitation, making space for another, and God can be thought of as supremely loving in this way.

6. This model understands creation as a relationship that affects God as well as creatures. This means that the relationship is real on the side of God as well as that of creatures. Each affects the other in a reciprocal relationship,[37] but a relationship that is asymmetrical: the world is dependent on God in a way that God is not dependent on the world.

The curious world of quantum reality with its nonlocal actions, complementarity and superposition (your observation determines what you see) in effect offers an insight into the divine realm, a way of understanding the relationships among and activities of the Trinity. Unknowingly quantum physicists have provided theologians with a host of new metaphors and new ways of conceiving how God works within creation.

> Entanglement gives metaphorical identity to the manner in which panentheism models God's relationship to the creation. The foundational interconnectivity between God and creation is such that not only does one influence the other, but they also exist in a communitarian relationship that mirrors the divine communion of the internal Trinity.[38]

---

37. Denis Edwards, "A Relational and Evolving Universe Unfolding within the Dynamism of the Divine Communion," in *In Whom We Live and Move and Have Our Being*, ed. Philip Clayton and A. R. Peacocke (Grand Rapids, MI: Eerdmans, 2008), 200–202. Quoted in Simmons, *The Entangled Trinity*, 158.

38. Simmons, *The Entangled Trinity*, 160.

## Conclusion

I feel a bit relieved when I read that Einstein among other luminaries found the emerging findings of quantum physics "incomplete," "spooky," and "unpredictable." We like the here and now. We like that the principles of cause and effect underlie our visible world. We like predictability. The quantum world will have none of that! Though physicists and mathematicians understand its inner beauty and order, for most of us, the quantum realm of quarks is, indeed, quirky.

> In the quantum phenomena the universe has opened again; the mechanistic part of reality is only the cortex of something deeper and wider that has room for the spiritual, and religious faith is not in conflict with objective science.[39]

What the quantum world does reveal is that at the smallest level of creation, cause and effect no longer function. Instead, we have the probability of an event. When we consider the actions of the Spirit described in Scripture, we see a similar pattern of potential action. Some receive gifts of prophecy, some gifts of teaching, administration, etc. (1 Cor 12:27-31).

The probability that a photon or an electron will demonstrate properties of a particle or a wave is directly connected to its observation. This ability to "affect" the state of a subatomic particle sheds light on how the Spirit is able to assist us in our prayer. We aren't changing God's mind by our prayer, but perhaps the potentiality of creation allows for our free will to direct the "state" of affairs, so to speak. In other words, intercessory prayer is similar to the observation of quantum elements. We can make a difference through our prayer.

Interestingly, most of the survey descriptions of the role of the Holy Spirit reflect these insights. How the Spirit directs, enlivens, and inspires appears random but actually adheres to a deeper unity, reflecting an internal/eternal connection much like we envision the relationship shared among the Persons of the Trinity. In our next chapter we'll explore the "Second Big Bang" of evolution and the role of Jesus Christ in this emerging, expanding, and complexifying cosmos.

---

39. Schäfer, "Quantum Reality," 528.

# Chapter Six

## Evolution and the Jesus Singularity

### Introduction

Sassy the shi tzu suits her name. At twelve pounds and fifteen inches, she sits on the throne that is my mother's lap as if she were born to rule. And then there is Yofi, my collie-beagle mix, whose love-hate relationship with the mail carrier is the stuff of legends. With the exception of Sassy's assertiveness and Yofi's howl, there is nothing that obviously links these two dogs to their gray wolf ancestor with whom they share 99.9 percent of their DNA. But some 40,000 years ago, the *Canis familiaris* emerged in eastern Asia. This genetic ancestor of all dogs realized that it was more advantageous to scavenge around the encampments of humans than to risk the dangerous and often fruitless hunt for prey. Fast forward: in 2018, Americans spent more than thirty billion dollars on pet food, indicating that the dogs knew a good thing when they saw it. How the ancestor of the wolf became humanity's best friend is just one of the interesting facets of evolution, the topic to which we now turn.

### Following the Footprints of the Past

Evolution describes the biological development of all organizations from less complex to more complex species, a development governed by natural law. However, "if one wanted to extend from the biological to the cosmological, one would see the fact of evolution as including all developmental change from the time of the Big Bang."[1] In fact, discussions on evolution in the seventeenth century centered on the emergence of suns and planets from gaseous nebulae. It would be more than a hundred years later when Charles Darwin (1809–1882) among others began their research on biological evolution. Though the concept of evolution was discussed prior to Darwin's work, it met with little support, owing to the fact that "it was seen to be a reflection of the ideology of progress—upward change in the human social world, and upward change in the history of life, from 'monad' to 'man.' "[2] This idea of evolution left little room for divine providence.

Charles Darwin was not the first in his family to be curious about the possibility of evolution, then called "transmutation." Physician and naturalist Erasmus Darwin, Charles' grandfather, had written on the topic. But in the nature versus nurture debate, Charles' life experience most definitely aided in his research. He spent five years as an unofficial naturalist onboard HMS *Beagle*, charting the coast of South America. He would credit this experience as foundational to his thinking on evolution:

> When on board the H.M.S. "Beagle," as naturalist, I was much struck with certain facts in the distribution of the inhabitants of South America, and the geological relations of the present to the past inhabitants of that continent. The facts seemed to throw some light on the origin of species—that mystery of mysteries . . .[3]

*On the Origin of Species*, first published in 1859, presented Darwin's theory of evolution, backed by evidence from paleontology, embryology, and geography. With this publication, Darwin "made the fact of evolution empirically plausible and no longer reliant on an underlying social philosophy for acceptance."[4]

---

1. Michael Ruse, "Evolution," in *Encyclopedia of Science and Religion*, vol. 1 (New York: Macmillan, 2003), 280.

2. Ruse, 280.

3. Charles Darwin, *The Annotated Origin: A Facsimile of the First Edition of "On the Origin of Species,"* ed. James Costa (Cambridge, MA: Harvard University Press, 2009), 1.

4. Ruse, "Evolution," 280.

It's a good thing that the adage, "leave nothing behind but footprints" didn't apply to the development of life, for it is literally the remnants of the past that shed light on our present. "Nearly all fossils can be regarded as intermediaries in some sense; they are life forms that come between ancestral forms that preceded them and those that followed."[5] The path of evolution, or phylogeny, refers to the history of the past discoverable from the fossil record, anatomical and embryological changes, and more recently molecular biological evidence. We now know with some certainty that the big bang occurred almost 14 billion years ago, the Earth is 4.5 billion years old, life on earth began forming 3.9–3.7 million years ago,[6] the age of mammals started 65 million years ago, and *Homo sapiens* appeared around 300,000 years ago. And along with our timeline, biologists can also confirm that all life shared a common ancestor. From that origin, more than 250,000 species of living plants, 100,000 species of fungi, and 1.5 million species of animals and microorganisms have been described and named. Taxonomists propose that an additional 86 percent of living organisms have not even been discovered. "Globally, our best approximation to the total number of species is based on the opinion of taxonomic experts, whose estimates range between 3 and 100 million species."[7] Dwarfing these numbers, an estimated five billion species that ever lived on earth have gone extinct.[8]

## Natural Selection

Darwin and others recognized the growth of diversity and could trace that development over time, but the question became: how? By what mechanism did evolution work? Why did changes occur over

5. Francisco J. Ayala, "Evolution, Biological," in *Encyclopedia of Science and Religion*, ed. J. Wentzel Vrede van Huyssteen, vol. 1 (New York: Macmillan, 2003), 292.

6. Ben K. D. Pearce et al., "Constraining the Time Interval for the Origin of Life on Earth," *Astrobiology* 18 (2018): 343.

7. Camilo Mora et al., "How Many Species Are There on Earth and in the Ocean?," *PLoS Biology* 9 (August 2011), https://www.ncbi.nlm.nih.gov/pmc/articles/PMC3160336.

8. Beverly Peterson Stearns and Stephen C. Stearns, *Watching, from the Edge of Extinction* (New Haven, CT: Yale University Press, 1999), x.

time in specific species and why did other species become extinct? Darwin's answer: natural selection.

> I have called this principle, by which slight variation, if useful, is preserved, by the term of Natural Selection, in order to mark its relation to [the hu]man's power of selection. We have seen that [the hu]man by selection can certainly produce great results, and can adapt organic beings to his own uses, through the accumulation of slight but useful variations, given to him by the hand of Nature.[9]

This process of natural selection took a great deal of time, with variations eventually leading to the development of new species. For example, the first mammals likely appeared about 65 million years ago. Approximately 2.5 to 2 million years ago the genus *Homo* emerged, with skeletons found in East Africa and China. Various species of genus *Homo* developed, some of which existed simultaneously. Eventually the *Homo sapien*s appear in the fossil record 300,000 years ago. Twelve thousand years ago, *Homo sapiens* supplant all archaic humans, becoming the only remaining species of the genus. Sixty-five million years to get from mammal to me!

More recently, Darwin's slow multiple-generational evolutionary model has been challenged. Molecular biologists have argued that much of evolution is the result of singularities, one-off occurrences that are inexplicable to what occurs before them. These singularities propel evolution exponentially, hastening development, and shortening the evolutionary timeline. For example, the meteor that struck Earth sixty-five million years ago led to the demise of the dinosaurs and made room for newer species. For the genus *Homo*, "The brain size increased only moderately during the first three million years of hominization, approximately up to the time of the famous Lucy."[10] Then about 800,000 years ago the human brain developed rapidly, some suggest due to dramatic changes in climate.

Whether following the slow winding route of natural selection or taking an unexpected shortcut, at the root of living things is the

9. Darwin, *The Annotated Origin*, 61.
10. Christian de Duve, *Singularities: Landmarks on the Pathways of Life* (Cambridge: Cambridge University Press, 2005), 224.

instinct to survive. As the environment changed or new predators emerged, those plants and animals that adapted survived. Over time those adaptations were inscribed into the plant or animal's DNA and passed on to its progeny.

> Given naturally occurring variation, and the fact that those that survive will tend on average to be different from those that do not, there will be a *differential reproduction*, natural selection. In time this leads to full-blown evolution, and evolution of a particular kind, for selection produces organisms with *adaptations*. The eye and the hand come naturally as a result of Darwin's causal process.[11]

I, for one, am particularly grateful that our tails receded, and our thumbs emerged! But the downside is the astounding number of species that become extinct as a result of natural selection.

### Natural Disaster

In 2020, climate change-induced drought led to massive wildfires in Australia that burnt an area the size of West Virginia. An estimated one billion animals lost their lives. While this devastating horror had its roots in human culpability, Mother Nature is not beyond dealing a lethal blow to her creatures. And Darwin would say that this is part of the larger mechanism of natural selection. Death begets life and makes room for newer more adaptive species. With an almost cavalier attitude, Darwin wrote:

> It is interesting to contemplate an entangled bank, clothed with many plants of many kinds, with birds singing on the bushes, with various insects flitting about, and with worms crawling through the damp earth, and to reflect that these . . . have all been produced by laws acting around us. These laws . . . being growth with reproduction; inheritance which is almost implied by reproduction; variability from the indirect and direct action of the external conditions of life, and from use and disuse; a ratio of increase so high as to lead to a struggle for life, and as consequence to natural selection, entailing divergence of character and extinction of less-improved forms. Thus,

---

11. Ruse, "Evolution," 281; italics in the original.

from the war of nature, from famine and death, the most exalted object which we are capable of conceiving, namely, the production of the higher animals, directly follows. There is a grandeur in this view of life, with its several powers, having been originally breathed into a few forms or into one; and that, whilst this planet has gone cycling on according to the fix law of gravity, from so simple a beginning endless forms most beautiful and most wonderful have been and are being, evolve.[12]

By Darwin's reckoning, death is a prerequisite for evolution and complexity.

> In what Darwin called the "entangled bank" of ecological intercon-nections and die-offs, he found the origin of species. The proximate cause of life was (some animal's) death. The proximate cause of death was (some animal's) life.[13]

But what Darwin didn't know at the time was that in Earth's history, five mass extinction events had already greatly affected the evolution and diversity of living organisms. The first, known as the Ordovician-Silurian, occurred 439 million years ago during the Paleozoic period, when global warming caused mass fluctuations in the sea level. Scientists estimate that approximately "25% of the families and nearly 60% of the genera of marine organisms were lost."[14] The second, the Late Devonian Extinction, occurred 364 million years ago and resulted from a global cooling. In this event, "22% of marine families and 57% of marine genera, including all jawless fish, disappeared."[15] The Permian-Triassic Extinction (251 million years ago) may have been initiated by a meteor impact that led to volcanic activity. This bio-catastrophe resulted in the loss of "95% of all species (marine as well as terrestrial) . . . and 70% of

12. Darwin, *The Annotated Origin*, 489–90.

13. Adriana Petryna, "The Origins of Extinction," *Limn* 3 (2013), https://escholarship .org/uc/item/7bt3q2q4.

14. D. B. Wake and V. T. Vredenburg, "Are We in the Midst of the Sixth Mass Extinc-tion? A View from the World of Amphibians," *Proceedings of the National Academy of Sciences* 105 (2008): 11466.

15. Wake and Vredenburg, 11466.

land plants, insects, and vertebrates."[16] It was almost as if life had to begin again. Between 199 and 214 million years ago, the End Triassic Extinction in the Mesozoic period resulted from massive lava flow in the Atlantic Ocean which again caused global warming. "Marine organisms were most strongly affected (22% of marine families and 53% of marine genera were lost), but terrestrial organisms also experienced much extinction."[17] Finally, the Cretaceous-Tertiary Extinction (65 million years ago) may have been caused by dual factors: volcanic floods in India and a massive asteroid impact in the Gulf of Mexico. The loss of global biodiversity included "16% of families, 47 % of genera of marine organisms, and 18% of vertebrate families."[18] And thus the dinosaurs met their demise. And mammals could emerge.

Arguing with Darwin, scientists propose that:

> The great mass extinctions of the fossil record were a major creative force that provided entirely new kinds of opportunities for the subsequent explosive evolution and diversification of surviving clades.[19]

But scientists warn, we haven't seen the last of these mass extinction events. In fact, we may be living in one right now. In the last 500 years, scientists estimate that 322 known animals have gone extinct due to human causes. "Today, the synergistic effects of human impacts are laying the groundwork for a comparably great Anthropocene mass extinction . . . with unknown ecological and evolutionary consequences."[20] The Anthropocene is a new geological epoch in which global human activities are affecting the earth and atmosphere. And not for the good. "Human activities are associated directly or indirectly with nearly every aspect of the current extinction spasm."[21] The most impactful human activities

---

16. Wake and Vredenburg, 11466.
17. Wake and Vredenburg, 11466.
18. Wake and Vredenburg, 11466.
19. J. B. C. Jackson, "Ecological Extinction and Evolution in the Brave New Ocean," *Proceedings of the National Academy of Sciences* 105 (2008): 11458.
20. Jackson, 11458.
21. Wake and Vredenburg, "Are We in the Midst?," 11472.

include destroying habitats, overexploitation of species, the spread of invasive species, pollution, and climate change.[22]

An estimated 80 percent of the habitat of 50 threatened animal and plant species was destroyed by the Australian fires. According to Professor Sarah Legge of the Australian National University, "It feels like we have hit a turning point that we predicted was coming as a consequence of climate change. We are now in uncharted territory."[23] In the past 200 to 300 years, the global species extinction rate has increased to 100–1,000 times Earth's historical geological background rate, directly due to human activity. Little could Darwin have anticipated that the "crowning achievement of evolution" could be the direct cause of another impending mass extinction event.

### Darwin Updated

*On the Origin of Species* set in motion a 160-year-old conversation on the deep relationship among all living organisms. A conversation that was often met with ridicule and religious fundamentalism. In the 1920s, the Scopes Monkey Trial pitted William Jennings Bryan against Clarence Darrow as they argued about recent anti-evolution legislation in Tennessee. Some eighty years later, evolution was still being debated in the courts. The 2005 case of Kitzmiller v. Dover Area School District centered around the teaching of "intelligent design" as a viable alternative to evolution.

Outside the courtroom and state legislatures, the evolution advocated by Darwin has been updated, critiqued, and enhanced by various scientific discoveries so that we now speak of "neo-Darwinism." Perhaps the most significant of these advances is found in the field of genetics, which has successfully demonstrated that "the fundamental evolutionary event is a change in the frequency of genes and chromo-

22. Ron Wagler, "The Anthropocene Mass Extinction: An Emerging Curriculum Theme for Science Educators," *The American Biology Teacher* 73 (February 2011): 79.

23. Reported by Graham Readfearn, "'Silent Death': Australia's Bushfires Push Countless Species to Extinction," *The Guardian*, January 3, 2020, https://www.theguardian .com/environment/2020/jan/04/ecologists-warn-silent-death-australia-bushfires-endangered -species-extinction?CMP=Share_iOSApp_Other.

some configurations in a population."[24] The sequencing of DNA has allowed scientists to trace how characteristics and diseases are passed on to successive generations.

Genetics may have confirmed Darwin's proposal of natural selection, but other discoveries have challenged the rate at which that selection occurs. "Evolution is absolutely a phenomenon of populations. Individuals and their immediate descendants do not evolve. Populations evolve, in the sense that the proportions of carriers of different genes change through time."[25] But the twenty-first century has seen more rapid changes among certain species for whom their environment has been dramatically altered. Similarly, "punctuated equilibrium" occurs when there is "a pattern of alternating rapid and slow evolution, especially when the rapid phase is accompanied by species formation."[26] Not every organism follows Darwin's slow steps toward progress.

In the early twentieth century, the theory of continental drift helped explain the location and diversity of many living organisms. As Alfred Wegener (1880–1930) presented in his 1912 book, *The Origin of Continents and Oceans*, the seven continents had once formed a single body, which eventually separated and drifted to their present locations. In the 1960s, advances in seismic imaging techniques and geophysical observations led to a confirmation of Wegener's original theory, now known as plate tectonics. The extraordinary and unique development of marsupials in Australia and the utter lack of either indigenous marsupials or mammals in New Zealand are owed to this separation of land mass and volcanic activity.

Far from discrediting Darwin's fundamental insights on the origin and diversity of the species, the more recent work of geneticists, biologists, paleontologists, and geologists confirms, enhances, and/or enlightens those original theories.

What drives evolution? This is the question that Darwin answered in essence and the twentieth-century biologists have refined to produce

24. Edmund O. Wilson, *The Diversity of Life* (New York: Norton, 1999), 75.
25. Wilson, 75.
26. Wilson, 89.

the synthesis, called neo-Darwinism, with which we now live in an uneasy consensus.[27]

## The Evolution of Humanity

The Dr. Seuss book, *Are You My Mother?*, follows the journey of a tiny hatchling through the barnyard of other animals, wistfully searching for its mother. [Spoiler alert: the bird baby and mother are reunited at book's end.] Similarly, the search for our human origins has sometimes played out like a mythic tale. Aristotle argued that we were godly creations and animals were designed for our use. Both creation stories in the book of Genesis place the creation of humans as the pinnacle (Gen 1:27), or the first and best model (Gen 2:7) of God's creative actions. In both stories, the flora and fauna are either a first act or an afterthought. The psalmist, too, claims humanity stands in a divinely designed position above all of creation (Ps 8). No wonder Darwin was none too eager to turn his evolutionary lens on the origins of humans. "Keenly aware of the controversy it would generate, the retiring Darwin minimized any reference to humans in his publication, and did not broach the problem of human origins until many years later."[28] However, the discovery of a human-like fossil, later called *Homo neaderthalensis*, in 1856 pushed the question of human origins into the limelight. No longer could evolutionary theory remain an interesting conversation about other living organisms. We human beings found ourselves on the evolutionary tree of life. Like it or not.

Religious belief forged much of the resistance against accepting the theory of human evolution. In neither Genesis creation account did apes appear. Enter Jesuit paleontologist, Teilhard de Chardin (1881–1955). His research on "Peking Man," a group of human fossils discovered between 1929 and 1937, "helped Teilhard to reconcile his now expansive knowledge of the human fossil record with his Christian belief."[29] His article, "The Phenomenon of Man,"

27. Wilson, 75.

28. Kenneth Mowbray and Ian Tattersall, "Evolution, Human," in *Encyclopedia of Science and Religion*, ed. J. Wentzel Vrede van Huyssteen, vol. 1 (New York: Macmillan, 2003), 300.

29. Mowbray and Tattersall, 300.

first published in 1930, explained Teilhard de Chardin's theory of human origins and human destination. A fuller treatment of his work with the same name was published in 1955, appearing just after his death.

With Darwin, Teilhard de Chardin argued that evolution moved in the direction of greater complexity. The pinnacle of this movement was human consciousness. Borrowing the phrase from Julian Huxley, Teilhard de Chardin described the human being as "evolution become conscious of itself."[30]

> Are we not at every instant living the experience of a universe whose immensity, by the play of our senses and our reason, is gathered up more and more simply in each one of us? . . . Are we not experiencing the first symptoms of an aggregation of a still higher order, the birth of some single centre from the convergent beams of millions of elementary centres dispersed over the surface of the thinking earth?[31]

This convergence of evolutionary consciousness would lead to the development of a new evolutionary layer: the noosphere, (from the Greek, *nous*, for "mind,"), the collective consciousness of all humanity. And from this, "followed in the right direction, must somewhere ahead become involuted to a point which we might call Omega."[32]

While concepts like the noosphere and Omega Point would be discussed by theologians and scientists alike, most would agree that "evolution navigates to increasing levels of complexity, including the discovery of consciousness."[33] But from where exactly did that consciousness emerge? Darwin himself was unsure. "In what manner the mental powers were first developed is as hopeless an enquiry as how life itself first originated. These are problems for the distant future, if ever they are to be solved by [hu]man."[34] Neuroscience

30. Pierre Teilhard de Chardin, *The Phenomenon of Man* (New York: Harper & Row, 1961), 220.

31. Teilhard de Chardin, 259.

32. Teilhard de Chardin, 259.

33. Simon Conway Morris, "Evolution and the Inevitability of Intelligent Life," in *The Cambridge Companion to Science and Religion*, ed. Peter Harrison (Cambridge: Cambridge University Press, 2010), 153.

34. Charles Darwin, *The Descent of Man* (London: John Murray, 1871), 237.

has come to Darwin's rescue, shedding new light on human brain development and demonstrating that evolution may not have followed quite as linear a path as early theorists had proposed. "The emergence of consciousness could be a result of the progressive integration of previous generic systems becoming faster or more specialized, but above all differentiated. This biological differentiation does not always mean complexification, inasmuch as we can easily show that the thresholds reached by any two species may be high although differentially expressed."[35]

While the origin and end of human consciousness is variously debated, the development of the human brain is more straightforward. The expansion of the brain, particularly the neocortex, led to an increase in the brain's functional areas.[36] Though most living organisms have some stimulus response, the mammalian neocortex was truly an evolutionary innovation.

> Mammals had the highest brain-to-body ratio and ended up with intelligence in excess of what was needed for controlling the body and managing the immediate environment . . . The mammals with the highest brain-to-body ratio, the Homo sapiens appeared on earth about two million years ago and then further transformed into Homo Sapien sapiens about six hundred thousand years ago.[37]

Our brains are not only larger than our hominoid ancestors and other primates, they have areas not present in these other species. The large part of the temporal lobe and sections of the frontal lobe of the left hemisphere are specialized for human language while regions of the right hemisphere allow for spatial reasoning. Our brains are designed for social interactions. One part of the ventral temporal lobe allows us to recognize faces, while our frontal lobes help us sense the intentions of others and understand the conse-

---

35. Marc-Williams Debono, "From Perception to Consciousness: An Epistemic Vision of Evolutionary Processes," *Leonardo* 37 (2004): 244.

36. Jon H. Kaas, "The Evolution of the Neocortex from Early Mammals to Modern Humans," *Phi Kappa Phi Forum* 85 (Spring 2005): 14.

37. Mayank N. Vahia, "Evolution of Science I: Evolution of Mind," *Current Science* 111 (November 2016): 1456.

quences of our actions. To paraphrase Descartes: I think, anticipate, remember, love and hate, therefore I am human.

## The Role of Jesus Christ in an Unfinished Evolving Universe

> For theology to have traction, we need to get the story straight.
> —Elizabeth A. Johnson, *Ask the Beasts*[38]

In her monumental book, *Ask the Beasts: Darwin and the God of Love*, Johnson endeavors to "get the story straight" as it relates to theology's engagement with science, specifically evolution. In her preface, she distinguishes several "big bang" moments. The first, the one of cosmic proportions, resulted in the creation of the universe some 13.77 billion years ago. The second big bang resulted in the creation of life on Earth 10 billion years later. "Here began the evolutionary process that now covers our planet with beautiful, complex creatures interacting in life-sustaining ecosystems," Johnsons writes.[39] Finally, in what is a blink of an eye in cosmic history, the third big bang resulted in the evolution of *Homo sapiens*, "mammals with mind and wills who think symbolically and act with deliberate, free intent."[40] Seen today, evolution now involves culture, communities, and consciousness.

> From matter to life to mind: from physical matter to biological life to linguistic consciousness; from galaxies to living species to human persons: though connected, these explosions form no simple, predictable unfolding but a fascinating, unexpected story.[41]

In this "unexpected story," God is understood as the prime mover or first cause of creation (*Summa Theologiae*, I.45.1), who remains actively involved, so that "the relation of the creature to the Creator is the principle of its very being." (*Summa Theologiae*, I.45.3). As

---

38. Elizabeth A. Johnson, *Ask the Beasts: Darwin and the God of Love* (London: Bloomsbury, 2014), xvi.

39. Johnson, xiii.

40. Johnson, xiii.

41. Johnson, xiv.

Rahner presented, creation is "not something that happens at the beginning of time but is rather the continuing relationship of the world to its transcendent ground."[42] God is "the dynamic power which enables evolutionary change to occur. Creation is understood, now, not as a relationship between the absolute being of God and a static world, but as a relationship between the dynamic being of God and a world in process of coming to be . . . In the history of evolution, creatures become more than they were."[43]

In fact, biologist Julian Huxely, paleontologist Teilhard de Chardin, theologian Karl Rahner, biochemist Arthur Peacocke, and historian Thomas Berry all recognize that the goal of evolution is self-transcendence and that human beings are literally the cosmos come to consciousness. From Rahner's perspective, this is a statement about God's relationship to matter.

> If [humankind] is thus the self-transcendence of living matter, then the history of nature and of spirit form an intrinsic and stratified unity in which the history of nature develops towards [humankind], continues in [them] as [their] history, is preserved and surprised in [them], and therefore reaches its own goal with and in the history of [humankind's] spirit.[44]

But lest we slip into anthropocentric thinking and self-congratulations at having arrived, we aren't the end of the evolutionary story. As Edwards explains, "The evolutionary history of the cosmos reaches its climax only when the creative Ground of the whole cosmic process engages in self-giving love with the free human person . . . We live in a world of grace, a world in which God is present in self-offering to human beings at every point."[45] Our self-transcendence allows for experiences of wonder, loss, death, suffering, friendship, solitude, and bounty, giving us a glimpse into the mystery at the heart of human

---

42. Karl Rahner, "Natural Science and Reasonable Faith," in *Theological Investigations* 21 (New York: Crossroad, 1988), 31.

43. Denis Edwards, *Jesus and the Cosmos* (New York: Paulist Press, 1991), 36.

44. Karl Rahner, *Foundations of Christian Faith: An Introduction to the Idea of Christianity* (New York: Seabury Press, 1978), 187.

45. Edwards, *Jesus and the Cosmos*, 29.

existence. That mystery is "God present, reaching out toward us in self-offering . . . It is God bent over us in love. The life of faith is simply the free response to this love, directed toward us from every point of the universe."[46]

As Edwards opines, "it is obvious that theology must listen to what science has to tell us about the story of the universe . . . the next major step . . . will be to ask: What does this story of the emerging universe have to do with Jesus?"[47] In this section, we will focus on one particular and significant ongoing episode in that unfolding story of God's relationship with creation: the singularity that is Jesus of Nazareth.

> The one who was totally centered on a gracious God upholding all creation, the one who interpreted God's law in a "humanizing" way, the one who ate scandalous meals with public sinners, who delighted and challenged his hearers with the artistry of his parables, who taught the impossible, like love of the enemy, the one who vigorously confronted those in authority, the one whose presence brought joy and happiness, the one who called his followers to a new family, the one who faced failure and death because of the positions he took, the one who has been raised up and vindicated by God. This very specific Jesus is the symbol and the reality of God's radical commitment to the cosmos. And this same Jesus is the symbol and the reality of the cosmos returning God's embrace with a definitive "yes."[48]

How do we understand the theological concepts of incarnation, redemption, and the cosmic Christ in light of this Jesus of Nazareth and evolutionary thinking? What follows are brief summaries of complex theological concepts and are meant only to indicate the impact science can have on our understanding of Christology.

### Incarnation as a First Thought

Two theological traditions concerning the incarnation find their source in different scriptural passages. Building on Paul's assertion

46. Edwards, 29.
47. Edwards, 7.
48. Edwards, 76.

that Jesus Christ redeemed us from our sins, acting as a second Adam as it were (e.g., Rom 5:12-21; Gal 4:4-5), Thomist Christology "maintains the Traditional attitude of the Old Testament wherein Adam's sin impeded God's plan until 'when the fullness of time came, God sent his Son, born of a woman, born under the law, that we might receive the adoption of sons.' (Gal 4:4)."[49]

As a good Dominican, I feel a particular loyalty to Aquinas, but on this topic, the Franciscans offer the most helpful insights. Here Christ isn't an antidote to sin but rather the predestined perfection of love. John Duns Scotus (1266–1308) drew from Exodus and 1 John.

> The first one tells us *that* God is (Ex. 3:14) and the second one tells us *what* God is, that is, love (1 John 4:8). Scotus concludes that from the love that God is, that Christ is the first predestined in the mind of God; he is God's *summum opus dei*.[50]

According to Scotus, Jesus isn't an afterthought sent to fix humanity's sinful state. The incarnation would have occurred regardless of the missteps of our primal parents, because "love seeks union with the beloved; this union occurs in the incarnation when the divine Word enters into personal union with the created world in Jesus Christ."[51]

Similarly, for Bonaventure (1221–1274) the incarnation didn't occur solely as a response to sin. It was also to witness to the primacy of love and the fulfillment of creation. "Christ does not save us *from* creation; rather, Christ is the reason *for* creation . . . Christ is first in God's intention to love; love is the reason *for* creation."[52] Long before an understanding of evolution, Bonaventure enumerated the connection between Christ and all creation in a sermon on the transfiguration.

> All things are said to be transformed in the transfiguration of Christ, in as far as something of each creature was transfigured in Christ.

---

49. Abbott, "Eric Doyle OFM: Blessed John Duns Scotus, Teilhard De Chardin and a Cosmos in Evolution," *Franciscan Studies* 75 (2017): 503.

50. Abbott, 502.

51. Johnson, *Ask the Beasts*, 226.

52. Ilia Delio, *Christ in Evolution* (Maryknoll, NY: Orbis Books, 2008), 6.

For as a human being, Christ has something in common with all creatures. With the stone he shares existence; with plants he shares life; with animals he shares sensation; and with the angels he shares intelligence. Therefore, all things are said to be transformed in Christ since—in his human nature—he embraces something of every creature in himself when he is transfigured.[53]

Bonaventure could have also cited Colossians 1:13-20 with regard to Christ's role in creation. While Colossians is attributed to Paul and shares some similar themes (note the forgiveness of sins), it was written between 70 and 100 CE and thus reflects a later Christology.

[God] has rescued us from the power of darkness and transferred us into the kingdom of his beloved Son, in whom we have redemption, the forgiveness of sins. He is the image of the invisible God, the first-born of all creation; for in him all things in heaven and on earth were created, things visible and invisible, whether thrones or dominions or rulers or powers—all things have been created through him and for him. He himself is before all things, . . . the firstborn from the dead, so that he might come to have first place in everything. For in him all the fullness of God was pleased to dwell, and through him God was pleased to reconcile to himself all things, whether on earth or in heaven, by making peace through the blood of his cross. (Col 1:13-20)

Christ is the image (*eikon*, from which we get "icon") of the invisible God and also the firstborn, (*prototokos*, literally the oldest child in the family). The evangelists Matthew and Luke will use narrative to explain the incarnation; the evangelist John will borrow poetic imagery from Wisdom literature, but here in Colossians, the author provides a more universal explanation. Jesus is firstborn among all creation and through him God became reconciled to all things (*ta panta* in Greek, the whole of everything). Thus, the kinship of Jesus with creation leads to the divinization of *ta panta*. Drawing on Rahner, Edwards noted, "The history of the cosmos is a history of self-transcendence into the life of God . . . The incarnation is understood as the beginning of the divinization of the world as a whole."[54]

---

53. Bonaventure, Sermo I, Dom. II in Quad. (IX, 215–219).
54. Edwards, *Jesus and the Cosmos*, 67.

In the Scotistic interpretation . . . the Messiah is no longer seen only as a Redeemer whose function it is to remedy the disaster of Adam and his children, but they affirm the absolute supremacy of Christ over all creation, that is, the entire cosmos, and see the mystery of Christ in a dimension that is outside chronological earthly history. Here Christ is not the second Adam merely coming as one who repairs the sin of Adam. He is the centre of God's plan, willed by God for his own sake, because of his intrinsic worth, and for his sake all the universe is willed, all people and all angels.[55]

Later theologians drew on the Scotistic interpretation, recognizing that creation and incarnation are "related dimensions of God's self-communication to the world."[56] Even if there had been no sin in the world, and thus no need to be "redeemed" from sin, the incarnation would still have occurred. "It was always God's plan to give God's self to creatures in love through the incarnation. God's self-giving, in Jesus of Nazareth, is primarily to be understood simply as an expression of God's boundless love for creation."[57]

## Redemption in an Evolutionary Creation

The primary elements of evolution are change, the movement toward greater complexity, and the incompleteness and ongoing nature of the process. This throws a pretty big wrench into the concept of original sin and an expiatory understanding of the incarnation, which are both based on a steady, complete and ordered creation. If we are still a work in progress, how do we envision sin and evil, and what does redemption look like through an evolutionary lens?

Here we again turn to the Franciscans. Bonaventure acknowledged the historical reality of sin but didn't limit the effects of Christ to redemption from sin. "From eternity God included the possibility of a fall of the human race and therefore structured the human person with a view to redemption."[58] Scotus "locates [Jesus'] redeeming power not in satisfaction rendered to a God whose honor has been

---

55. Abbott, "Eric Doyle OFM," 503.
56. Edwards, *Jesus and the Cosmos*, 70–71.
57. Edwards, 71.
58. Delio, *Christ in Evolution*, 7.

violated, but in the presence of divine love in the flesh enacting an historical solidarity with all who suffer and die."[59]

In the eastern church's theology, the focus of redemption is not solely to save us from sin but to open fullness of life for all. It is death—the shared fate of all the living—from which Christ redeems us. Here is the theology of the Colossians' hymn writ large. All the cosmos is redeemed.

> This idea of cosmic redemption is based . . . upon a right under-standing of the Incarnation: Christ took flesh—something from the material order—and so has made possible the redemption and metamorphosis of all creation—not merely the immaterial but the physical.[60]

Though Teilhard de Chardin "argued that moral and physical evil are inevitable byproducts of a developing universe that is moving from a condition of multiplicity and disorganization toward a state of unification,"[61] that doesn't make the suffering and pain that results any easier to comprehend or endure. Theologians distinguish between "natural evil"—that which results from naturally-occurring events such as floods, earthquakes, etc., and "moral evil"—the human propensity to sin. Much of our traditional theological thinking has focused on how Christ redeems us from sin or moral evil. But how do we understand the pervasive presence of pain, suffering, and death in the natural world? For the believer, this has often led to questions of theodicy; how does God allow suffering in God's creation and what role does Jesus Christ play in this evolutionary inevitability of anguish and mortality? In other words, how does Jesus redeem us from entropy, the naturally occurring disorder in a system? It begins with his humanity, his creatureliness. And is transformed through his death by his resurrection.

---

59. Johnson, *Ask the Beasts*, 226.

60. Kallistos Ware, *The Orthodox Church* (Hammondsworth: Penguin, 1963), 239–40.

61. Robin Ryan, *Jesus and Salvation: Soundings in the Christian Tradition and Contemporary Theology* (Collegeville, MN: Liturgical Press, 2015), 152.

In Christ, the living God who creates and empowers the evolutionary world also enters into the fray, personally drinking the cup of suffering and going down into the nothingness of death, to transform it from within. Hope springs from this divine presence amid the turmoil.[62]

We believe this. We experience this in the Eucharist. We know this to be true. Through an evolutionary lens, we see the cross not as sacrifice and expiation, but as a way forward toward unification with God not only for us but for all of creation. "Biologically speaking, new life continuously comes from death, over time. Theologically speaking, the cross gives grounds to hope that the presence of the living God in the midst of pain bears creation forward with an unimaginable promise."[63] Theologian Niels Gregersen coined the term "deep incarnation" to express the cosmic implications of the cross:

> The incarnation of God in Christ can be understood as a radical or "deep" incarnation, that is, an incarnation into the very tissue of biological existence and the system of nature. Understood this way, the death of Christ becomes an icon of God's redemptive co-suffering with all sentient life as well as with the victims of social competition. God bears the costs of evolution, the price involved in the hardship of natural selection.[64]

Similarly, Teilhard de Chardin saw that "the cross does not assume the role of expiation but is the very sign of evolution, as suffering and death yield to greater union."[65]

The manifestation of that greater union occurred on the first Easter. All four gospels agree that the women disciples visit the tomb. In John's Gospel, Mary actually encounters the Risen Jesus. Modern readers are sometimes shocked by what appears to be Jesus' rebuke of Mary: "Do not hold on to me" (John 20:17). Jesus tells Mary

---

62. Johnson, *Ask the Beasts*, 192.

63. Johnson, 210.

64. Niels Gregersen, "The Cross of Christ in an Evolutionary World," *Dialgoue: A Journal of Theology* 40 (2001): 205.

65. Delio, *Christ in Evolution*, 141.

that he has not ascended to the Father, but she is to announce to the others that he is ascending "to my father and your father, to my God and your God"—a visual if not verbal parallel to the ancient custom of being gathered to one's ancestors, but in a wholly new way.

All we hear in Mark is "So they went out and fled from the tomb, for terror and amazement had seized them; and they said nothing to anyone, for they were afraid" (Mark 16:8). Three days earlier, they were with Jesus at his death. They saw where his body had been placed. And now, after the Sabbath, they have come to prepare him properly for burial. But the stone is moved. The body is gone. And a figure in white tells them that Jesus of Nazareth, indeed the one who was crucified, has been raised. According to the Old Testament, resurrection was a sign of the coming reign of God. The prophet Isaiah announces, "Your dead shall live, their corpses shall rise. / O dwellers in the dust, awake and sing for joy! / For your dew is a radiant dew, / and the earth will give birth to those long dead" (Isa 26:19). The psalmist trusts that God will rescue him, "You who have made me see many troubles and calamities / will revive me again; / from the depths of the earth / you will bring me up again" (Ps 71:20). And Daniel promises, "Many of those who sleep in the dust of the earth shall awake, some to everlasting life, and some to shame and everlasting contempt" (Dan 12:2). But not until Jesus' resurrection had one returned from the dead, physically present but somehow altered.

> This person, Jesus of Nazareth, was composed of star stuff and earth stuff; his life formed a genuine part of the historical and biological community of Earth; his body existed in a network of relationships drawing from and extending to the whole physical universe. If in death this "piece of this world, real to the core," as Rahner phrases it, surrendered his life in love and is now forever with God in glory, then this signals embryonically the final beginning of redemptive glorification not just for other human beings but for all flesh, all material beings, every creature that passes through death. The evolving world of life, all of matter in its endless permutations, will not be left behind but will likewise be transfigured by the resurrection action of the Creator Spirit.[66]

66. Johnson, *Ask the Beasts*, 209.

### The Cosmic Christ

Let's clear the air. The term "Cosmic Christ" is perhaps one of the most misunderstood aspects of the New Cosmology. As the survey results showed, some sisters fear that the Cosmic Christ overshadows Jesus. In fact, "we rarely speak of Jesus or Christ in community prayer outside of Mass. We forgo scripture in favor of more general cosmic material." Another responded, "Where does 'Son of God' fit into the Universe Story? How is God's Messiah sent for the whole of the universe?" Some respondents found the term "too impersonal" for them, "a bit out there," but others reported that the concept deepens their spirituality.

> For me the Cosmic Christ is the Christ who is in all, above and below all. Always present, always embracing all of creation, all of the cosmos. Christ offers us incredible presence and love. This concept inspires my prayer and also my interactions with others as I am assured of Christ's presence.

When asked to define the term "Cosmic Christ," many sisters drew from Scripture. Following a Johannine thread, one sister defined the term Cosmic Christ thus: "Jesus as the Incarnation of the preexisting eternal Wisdom/Word of God who by becoming flesh (*sarx*) and rising assumes & redeems the entire cosmos." Other definitions intertwine scriptural imagery and theological insights to create the portrait of the Comic Christ. "I first remember reading this term in connection with Teilhard de Chardin. Of course, it's also connected with John's gospel and Paul's writings in the New Testament. It implies a certain mystical connection between Jesus and all of creation/cosmos/universe," one respondent synthesized. Another sister interpreted the term through the lens of the New Cosmology:

> The Christian term for the God-life which has permeated all reality since the first Flaring Forth (the Big Bang). All creation (even in its magnificent diversity) is drenched in the Divine (the Cosmic Christ) and is a manifestation of the goodness of the Divine. The Cosmic Christ embodies (without a literal body!) the unity in diversity/the diversity in unity of everything that exists. Because of that presence, everything is entitled to reverence, respect and care.

These varied portraits of the Cosmic Christ demonstrate the variety of sources from which we draw when reflecting theologically: Scripture, tradition, and experience. But our interpretations of Scripture and tradition are mutable; our experiences change. In other words, we are a work in progress. We are going somewhere. But when we look at the long arc of cosmic history, our small transitory lives don't seem to cover much ground. But that's the point of evolution. Small alterations over time lead to greater complexity. When pondering the Cosmic Christ, we recognize that this process isn't just about our individual or even congregational journeys. It isn't even about the destiny of humanity. It's about the emergence of our communal spirit.

> The law of complexity-consciousness reveals that ever more intricate physical combinations, as can be traced in the evolution of the brain, yield ever more powerful forms of spirit. Matter, alive with energy, evolves into spirit. While distinctive, human intelligence and creativity rise out of the very nature of the universe, which is itself intelligent and creative. In other words, human spirit is the cosmos come to consciousness.[67]

For Teilhard de Chardin, Christ is present throughout this entire process, "from the least particle of matter to the convergent human community. The whole cosmos is incarnational."[68] As Teilhard de Chardin pondered progression in evolution, he recognized that the destination was the ultimate fulfillment of God's desire for creation and the cosmos, the Omega Point, and proposed that one of the final steps of evolution was the development of a noosphere, "the formation of a collective human organism [that] conforms to the general law of recurrence which leads to the heightening of Consciousness in the universe as a function of complexity."[69] This

67. Elizabeth Johnson, *Women, Earth, and Creator Spirit* (New York: Paulist Press, 1993), 37.

68. William D. Dinges and Ilia Delio, OSF, "Teilhard de Chardin and the New Spirituality," in *From Teilhard to Omega: Co-Creating an Unfinished Universe* (Maryknoll, NY: Orbis Books, 2014), 173.

69. Teilhard de Chardin, *The Future of Man* (New York: Doubleday, 1964), 169.

supreme consciousness would be the final stage of evolution and would culminate in the Omega Point. Christ was the fullness of the evolutionary process as the "contrasting principle," "Pleroma" and "Omega Point" at which humanity—individually and communally—and the cosmos find their end and fulfillment.

As Delio argues, "If it is true that it is through Christ-Omega that the universe in movement holds together, then it is from his concrete germ, the man of Nazareth, that Christ-Omega derives his whole consistence."[70] The Cosmic Christ is the fulfilled potentiality seeded in the creation, germinated in the human Jesus, and blossomed in evolutionary consciousness. "The whole concept of evolution has liberated Christ from the limits of the man Jesus and enabled us to locate Christ at the heart of creation: the primacy of God's love, the exemplar of creation, the centrating principle of evolution, and the Omega point of an evolutionary universe."[71]

The Cosmic Christ is the ultimate both/and. Described in Scripture, born out in tradition, and verified in our personal experiences of prayer and encounter. But the Cosmic Christ is also the direction forward. Teilhard de Chardin used Christogenesis to describe "evolution as the genesis of the total Christ" and "urged Christians to participate in the process of Christogenesis, to risk, get involved, aim toward union with others, for the entire creation is waiting to give birth to God."[72] The Omega Point isn't simply a destination at which to arrive. It is a process that demands our participation. "We are to harness the energies of love for the forward movement of evolution toward the fullness of Christ."[73]

## Conclusion

Darwin drew on the science of his day to develop his theory of natural selection and the slow evolution of life on Earth. Today, scientists extend his theories so that "the idea that life unfolds from

70. Dinges and Delio, "Teilhard de Chardin," 173.

71. Delio, *Christ in Evolution*, 174.

72. Ilia Delio, *Making All Things New: Catholicity, Cosmology, Consciousness* (Maryknoll, NY: Orbis Books, 2015), 93.

73. Delio, 94.

more simple to complex structures now holds true not only on the level of biology but on the levels of cosmology, culture, and consciousness as well."[74] That understanding has led a community of researchers to recognize a universal cosmic-evolutionary narrative.

> The result is a grand evolutionary synthesis bridging a wide variety of scientific specialties—physics, astronomy, geology, chemistry, biology, anthropology, among others and including the humanities—a genuine epic of vast proportions extending from the very beginning of time to the present—and presumably beyond in both space and time.[75]

Though with roots in biology, the process of evolution is a subject of all fields of science, endeavoring to answer the questions "how does order emerge out of chaos?" and "how do we reconcile the constructiveness of cosmic evolution with the destructiveness of thermodynamics?"

> And if Darwinism created a revolution of understanding by helping to free us from the notion that humans differ from other lifeforms on our planet, then cosmic evolution extends that intellectual revolution by treating matter on Earth and in our bodies no differently from that in the stars and galaxies beyond.[76]

Indeed, as the scientists conclude, we are all part of a larger cosmic narrative and so we are not necessarily the end of the story. As Teilhard de Chardin saw this trajectory, we are heading to the Omega Point. In his book, *Jesus and Salvation*, Robin Ryan provides a helpful summary of the implications of Christ in this evolving universe.[77]

a) The incarnation links God with humanity and the cosmos.

b) In his public ministry, Jesus touched the whole person, healing spirit and body, leading to the flourishing for all creation.

74. Delio, *Christ in Evolution*, 16.
75. Eric J. Chaisson, "A Singular Universe of Many Singularities: Cultural Evolution in a Cosmic Context," in *Singularity Hypotheses: A Scientific and Philosophical Assessment*, ed. A. H. Eden et al. (Berlin: Springer, 2012), 416.
76. Chaisson, 417.
77. Ryan, *Jesus and Salvation*, 159.

c) In his death, "God entered into the darkness and suffering of death; God has known this experience from the inside . . . From an evolutionary perspective, theologians extend this solidarity of God beyond humanity to all creatures . . . While this divine solidarity does not resolve the mystery of suffering within creation, it does make the bold claim that no creature, human or nonhuman, is ever alone in its suffering. God is always present in divine compassion." [78]

d) In the resurrection, Rahner recognized that the risen Jesus, "a piece of this world, real to the core," is now with God in glory.

According to Teilhard de Chardin, "God enters into the evolutionary process in Jesus Christ, initiating a new incarnational dynamic that moves laterally rather than upward. The historical event of Christ is a divine 'Big Bang' in the history of the universe."[79] As reconciler and God-made-visible, the incarnate Jesus stands as a response to entropy. Jesus' presence and attention to the broken, ephemeral, displaced, forgotten, and dying assured that the inevitable passing from this state of matter back to spirit was not the result of sin or disobedience, but was simply and painfully the cost of the evolution. "Those who believe in Christ make a wager that love as Jesus enfleshed it in a human way reveals the ineffable compassion of God; this love is the meaning encoded at the core of human life and at the heart of the universe itself."[80]

Our focus in this chapter has been to highlight how we might understand the incarnation, resurrection, and the Cosmic Christ in light of evolutionary theory, each element itself a topic of numerous theological tomes. What we attended to only slightly was the historical character of Jesus of Nazareth and the communal experience of his disciples as presented in the gospels. With an evolutionary hermeneutical lens, we would no doubt consider that his parables, teachings, healings, and prophetic actions had then and continue to have now cosmic implications, but that is the subject of a different book.

78. Ryan, 159.
79. Delio, *Christ in Evolution*, 126.
80. Johnson, *Ask the Beasts*, 201.

Section Three

# *Chapter of Elections*
## Choosing a Future for Religious Life

The scientific trinity of cosmology, quantum mechanics, and evolution presents an understanding of the origins of our universe, the unpredictable actions of the subatomic particles that make up our reality, and the process by which life itself emerged on this one celestial globe circling our medium-sized sun. As Rolston suggested, we might think of these as birthing remarkable singularities.

> There have been three big bangs: generating matter-energy, generating life, generating the human mind. These explosions form no simple continuum but a complicated, diffracted, exponential story. "Big bang" is here a metaphor for critical, exponential, nonlinear bursts with radical consequences for exploring new state spaces with novel combinatorial possibilities.[1]

And though each "big bang" entails a specific area of scientific inquiry, many of the lines of investigation were occurring contemporaneously and drawing on the work of the same notable figures like

---

1. Holmes Rolston, *Three Big Bangs: Matter-Energy, Life, Mind* (New York: Columbia University Press, 2011), ix.

Albert Einstein, Niels Bohr, and Max Planck. The interrelationship among cosmology, quantum theory, and evolution witnesses to a deep interconnectedness, so that "today, the origin of life, together with the finely tuned universe that supports it, has to be likewise traced back to the quantum world."[2]

Though science investigates what can been seen, measured, and tested, it cannot answer the existential questions. "Most scientists give the impression that they can explain the whole universe with science, but the more we get to know about it, the more miraculous it appears."[3] As people of faith, we've never doubted the miraculous.

In fact, we recognize the importance of both faith and reason. In the last section, "Chapter of Affairs," we explored the relationship between science and theology in light of the cosmos, creation, and the cross. We pondered questions like, What or who existed at time zero ($t_0$, the moment before the big bang? If the principle of cause and effect does not operate in the quantum world as it does in the macroworld, how do we live in what is truly a world built on probability and not precision? What is the final stage, the Omega Point, of evolution and where do our religious traditions fit within this understanding? Our exploration of the scientific trinity of cosmology, quantum mechanics, and evolution offered interesting insights into our belief in God as Creator and Sustainer, the role of the Holy Spirit, and how Jesus Christ redeems in the unfinished, evolving universe.

In any chapter of affairs, we discuss proposals, weigh directions, and negotiate compromise. The enactments we write, vote for, and affirm become direction-setting for our life and mission—until the next chapter of affairs. And for most of us, once we conclude the chapter of affairs, we then open the chapter of elections. Here we choose our leadership, the women who are entrusted with the institutional responsibilities for sustaining, promoting, and growing our life and mission. As regards the study in this book, we are using the chapter of elections metaphorically. In light of the survey results and

---

2. Alex Williams, "Improbable Singularities—Evolution Is Riddled with Them," *Journal of Creation* 29 (2015): 92.

3. Williams, 95.

our generational differences, the scientific findings and the emerging theology, how might we elect to revitalize our religious lives and to respond to the emerging signs of the times?

Since Vatican II, women religious have taken to heart the call to respond to "the signs of the times." As theologian Susan Smith, RNDM, noted,

> Faith against culture was out, and the need for a positive relationship between faith and the culture in which a religious congregation lived and worked was emphasized. This important shift could be seen, for example, . . . in the de-institutionalization of religious life, and the individualizing of ministries and its corollary, the loss of corporate apostolates such as teaching in the local Catholic school. These developments could be interpreted as a certain accommodation with the dominant cultures of English-speaking countries in the Western world, or as most women religious did, a commitment to discerning, and responding to, the "signs of the times" (*Gaudium et Spes*).[4]

In the half century since Vatican II, we have been attentive to changing societal needs that called for new ministerial responses. As educators, some of us moved from traditional school ministry to adult literacy, General Educational Development (GED) training, and prison ministry. Those congregations in health care who once operated large Catholic hospitals saw new needs and opened AIDS clinics, staffed mobile health clinics for the homeless, and created drug rehabilitation programs. As the needs of the people of God evolved, so did the sisters' response to meet those needs. As Sandra Schneiders reported,

> In the wake of the Council, and very quickly in ecclesiastical time, we emerged from our habits and horaria, our convents and schools into the inner city, under-served parishes, ecumenical retreat centers; we became advocates for women and children and for our endangered earth; we undertook political organizing, relief work, immigration

---

4. Susan Smith, "Whither Religious Life? Reflections from New Zealand," *Global Sisters Report* (August 5, 2020), https://www.globalsistersreport.org/news/whither-religious -life-reflections-new-zealand.

mediation, peace work, prison chaplaincies, hospice work, social justice projects, cross cultural ministries among the poor, substance abuse rehabilitation, poverty law, theological research and education, mission effectiveness for institutions, the arts and public speaking, and so on.[5]

We have also attended to structural changes. Our sponsored institutions were given over to capable lay leadership. Our motherhouses retrofitted to be more "green" and eco-friendly. Our understanding of membership broadened to include associates who desired to share in our mission. Many of us have continued our theological study, broadening our interests to include interreligious dialogue, ecumenicism, ecology, feminism, and the New Cosmology. And we've even experimented with leadership structures, redefined local chapters, and broadened how we define "community living." But have all of these been responses to the signs of the times or are some reactions to our declining and aging membership? Or is diminishment the new sign of the times? Perhaps with Pope Francis we might ask how open are we to God's surprises?

> When we set out on a journey, when we are on our path, we always encounter new things, things we did not know. And this should make us think: am I attached to my things, my ideas, [are they] closed? Or am I open to God's surprises? Am I at a standstill or am I on a journey? . . . Am I able to understand the signs of the times and be faithful to the voice of the Lord that is manifested in them?[6]

What seems to be missing in our response to the "signs of the times"—whether ministerial, corporate, or structural—is a deeper renewal that comes from an integrated communal discernment. As the survey results indicated, we aren't listening well to each other at least with regard to the New Cosmology. If we hope to have a

5. Sandra Schneiders, "Vowed Religious Life," Presentation to the IHM Congregation (June 14, 2009), 9, https://anunslife.org/sites/www.anunslife.org/files/assets/blogimages/SSchneidersLecture2009.pdf.

6. Pope Francis, "Homily," October 13, 2014, http://www.archivioradiovaticana.va/storico/2014/10/13/pope_at_santa_marta_holy_law_is_not_an_end_in_itself/en-1108446.

future that is relevant and responsive to the people of God while nourishing our vocation, now might be the time to imagine, envision, and plant seeds for that future. In the chapters that follow, we will build on our study of science and theology to envision how formation, the vows, and mission might evolve in this unfinished universe. It will be up to you whether you elect this new direction.

# Chapter Seven

## *The Emergent Disciple*

### *Formation in an Unfinished Universe*

Full disclosure: I am probably the last person to write about formation. I was, without exaggeration, a formator's worst nightmare. To be honest, I don't think it was all my fault. It was the late eighties—early nineties. I had little or no catechesis. I only met sisters as a young adult, and my interest in vocation was deeply entwined with my interest in social justice. In the course of my vocational search, I met with five different vocation directors, two of whom left their respective congregations (I don't think it was because of me!). I entered one Dominican congregation only to be asked to leave shortly before first vows. Nothing nefarious, I promise. I then entered my current congregation, but because I had not made vows with the first group, I now had the pleasure of re-doing the canonical novitiate. That none of my formation directors left the congregation is a testament to the depth of their vocation!

On the cusp of Generation X, I had already served as a lay missioner, possessed an MA in Theology, and had extensive ministerial experience. In a word, I considered myself a fully formed adult who was now to be "formed" as a woman religious. My experience of frustration, tension, conflict, and infantilization is not singular. What is surprising is that as collectively the best educated, theologically astute, and ministry-minded cohort of Catholic women in the United States, when it comes to formation, we're still a work in progress. This is no reflection on the hard work of organizations like the Religious Formation Conference and the Institute for Religious Formation. We are all responsible for "forming" the next generation. Our language (formator?), our expectations of new members, our personnel, and our theology often reflect a mode of incorporation that is oddly out of sync with today's candidates. "You think you had it bad, let me tell you about my novitiate . . ." may make a good story but it is not the reason for continuing unhelpful practices. "Punitive," "rote," "unimaginative" are not adjectives that should describe the process of welcoming new life into a religious congregation whose heart is set on the kingdom. This is a holy endeavor—our vocation—and it is both an individual and a communal undertaking that doesn't end with final vows. As the Code of Canon Law canon 659 notes, formation is a life-long process for all religious, "so that they lead the proper life of the institute more fully and carry out its mission more suitably." In that light, in our conversation on formation, while we most immediately think of new members, we all should also consider ourselves *formandi* (we definitely need new language!).

In her book *Social Analysis for the 21st Century*, Maria Cimperman, RSCJ, describes the complexity of global problems, reminding us of "the important difference between responding to symptoms and seeking out the cause of a situation."[1] The larger picture provides the context for complex underlying structures than give rise to the symptoms. She outlines five significant points to keep in mind when dealing with the larger view:

1. It is helpful to understand that problems usually have layers upon layers of complexity that must be considered in order to gain some perspective.

2. At every stage it is important to spend some time exploring, researching, and reflecting on what is actually happening. Humility (seeking truth) and curiosity are most helpful. This step, like every other step in social analysis, requires some reflection instead of immediate action; we must hold back from early action.

---

1. Maria Cimperman, *Social Analysis for the 21st Century* (Maryknoll, NY: Orbis Books, 2015).

3. We need others working with us. In order to see a situation clearly, we must be attuned to as many of the layers of inter-relationships as we can, and we do this best when working with others.

4. Creating alternatives to a problem requires that we allow new insights to emerge and that we free ourselves to see different patterns.

5. At some point we must act, even as other layers of response probably will emerge as we act.[2]

As we discuss formation in light of emerging science, let us keep in mind that the incorporation of new members and vivification of vowed members (1) is complex and layered, (2) requires deep reflection, (3) necessitates interrelationship and collaboration, (4) asks for a freedom and openness to new insights, and (5) is an ongoing, evolving activity. In a word, we cannot do as we have always done. If we accept that we live in an unfinished universe, in the midst of evolution, where at the very heart of matter is probability not certainty, then our very structures, processes, and programs must reflect our emerging reality. Far from upsetting the apple cart, we might come to realize that at our best, we women religious have always demonstrated such flexibility, mobility, and responsiveness with regard to our apostolic lives. We just haven't always transferred that social analysis and theological insight to some of our internal structures.

In what follows, we will discuss the theological implications of the study of emergence before exploring how our Scriptures—read through the lens of emergence—offer insights into incorporating new members and revitalizing vowed members. Finally, we will discuss a nested hierarchy of charism as a metaphor for formation in an unfinished universe.

## Emergence: More Than the Sum of Its Parts

As Gregersen explained, "In ordinary language 'emergence' refers to processes of coming forth from latency, or to states of things arising

2. Cimperman, 9.

unexpectedly."[3] How would our programs look if we thought of the formation of each candidate as bringing forth from latency the potential that was always there? I will offer a brief historical note on the origins of the metaphysical understanding of emergence, before we attempt to apply the concept to our religious context.

We begin with Robert Boyle (1627–1691), the "father of chemistry," and Isaac Newton (1642–1727), the "father of modern science," who both used the term "emergence," though differently depending on their field. Boyle understood emergence "to refer to the rising of substances to the surface of liquids," while Newton used it "to designate the appearance of light refractions."[4] But it wasn't until the early twentieth century that emergence theory became a way of interpreting the results of cosmic, biological, mental, and cultural evolution. Australian-born philosopher Samuel Alexander (1859–1938) became part of a collection of British emergentists in the 1920s who conceived of "the world as a hierarchy of levels: space and time sit at the lowest level, and through a process of emergence give rise to the levels of matter, life, mind, and deity."[5] In modern parlance, the term "emergent evolution" was coined by psychologist C. Lloyd Morgan (1852–1936), who in his 1922 Gifford lecture at St. Andrews stated:

> Evolution, in the broad sense of the word, is the name we give to the comprehensive plan of sequence in all natural events. But the orderly sequence, historically viewed, appears to present, from time to time, something genuinely new. Under what I here call emergent evolution stress is laid on this incoming of the new. Salient examples are afforded in the advent of life, in the advent of mind, and in the advent of reflective thought.[6]

---

3. Niels Henrik Gregersen, "Emergency and Complexity," in *The Oxford Handbook of Religion and Science*, ed. Philip Clayton and Zachary Simpson (New York: Oxford University Press, 2006), 767.

4. Gregersen, 767.

5. Emily A. E. Thomas, "Samuel Alexander," in *The Stanford Encyclopedia of Philosophy*, ed. Edward N. Zalta (Spring 2018 Edition), https://plato.stanford.edu/archives /spr2018/entries/alexander.

6. C. Lloyd Morgan, *Emergent Evolution* (New York: Henry Holt, 1923), 1.

Most emergent theories hold three tenets in common: (1) that which emerges is a qualitative novelty, (2) nature is a nested hierarchy of ontological levels, and (3) higher levels of emergence are not predictable based on their constituent parts. By qualitative novelty, we mean that what emerges is more than the end result of simply adding parts together. Gregersen offered the following example:

> "Weight," for example, is a resulting property of aggregating matter, whereas the liquidity and surface tension of water are new, emergent qualities in relation to the chemical compounds of hydrogen and oxygen.[7]

In evolution, qualitative novelties include the shell of turtles, flowers, eyes, hearts, and bipedalism. "Evolutionary novelties are new traits or behaviors, or novel combinations of previously existing traits or behaviors, arising during the evolution of a lineage, and that perform a new function within the ecology of that lineage."[8] These novelties can cause evolutionary advancements. A component of true novelty is its ability to enhance the function of the organism over time, so the actual novelty may not be immediately apparent when it first emerges.

Of particular interest to us is the idea of nested ontological levels, in which "the higher emergent levels (e.g. living organisms) include the lower levels (e.g. inorganic chemistry), on which they are based."[9] Nested hierarchies imply that an emergent novelty does not have a sui generis origin. In other words, novelty has a history, a connection to what has developed prior, and builds on that.

> In the emergent universe, gravitational attraction of dust and gasses has produced planets; molecular and chemical interactions have led to living cells; the process of natural selection has acted on living systems to create organisms with high-functioning consciousness. In

---

7. Gregersen, "Emergency and Complexity," 767.

8. Massimo Pigliucci, "What, If Anything, Is an Evolutionary Novelty?," *Philosophy of Science* 75 (2008): 890.

9. Gregersen, "Emergency and Complexity," 767.

each case the emergent phenomenon gathers up what has preceded it, shaping this material into a new, more complex unity.[10]

Finally, in evolutionary emergence, what arises is quite frankly a surprise. "Higher levels are not predictable from our knowledge of their constituent parts, and their operations are often in principle irreducible to the lower levels."[11] Early theorists attributed this aspect of emergence to an evolutionary tendency toward whole-making, or what Jan Smut termed "holism." He explained:

> The creation of wholes, and ever more highly organized wholes . . . is an inherent character of the universe. There is not a mere vague indefinite creative energy or tendency at work in the world. This energy or tendency has specific characters, the most fundamental of which is whole-making . . . Wholeness is the most characteristic expression of the nature of the universe in its forward movement in time. It marks the line of evolutionary progress. And Holism is the inner driving force behind that progress.[12]

This movement toward wholeness "portrayed the evolutionary process as an unfolding of inherent tendencies, which he associated with a creative divinity" not dissimilar to the thoughts of Teilhard de Chardin.[13]

More recently, a re-emergence of emergence has "roughly coincided with the growth of scientific interest in the phenomenon of complexity and the development of new, non-linear mathematical tools—particularly chaos theory and dynamical systems theory—which allow scientists to model the interactions within complex, dynamic systems in new and insightful ways."[14] Not all forms of emergence follow the same path or relate to their individual parts in a similar way. Terrence Deacon has proposed a typology of three

---

10. Johnson, *Ask the Beasts*, 175.

11. Gregersen, "Emergency and Complexity," 767–68.

12. J. C. Smut, *Holism and Evolution* (New York: Macmillan, 1926), 99.

13. Peter A. Corning, "The Re-Emergence of Emergence, and the Causal Role of Synergy in Emergent Evolution," *Synthese* 185 (2012): 298.

14. Corning, 300.

forms of emergence.[15] In the first-order emergence, the higher-order systems depend on their lower levels from which they emerged. For example, the viscosity of water emerges from multiple elements of water itself: the chemical bonding between the molecules of hydrogen and oxygen, the quantity of molecules, and the right thermal environment.

The second-order emergence includes the first. For example, snow crystals are the result of both first-order properties of ice and additional interactions such as the history of temperature and humidity and the initial form of the snow. As Gregersen explained, the "second-order variant of emergence takes place through chaos and self-organization, where the environmental conditions play a formative role in combination with the concrete history of the system."[16] Finally, the third-order emergence can properly be called evolutionary, where the novelty is passed on to the next generation. All three orders recognize a bottom-up causality. But "once the emergent systems have been established, they are able to perform additional causal roles by constraining and channeling ('from above') what is dynamically possible ('from below')."[17] Gregersen adds to Deacon's typology suggesting that what develops can be further categorized as either weak emergence or strong, depending on its capacity to influence its constituent parts. Weak emergence is when features at a higher level cannot be anticipated in their pre-emergent stage, while strong emergence makes "it possible that higher-level or more comprehensive systems can exert a top-down, selective influence on the lower-level (or local)."[18]

To say that emergent theory is complex is an understatement, but for our purposes, we should keep in mind these general concepts: qualitative novelty, nested hierarchy, and the tendency toward whole-making or holism. The novelty that emerges is both in con-

15. Terrence Deacon, "The Hierarchical Logic of Emergence: Untangling the Interdependence of Evolution and Self-Organization," in *Evolution and Learning: The Baldwin Effect Reconsidered*, ed. Bruce H. Weber and David J. Depew (Cambridge, MA: MIT Press, 2003), 273–308.

16. Gregersen, "Emergency and Complexity," 773–74.

17. Gregersen, 774.

18. Gregersen, 775.

tinuity and discontinuity with what preceded it. It is more than simply the sum of its parts, but at the same time these parts are incorporated into what emerges (nested hierarchy). Back to our snowflake. It is still composed of hydrogen and oxygen (parts), but environmental forces have transformed it into something new, unique, and beautiful (it is more than the sum of its parts). Thus, "emergence refers to layers or levels of reality that fit with each other and form new systems" (holism).[19]

Various theologians have attempted to understand how emergence may reflect the activities of the divine. One proposal is that "God acts directly at the quantum level both to sustain the development of elementary processes and also to determine otherwise indeterminate quantum events."[20] Through this process, God brings about "special, providential and revelatory events at the macrolevel."[21] Thus God's actions are not contrary to natural law, since those actions evidence "a continuous creative (divine) presence within each (quantum) event, co-determining the outcome of these elementary physical processes."[22] Reflecting of a theistic view of emergence, physicist Paul Davies argued that,

> by selecting judiciously, God is able to bestow a rich creativity on the cosmos, because the actual laws of the universe are able to bestow a remarkable capacity to canalize, encourage, and facilitate the evolution of matter and energy along pathways leading to greater organizational complexity.[23]

19. Roger Haight, SJ, *Faith and Evolution: A Grace-Filled Naturalism* (Maryknoll, NY: Orbis Books, 2019), 20.

20. Nancy Murphy, "Divine Action, Emergence and Scientific Explanation," in *The Cambridge Companion to Science and Religion*, ed. Peter Harrison (Cambridge: Cambridge University Press, 2010), 256.

21. Murphy, 256.

22. Robert J. Russell, *Cosmology: From Alpha to Omega: The Creative Mutual Interaction of Theology and Science*, Theology and the Sciences (Minneapolis: Fortress Press, 2008), 156.

23. Paul Davies, "Teleology without Teleology," in *Evolutionary and Molecular Biology: Scientific Perspectives on Divine Action*, ed. Robert John Russell, William R. Stoeger, SJ, and Fransisco J. Ayala (Vatican City State: Vatican Observatory Publications; Berkeley: Center for Theology and the Natural Sciences, 1998), 158.

In an unfinished universe, the capacity for novelty is not only ever present, it is also ever-expanding. While most often the purview of science and metaphysics, the theme of emergence has deep biblical roots.

> By urging us to wait upon the Lord, to live in trust and hope, the biblical vision inevitably locates the fullness of being in an area that we can locate only "up ahead" and not "up above" in a timeless heaven of total perfection, nor behind us in the fixed routines of past physical causation.[24]

## "Behold, I Make All Things New" (Rev 21:5): The Emergent Disciple

As the Book of Revelation culminates, the visionary proclaims:

> Then I saw a new heaven and a new earth; for the first heaven and the first earth had passed away, and the sea was no more. And I saw the holy city, the new Jerusalem, coming down out of heaven from God, prepared as a bride adorned for her husband. And I heard a loud voice from the throne saying,
> "See, the home of God is among mortals.
> He will dwell with them;
> they will be his peoples,
> and God himself will be with them;
> he will wipe every tear from their eyes.
> Death will be no more;
> mourning and crying and pain will be no more,
> for the first things have passed away."
> And the one who was seated on the throne said, "See, I am making all things new." (Rev 21:1-5)

In these five verses, the word "new" appears four times. But this isn't the Greek word *neos*, which can mean "recent" when referring to time, or "young" when referring to things or people. The word translated as "new" in these verses is *kainos*. It has the connotation of "freshness," of something "newly-invented" or "novel." This new

---

24. John F. Haught, *God After Darwin: A Theology of Evolution*, 2nd ed. (New York: Routledge, 2018), 106.

thing isn't a break from the old, but a fresh revision of the old, a novel take of what has been. That which had been created—the old—remains the work of God, but now it is fully glorified.

The vision of a renewed world with a renewed relationship with the divine is at the heart of our Scriptures. In our vocabulary borrowed from metaphysics, we can say that the Bible is a chronicle of the emergence of faith, a composite of our trials, tribulations, missteps, misgivings, heartbreaks and heroism, and ultimately our reconciliation with God. From the call of Abraham to leave his homeland to Moses' mission to free the Hebrew slaves. From the rise of kings in Israel to the messianic expectations after the exile. From the incarnation to the cross to the resurrection, Scripture recounts God's ever-faithful invitation to wholeness. Indeed, this verse from Second Isaiah sums up God's biblical presence and promise: "I am about to do a new thing; / now it springs forth, / do you not perceive it?" (Isa 43:19).

But we have the advantage of hindsight. We know it works out well for Abraham and Sarah—in the end. We know Moses brings the people to very edge of the Promised Land. We know the Messiah has come, and that the reign of God is dawning. It's a bit like saying to the younger generation, "This too will pass. Life will get better," because we have endured what is yet ahead for them. How might revisiting our Scriptures through the lens of emergence give us new insights for the incorporation of new members and the re-inspiration of our own vocation?

Our question is a focused one. It is not simply a renewal of faith that we seek but a deepened sense of mission. In other words, as apostolic women religious, we are bound to discipleship, and I would argue that the formation of a new member is essentially a mentoring for discipleship, creating opportunity for the gifts and desires of the candidate to emerge within the context of the congregation's charism. And as is the case with the disciples of Jesus, emerging disciples do not follow the same path, walk at the same speed, or even arrive at the same place. Such is the way of emergence. It cannot be planned, forced, facilitated, or hurried. It is a process that keeps to its own time and integrity. And yet there is a certain pattern that is discernible. As we view discipleship in the gospels, we see three stages of emergence:

- On the Way: Potential Qualitative Novelty

- In the Midst: A Nested Hierarchy toward Wholeness

- After Easter: Choosing Strong Emergence

## *On the Way: Potential Qualitative Novelty*

The entry level of discipleship—"On the Way"—roots a disciple in the daily following of Jesus. They are most often observers and not engaged participants. "On the Way" is a necessary step to a deeper relationship and commitment to Jesus. Two major questions seem to occupy the disciples of Jesus at this stage: What about our daily needs? and, more importantly: Who are we really following?

In Matthew 6, we read a prime example of the former:

> Therefore I tell you, do not worry about your life, what you will eat or what you will drink, or about your body, what you will wear. Is not life more than food, and the body more than clothing? Look at the birds of the air; they neither sow nor reap nor gather into barns, and yet your heavenly Father feeds them. Are you not of more value than they? And can any of you by worrying add a single hour to your span of life? And why do you worry about clothing? Consider the lilies of the field, how they grow; they neither toil nor spin, yet I tell you, even Solomon in all his glory was not clothed like one of these. But if God so clothes the grass of the field, which is alive today and tomorrow is thrown into the oven, will he not much more clothe you—you of little faith? Therefore do not worry, saying, "What will we eat?" or "What will we drink?" or "What will we wear?" For it is the Gentiles who strive for all these things; and indeed your heavenly Father knows that you need all these things. But strive first for the kingdom of God and his righteousness, and all these things will be given to you as well. So do not worry about tomorrow, for tomorrow will bring worries of its own. Today's trouble is enough for today. (Matt 6:25-34)

Repeatedly Jesus must remind the disciples that their needs, their status, their ambitions are no longer valid concerns. This reorientation takes time. The Sons of Zebedee, whom Jesus has previously named "Sons of Thunder" should more aptly be called "Dunderheads." Three times Jesus has announced his coming passion and death. And what is their response: "Grant us to sit, one at your right hand and one at your left, in your glory" (Mark 10:37). What's worse—even after encountering the resurrected Jesus and receiving the Holy Spirit, Peter and the disciples return to Galilee to their old ways as fishermen (John 21:3). Truly knowing and understanding Jesus is a process. And the attraction of our ordinary comfortable, predictable lives becomes ever more enticing.

Even though we are desirous of a deeper relationship with Jesus, we are beset with concerns about practical matters. I still recall quite vividly when three of us in initial membership first met with our congregation's treasurer to answer any financial questions we had. Our three questions: (1) if I win the lottery, who gets the money? (2) Who owns my clothes? and (3) If I die, who buries me? True emergent discipleship is a process. We recognize that our call and commitment sometimes founders. Sometimes tossed by the waves of self-doubt and uncertainty. Sometimes cast into the shoals of routine and apathy. What we sometimes forget, or overlook, is that our primary concern is not the mundane questions and our own needs, but our ability to recognize whom we follow. When Jesus asks his disciples who they think he is, Peter responds enthusiastically, "You are the Messiah." But that enthusiasm drains when Jesus explains

> that the Son of Man must undergo great suffering, and be rejected by the elders, the chief priests, and the scribes, and be killed, and after three days rise again. He said all this quite openly. And Peter took him aside and began to rebuke him. But turning and looking at his disciples, he rebuked Peter and said, "Get behind me, Satan! For you are setting your mind not on divine things but on human things." He called the crowd with his disciples, and said to them, "If any want to become my followers, let them deny themselves and take up their cross and follow me. For those who want to save their life will lose it, and those who lose their life for my sake, and for the sake of the gospel, will save it. (Mark 8:31-33)

At this stage of emergent discipleship, it's not what we have left behind that matters, but after whom we follow. This is the learning of "On the Way"—the coming to grips with the realization of what discipleship really costs and deciding if Jesus is worth following.

From a formation perspective, the potential for qualitative novelty—in this case, a candidate becoming a healthy, creative, contributing member of her congregation—is visible but not yet fully emerged. There is a reorientation of our lives, a regression and progression, steps forward and backward on the road to deeper conversion.

### In the Midst: A Nested Hierarchy toward Wholeness

After the excitement of the initial invitation to follow, after the ups and downs of life on the road with Jesus, the disciples settle into a deeper rhythm. They are "in the midst." While they are somewhere on the way to the cross, their focus is not on the destination, as much as it is on the person. This is best illustrated in John's Gospel. The disciples begin to recognize that the question is not "what am I getting out of this" but "how can I be present to this." Being present to the moment, to the encounter with Jesus brings profound insights, though the disciples will not understand them until after the resurrection. We read in John 13:

> Jesus, knowing that the Father had given all things into his hands, and that he had come from God and was going to God, got up from the table, took off his outer robe, and tied a towel around himself. Then he poured water into a basin and began to wash the disciples' feet and to wipe them with the towel that was tied around him. (John 13:3-5)

We often focus on the action of washing the feet and miss the impact of the narrator's comment: "he had come from God and was going to God." The Son of God strips himself, bows before the disciples, and cleans their feet. The profound act of humility will be repeated on the cross.

Later in John, we are told that we are branches of the true vine. We are to remain in Jesus and bear fruit.

> If you abide in me, and my words abide in you, ask for whatever you wish, and it will be done for you. My Father is glorified by this, that you bear much fruit and become my disciples. As the Father has loved me, so I have loved you; abide in my love. If you keep my commandments, you will abide in my love, just as I have kept my Father's commandments and abide in his love. I have said these

things to you so that my joy may be in you, and that your joy may be complete. (John 15:7-11)

The word translated as "remain" is *menō*, which also means "to dwell." Remaining in Jesus, dwelling in Jesus is John's way of describing true discipleship. As the name indicates, "in the midst" is an in-between moment. In the story of Jesus, "in the midst" is between life and death, death on the cross. "In the midst" accepts that destiny with profound peace. While John's Jesus approaches the cross with much aplomb, the entire Gospel depicts Jesus' willingness. His earthly life has always been "on the way" to the cross, but he has always been "in the midst" of the Father. And now with Good Friday, he has finally reached his goal.

In his prayer to the Father in John 17, Jesus described the communion that his death would create for his disciples:

> The glory that you have given me I have given them, so that they may be one, as we are one, I in them and you in me, that they may become completely one, so that the world may know that you have sent me and have loved them even as you have loved me. Father, I desire that those also, whom you have given me, may be with me where I am, to see my glory, which you have given me because you loved me before the foundation of the world. (John 17:22-24)

Shortly before his death, Jesus speaks of the disciples as his gift from the Father. One would betray him, and one would deny him. For us, "in the midst" on the way to the cross is an intimate being-with Jesus. At the foot of the cross, we stand weeping, overwhelmed by God's compassion, Jesus' generosity, and the companionship of the Holy Spirit.

At this stage of emergent discipleship, the candidate grows in commitment and begins to integrate the charism of the congregation with her own gifts, desires, and dreams. As Ellen Dauwer, SC, commented, "she is being incorporated into the midst of local community and into the larger congregation. In essence she is incorporating membership into her core identity, while deepening in relationship with Jesus."[25]

---

25. Personal correspondence, February 17, 2021.

She becomes a visible nested hierarchy that will culminate in wholeness. "That they may be one, as we are one."

## After Easter: Choosing Strong Emergence

I'm a Dominican, and I work with a Passionist. As you might imagine, we approach the Triduum through a decidedly different lens. He's all about Good Friday. I'm all about the empty tomb. We all have different responses to the passion, different ways of interpreting the experience and its meaning for us. This third and final section of emerging discipleship occurs "after Easter." Here a disciple must choose whether to be merely a follower with little causal effect on the mission or to be an apostle acting for the sake of mission. The focus is on a very necessary step that must occur before the disciples can truly experience Easter, and thus be sent on mission (Matt 28:19-20). Depending on your life and experience, it may be a nearly insurmountable step—that of reconciliation that leads to mission.

In all four gospels, Peter is named ahead of the remaining twelve indicating his prominence. And it is Peter who continually mis-steps—literally. He rebukes Jesus for announcing his impending passion (Mark 8:32). He steps onto the water only to lose his nerve. "Lord, save me!" (Matt 14:30). He refuses to have his feet washed (John 13:8). And most distressingly, he denies knowing Jesus three times (Mark 14:66-72; Matt 26:69-75; Luke 22:54-62; John 18:15-18, 25-27). But that isn't the end of the story.

In John 21, Jesus and Peter meet again. Three times Jesus asks Peter if he loves him. We see this as parallel to the three times Peter denied Jesus. But what may escape our notice is the vocabulary that Jesus uses. When we look at the words for "love" in the Greek text, we appreicate more fully the encounter between Jesus and Peter.

Jesus asks Peter if he loves him the first time, and uses the verbal form of the word *agape*: "Peter, do you *agapē* me more than these?" Peter responds, "Yes, Lord, you know that I *philō* you." Jesus is asking of Peter that type of love that lays down one's life for one's friend, the type of love that God has of us, an expansive love. That's *agapē*. Peter responds that he holds a friendship love, *philō*—one based on doing good, reciprocating and working toward the betterment of the friend. Again Jesus asks Peter, "Do you *agapē* me?"

Peter doesn't hear the distinction. He responds, "You know that I *philō* you." The third time Jesus asks, "Peter do you *philō* me?" And Peter responds, "You know that I *philō* you." Jesus changes his vocabulary. Peter is not yet ready to love as Jesus desires. Nonetheless, Jesus entrusts him with the care of the community, recognizing that friendship love leads to the kind of love that God asks of all God's children: *agapē*.

Reconciliation is not forgetting. Reconciliation isn't only forgiving. Reconciliation means meeting the other where the other is—in the other's imperfection. And loving the other anyway. Emerging discipleship must contain an element of reconciliation or we cannot live among the various imperfect human beings whom we are to call our brothers and sisters. The process of reconciliation is modeled by Jesus, who not only reconciles with the very disciple who denied him, but then commissions him. "Tend my sheep." Here is the invitation to choose how we will respond to our emergent discipleship. This intrinsic relationship between reconciliation and ministry is made explicit in Paul's Second Letter to the Corinthians:

> So if anyone is in Christ, there is a new creation: everything old has passed away; see, everything has become new! All this is from God, who reconciled us to himself through Christ, and has given us the ministry of reconciliation; that is, in Christ God was reconciling the world to himself, not counting their trespasses against them, and entrusting the message of reconciliation to us. So we are ambassadors for Christ, since God is making his appeal through us; we entreat you on behalf of Christ, be reconciled to God. For our sake he made him to be sin who knew no sin, so that in him we might become the righteousness of God. (2 Cor 5:17-21)

In the formation for emergent disciples, we are to take God's lead. "God sees our fullest potential—our redeemed and holy self—and God loves us in a way that beckons this self to life."[26] All along the way of becoming, God is urging, acting, inviting and loving us into this reconciled, emerging reality.

---

26. Paul J. Wadell, *The Primacy of Love: Introduction to the Ethics of Thomas Aquinas* (Eugene, OR: Wipf & Stock, 2009), 73.

Recently, I was asked to write a letter of recommendation for a temporary professed sister who was requesting final vows. In the invitation I was also given the "signs of readiness" by which this sister's request would be evaluated. As I acknowledged in my letter, I don't think even Jesus himself could have mastered the litany of "readiness." In fact, in John's Gospel, the only criteria Jesus sets for his disciples is love.

> No one has greater love than this, to lay down one's life for one's friends. You are my friends if you do what I command you. I do not call you servants any longer, because the servant does not know what the master is doing; but I have called you friends, because I have made known to you everything that I have heard from my Father. You did not choose me but I chose you. And I appointed you to go and bear fruit, fruit that will last, so that the Father will give you whatever you ask him in my name. I am giving you these commands so that you may love one another. (John 15:13-17)

What would our formation for emerging discipleship look like if the goals were to become friends with one's sisters and one's God, to grow in confidence that one has been chosen and has the capacity to bear fruit, and, finally to learn to love deeply and broadly. To love God who creates, Jesus who calls, and the Spirit that energizes. To love the people of God and all of creation and most especially, to love oneself.

## Conclusion: Charism as a Nested Hierarchy

The elements of emergence—qualitative novelty, nested hierarchy of ontological levels, and holism—provide a renewed way to envision the formation of new members and the ongoing formation of vowed members in an evolving universe. But as members of apostolic religious congregations with a long history of responding to the signs of the times, our goal isn't simply to draw out the latent potential in new members. We are forming folks for something. We hope for what Gregersen calls "strong emergence." Where the emergent properties "do not immediately fall prey to their changing environments (as snowflakes do). Causal capacities require the emergence of relatively stable systems that are able to follow their own programmatic 'ends' even under changing circumstances."[27] Though he is speaking of systems, we can translate a bit and envision membership and the mission of the congregation. Drawing from Maria Cimperman's social analysis,[28] we should keep in mind that the incorporation of new members and vivification of vowed members (1) is complex and layered, (2) requires deep reflection, (3) necessitates interrelationship and collaboration, (4) asks for a freedom and openness to new insights, and (5) is an ongoing, evolving activity.

In that light, Schneiders encourages that we adopt a "radical conversion, profound renewal in terms of a new theological vision" in light of the evolving universe in which we find ourselves.

> The primary focus that unifies all the efforts at renewal of contemporary Religious is this changed understanding of ministry and world engagement. Ministry in the reality of our times, i.e., in the world, has become absolutely central to our identity. We have grasped, or been grasped by, the unity of the one great commandment. Effective love of the whole world, especially of the human family for whom Christ died and rose, is not a consequence of love of God or a secondary end flowing from a primary commitment to our own sanctification.[29]

Mission and its activities (ministry) incarnate our love of God and love of neighbor. It is not what we do; it is for whom we do it. And the formation of new members is the process by which the charism of the congregation—its unique gift—is breathed into the next generation. In light of the science of emergence, I propose that we think of charism as the nested hierarchy from which emerges not only the future membership but the future mission. In a nested hierarchy the emergent levels contain the lower ones. Pope Paul VI recognizes this historical embeddedness in the Apostolic Exhortation on the

27. Gregersen, "Emergency and Complexity," 776.
28. Cimperman, *Social Analysis for the 21st Century*, 9.
29. Sandra Schneiders, "Vowed Religious Life," Presentation to the IHM Congregation (June 14, 2009), 5, https://anunslife.org/sites/www.anunslife.org/files/assets/blogimages/SSchneidersLecture2009.pdf.

Renewal of Religious Life According to the Teaching of the Second Vatican Council:

> It is precisely here that the dynamism proper to each religious family finds its origin. For while the call of God renews itself and expresses itself in different ways according to changing circumstances of place and time, it nevertheless requires a certain constancy of orientation. The interior impulse which is the response to God's call stirs up in the depth of one's being certain fundamental options. Fidelity to the exigencies of these fundamental options is the touchstone of authenticity in religious life. Let us not forget that every human institution is prone to become set in its ways and is threatened by formalism. It is continually necessary to revitalize external forms with this interior driving force, without which these external forms would very quickly become an excessive burden.[30]

When the process of formation is modeled on emergence then the charism of the congregation is historically situated (lower levels), evolutionary (emerging from a nested hierarchy), and responsive to the inchoate signs of the times in an unfinished universe. "See, I am making all things new" (Rev 21:5). Indeed!

30. Pope Paul VI, Apostolic Exhortation on the Renewal of Religious Life According to the Teaching of the Second Vatican Council (*Evangelica Testificatio*), June 29, 1971, I.12, https://w2.vatican.va/content/paul-vi/en/apost_exhortations/documents/hf_p-vi_exh_19710629_evangelica-testificatio.html.

# Chapter Eight

## Seeking the Whole

### The Vows through a Hermeneutic of Catholicity

Perspective affects what you see. Case in point: frequently I lead the Biblical Study and Travel Program, sponsored by Catholic Theological Union, which takes students and avid participants to Israel/ Palestine, Greece, and Turkey. A decade ago, when leading one of these programs, I was attempting to take the bus back from the Old City of Jerusalem to our hostel in Bethany. Before the completion of the security fence that separates Israel from the West Bank, we simply rode the number 36 bus, which stopped at the base of our hill before continuing its route to al-Eizariya, the Arabic name for the city of Lazarus (Bethany in the New Testament). Now two number 36 buses had to leave from the Arab bus station. One cost four shekels and would bring me to my stop, Shayyah Road. Another cost six shekels and circumnavigated the wall, passing through a checkpoint before arriving at al-Eizariya, directly on the other side of the security fence. I approached one 36 bus and inquired of the driver, "inside the wall?" The driver nodded. I handed over 4 shekels. "No," he responded. "Six." What I considered "inside"—in Israel, he understood as "inside"—in Palestine. What is inside and outside depends on one's vantage.

In chapter 5, we were introduced to two novices both reviewing a landscape through the lens of their own home geography. Where you stand, or have stood, affects what you see, or rather, how you interpret what you see. In chapter 3, we explored how generational differences and societal changes affect our ecclesiology. The church we knew in our young adulthood became imprinted on us, so to speak, as the template for our developing understanding of church, theology, liturgy, social action, etc. Given our generational geography and formative ecclesiology we should not be surprised that we view elements of our vowed religious lives differently. Two concepts, social location and hermeneutics—the first borrowed from anthropology and the second from textual studies—can help us appreciate these differences. Once we situate ourselves and recognize the variety of lenses through which we view ourselves and our world, we are ready to develop a new hermeneutical strategy that integrates emerging science and theology. As one sister stated, "How can we live a vibrant vowed life in the 21st century when the theology of religious life was originally developed by those who believed the world was flat?" We conclude by proposing how a hermeneutic that attends to emerging science—a hermeneutic of catholicity—can contribute to our vision of religious life, and particularly, our understanding of the evangelical counsels.

## Wherever You Go, There You Are

Jon Kabat-Zinn's book by the same name focused on the importance of recognizing the place in which we find ourselves in the here and now and its implications for practices of mindfulness.[1] As I invoke this phrase, the stress is not on the "there" but the "you." Wherever one goes in life, in ministry, in relationships, one brings oneself, but seldom does one ponder the whole package. Cultural anthropologists name the "whole package" our social location,

> which refers to the contexts within which human beings structure their lives, or the contexts that structure humans. Social location is a matrix or convergence of a number of thought systems that define a community and its reality. This matrix includes political, theological,

---

1. Jon Kabat-Zinn, *Wherever You Go, There You Are: Mindfulness Meditation in Everyday Life* (New York: Hyperion, 2014).

social, linguistic, aesthetic, literary, scientific, educational, and other systems that constitute a community's symbolic world. From within this social location, a person values, makes judgments and decisions, and knows as far as the conventions of the system allows. All human activity (including the construction of systems, the creative arts, writing, reading, and interpreting) occur *within* contexts.[2]

We are all situated in time and space, a particular time and a particular space that defines who we are within our larger group. This social location or matrix includes our gender, race, social class, age, ability, religion, sexual orientation, and geographic location. As Ada Maria Isasi-Diaz describes, "*Lo cotidiano* [everyday life] makes social location explicit for it is the context of the person in relation to physical space, ethnic space, social space."[3] When forming a new local community, one of the first questions that we ask of each other is "How do you spend the holidays?" The family and cultural rituals that each sister carries are important identity markers, and failing to recognize our experiences and our differences can lead to no little difficulty.

Our social location isn't baggage. It isn't a handicap. And it isn't "something to get over." It is the matrix in which we know ourselves as individuals within a larger group. "Our first ethical responsibility is to acknowledge and recognize how each of our own respective and specific *vidas cotidianas* (daily lives) impact and influence our individual methodologies, foundations and starting points for reflection."[4] Failing to recognize where we "stand" is part of the reason family arguments can devolve. For example, like many religious congregations, mine supports efforts toward comprehensive immigration reform but sharing that on Facebook unintentionally upset my sister-in-law. Only after a long conversation was I able to

2. W. Randolph Tate, "Post Modern Interpretation," *The Oxford Encyclopedia of Biblical Interpretation*, ed. Steven L. McKenzie (New York: Oxford University Press, 2013).

3. Ada Maria Isasi-Diaz, *Mujerista Theology: A Theology for the Twenty-First Century* (Maryknoll, NY: Orbis Books, 1996), 71.

4. Carmen Marie Nanko, "Elbows on the Table: The Ethics of Doing Theology, Reflections from a U.S. Hispanic Perspective," *Journal of Hispanic/Latino Theology* 10 (February 2003): 67.

hear her "social location" with regard to this issue. She is a legal immigrant who went through much time, trouble, and expense to secure her citizenship. I still support the humane care of asylum seekers, immigrants, and migrants, but understanding her social location helps me to appreciate her perspective and to engage in civil conversation.

Our social location evolves as we do. My gender and race will not change, but my understanding of what it means to be a woman and to be a White woman living in a North American context does change.

> While we inhabit this earth as soil, peoples, animals and spirits, we are marked by our social locations. Thus, our differences must be engaged based on this common sense of collectivity, of being together and sustaining both our strange commonalities and our irreducible differences.[5]

As we integrate new experiences and acquire knowledge, aspects of our social location are changed. This evolving wisdom—like our culture, race, gender, geography, economic setting, and education—provides a lens through which we view and understand our world. Deciphering this lens is properly understood as hermeneutics—the theory of interpretation.

## Creating a Hermeneutics of Catholicity

The word "hermeneutics" has its origins in Hermes, the god of language and interpretation, who "was able to bridge the gap between the divine and human realms, putting into words those mysteries which were beyond the capacity of human utterance."[6] Most often the term is used in reference to deriving meaning from texts, particularly the Bible. That meaning is always contextual since "*any* attempt at interpretation is a quest for meaning, and meaning

---

5. Cláudio Carvalhaes, "We Are All Immigrants! Imago Dei, Citizenship, and The Im/Possibility of Hospitality," *Practical Matters Journal* 11 (2018): 3.

6. David Jasper, *A Short Introduction to Hermeneutics* (Louisville, KY: Westminster John Knox Press, 2004), 7.

is always meaning for *someone*."[7] And an interpretation is "always made against a set of socially agreed upon canons and texts (albeit interpreted ones), which are themselves publicly accessible in the case of disputations."[8] Hermeneutics requires a continual return to the object of interpretation in what is called a hermeneutical cycle.

> It is circular because it involves a constant movement from us, the interpreter, to the interpreted, and back again, thereby also implying that every interpretation is itself interpreted. It is indeterminate because that loop of interpretation has no end. And it is perspectival because interpreters are embedded in their situations which makes their knowledge always partial and incomplete.[9]

Moving beyond the interpretation of texts, the hermeneutical approach is used in a variety of fields including anthropology, the history and philosophy of science, and economics.[10] The question becomes: Can the trifocals of cosmology, quantum theory, and evolution provide a new lens through which to view religious life? Such a hermeneutic finds its roots in the center of our faith: catholicity.

## Seeking the Whole

Little could the Greeks know that their introduction of space into the ancient Near Eastern two-tier cosmology would allow for a radical new understanding of the human and the cosmos. As Delio writes,

> The Greeks introduced the concept of space and conceived of the cosmos as a three-dimensional sphere with height, depth, and width. One could suggest that awareness of a spatial, three-dimensional cosmos impelled the ancient Greeks to separate the human from world in a way that allowed them to discover a cosmos.[11]

7. Sandra M. Schneiders, *Written That You May Believe: Encountering Jesus in the Fourth Gospel* (New York: Crossroad Publishing, 1999), 175.

8. "Hermeneutics," in *GeoDZ The Earth Encyclopedia*, http://www.geodz.com/eng/d /hermeneutics/hermeneutics.htm.

9. "Hermeneutics," in *GeoDZ The Earth Encyclopedia*.

10. "Hermeneutics," in *GeoDZ The Earth Encyclopedia*.

11. Ilia Delio, *Making All Things New: Catholicity, Cosmology, Consciousness* (Maryknoll, NY: Orbis Books, 2015), 8.

Standing outside (if only theoretically) of the world in which humanity dwelt became a starting point, the trajectory of which would lead to Teilhard de Chardin's affirmation of Huxley's insight, the human being was "evolution become conscious of itself."[12] The cognitive act of separation allowed for a deeper recognition of unity, which Delio, among others, names as "catholicity."

The word itself is not new to us. It comes from the Greek, *kata* (according to) *holos* (the whole) or a "sense of the whole." We are Catholic women religious, members of a universal church. We acknowledge the breadth of this ecclesial membership in both the Apostles' and the Nicene Creeds:

> I believe in the Holy Spirit, the holy catholic Church (Apostles' Creed).
> I believe in one, holy, catholic and apostolic Church (Nicene Creed).

Recently, systematic theologians have discussed the concept of catholicity, but in very different ways. Robert Schreiter, CPPS, describes a "new catholicity" that possesses three dimensions: the universal extension of the church, the fullness of faith, and new patterns of communication that respond to the genuine diversity of communities and cultures.

> While such worldwide extension is even more true today, in the twenty-first century, than it was through much of the Church's history, that "seeking of the whole" of the Church today will have to include aspects that have been discussed here as part of the second modernity: a cosmopolitan, rather than an ethnocentric view of humanity and human cultures; ways of including a sense of the "both-and" view of reality rather than the more familiar "either-or" attitude that has shaped much of our history; and ways to extend our sense of *communio* to include a *convivência* [living together] of peoples, where difference is not only recognized, but engaged.[13]

---

12. Pierre Teilhard de Chardin, *The Phenomenon of Man* (New York: Harper & Row, 1961), 220.

13. Robert J. Schreiter, CPPS, "A New Modernity: Living and Believing in an Unstable World," *Melintas: An International Journal of Philosophy and Religion* 21 (2005): 182.

Schreiter's "new catholicity" draws on the development of culture and communication in post-modernity, recognizing that creating a theology of culture builds on the moments of change.

> For it is the experience of moving from one place to another, of cobbling together new identities out of the old ones, of negotiating multiple identities and logics that insight into where God is at work in a globalized culture will be found. It will be a study in surprise, in turning up the unexpected, in celebrating the small victories, for the experience of a globalized world lies in is peripheries, in the moments of risk and change, in the celebration of survival of yet another day.[14]

As social scientists and anthropologists explain, the development of culture is the result of our human capacity to think, form language, and communicate. Culture is part of humanity's evolutionary trajectory.

> Cultures are shared worldviews, patterns of behavior, and affective understandings that are learned through a process of socialization. The transition into culture, a psycho-social phenomenon, occasions a non-linear, exponential jump in intellectual power . . . Human evolution proceeds by the interplay of two fronts: biological, governed by genetic variation and natural selection, and cultural, a mental and social realm rife with new freedoms.[15]

While Schreiter's new catholicity is chiefly ecclesial in its orientation, it nonetheless recognizes the evolutionary aspect of culture and the value of intercultural communication. It upholds the genuine diversity in the church and world and advocates for interculturality, solidarity, and *convivência*.

Another understanding of catholicity is cosmic in orientation. In this sense, "The word catholicity was coined to describe a consciousness of the whole cosmos, the whole physical order of things to which the human was connected but distinct from; cosmos was

14. Robert J. Schreiter, *The New Catholicty: Theology between the Global and the Local* (Maryknoll, NY: Orbis Books, 1997), 59.

15. Elizabeth A. Johnson, *Ask the Beasts: Darwin and the God of Love* (London: Bloomsbury, 2014), 239–40.

the source for guiding human action."[16] The way Delio presents it suggests that deep in our religious roots we have always held the potential for a larger reality, a universality that counters parochialism and anthropocentricism. This sense of catholicity isn't a place as much as it is a way of being.

> Catholicity is not a physical order or a spiritual one; it does not connote geographical extension . . . Catholicity belongs not to the phenomenal and empirical but to the noumenal and ontological plane; it describes the essential nature of reality, the external manifestations. Catholicity is what contemporary Jesuit philosopher Bernard Lonergan called "notional being," an orientation of being toward wholeness or leavening the stuff of life to create a greater whole.[17]

This concept of catholicity begins in a shared origin that confirms a deep unity connecting all of creation. It integrates cosmology and anthropology and is deeply evolutionary and emergent.

Drawing from the work of Schreiter and Delio, we find three elements of an integrated anthropological and cosmological understanding of catholicity: the role of interculturality, the shared origin of all creation and its unitive nature, and the evolutionary trajectory toward Omega/God. First, interculturality acknowledges the multiplicity of "places" that form our individual and corporate social location. It's important here to distinguish between multicultural and intercultural.

> Where different cultural groups coexist in the same region, we have a multicultural society and living conditions. But this is often as far as it goes. In general, people do not commit themselves— or seek— to build a new, integrated community. They may live in peaceful coexistence, with tolerance or mutual respect and even some degree of good-neighborliness . . . In fact, they remain "at home" while their neighbors of different cultures likewise remain "at home." So

---

16. Delio, *Making All Things New*, 8.

17. Delio, 9. Delio cites Longeran, *A Second Collection*, ed. William Ryan and Bernard Tyrrell, (Toronto: University of Toronto Press, 1996), 80.

we describe this kind of multiculturality as many people who are all equally at home but separately rather than together.[18]

The term, multicultural, admits to differences but does not cross boundaries so as to create a new synthesis. Rather, as Anthony Gittins writes of interculturality, "each is able to become a participating outsider and to bring his or her particular culture to the emerging reality."[19] Joanne Jaruko Doi, MM, adds, even "our full names illustrate the inherent interculturality and different webs of relationships to which we belong."[20] Interculturality enables "the subjects of any cultural universe to utilize the 'reserves' of their tradition of origin as a point of support for their own personal identity, without discriminatory consequences."[21] Recognizing and embracing interculturality is thus an act of hospitality and genuine respect.

Through a cosmological lens, our understanding of catholicity finds its origin in the Big Bang, which sent forth all the material that would one day—long into the future—form life on Earth. As chapter 4, "The Cosmos and Creation," recounted, all of matter living and inanimate finds its origin in that fraction of fraction of a second. Whether that Big Bang was the first or part of a continuing cycle of the universe's death and rebirth, it initiated a chain of events that would birth stars and galaxies. Eventually, the primordial hydrogen and helium under the pressure of a dying star exploded into heavier elements necessary for life—carbon, nitrogen, oxygen, phosphorous, and silicon. It is not an exaggeration to say that we—and all of creation—are made of star dust. Indeed, Francis of Assisi got it right. "The Canticle of Brother Sun and Sister Moon" reminds us of our shared relationship—billions of years in the making. Thus, our second aspect of catholicity is unitive, recognizing that "all

18. Anthony J. Gittins, CSSp, *Living Mission Interculturally: Faith, Culture, and the Renewal of Praxis* (Collegeville, MN: Liturgical Press, 2015), 34–35.

19. Gittins, 23.

20. Joanne Jaruko Doi, "Interculturality: A Foundation for U.S. Mission," in *The Gift of Mission: Yesterday, Today, Tomorrow: The Maryknoll Centennial Symposium*, ed. James H. Kroeger (Maryknoll, NY: Orbis Books, 2013), 205.

21. Gittins, *Living Mission Interculturally*, 23.

living beings on the planet are interrelated by common descent"[22] and move toward relationship and wholeness. "We must become inwardly whole by training our minds to become more integrated, a higher consciousness of oneness; to unify the partials of our lives, in our communities and in our world; to make an 'option for the whole.'"[23]

The third element of an integrated understanding of catholicity acknowledges this process toward wholeness.

> There is an impulse in nature toward greater wholeness and unity. Evolution discloses a dynamism of catholicity; every whole is part of a larger whole, and the whole process of evolution seems to yearn for ultimate wholeness.[24]

This striving for wholeness and final unity is directional, moving toward the Omega Point, which Teilhard de Chardin identified as God. Our task now is to see how these elements of catholicity—interculturality, union, and evolution—might form a lens through which to view the vows.

## The Vows in the Holocene

It came as a surprise sometime during my early formation as a Dominican Sister of Sinsinawa. We take only one vow—that of obedience. Having studied the evangelical councils and after spending many a tearful moment of discernment about how or if I could live poverty, chastity, and obedience, I suddenly learned I only had to vow obedience. And then the other shoe dropped: our obedience is to the prioress and her successors and to the Constitution into which is neatly and unequivocally tucked the evangelical councils. Back to tearful moments of discernment.

The vows, it seems, are indispensable:

---

22. Johnson, *Ask the Beasts*, 101.
23. Delio, *Making All Things New*, 197.
24. Delio, 176.

The purpose of the religious life is to help the members follow Christ and be united to God through the profession of the evangelical counsels.[25]

This is it, isn't it? The core of our life as religious—the vows. Many do good works, many pray, many share our various charisms. What makes our lifestyle different from that of the married or single laity is our profession of poverty, chastity, and obedience.[26] And through the lens of catholicity, these three are not so much separate as distinct parts of a larger whole. Physicist David Bohm (1917–1992) described an undivided wholeness in life in which each part is connected to every other part at the quantum level. "It is shown that both in relativity theory and quantum theory, notions implying the undivided wholeness of the universe would provide a much more orderly way of considering the general nature of reality."[27] Thus, Bohm proposed that holonomy counters autonomy, for at a deep quantum level, there is an undivided wholeness.

The term, "holon," was coined to describe the reality that all of individual elements in a living system are actually part of a larger whole, so that "a holon is simultaneously a whole and a part."[28] Through a lens of catholicity then, the vows of poverty, chastity, and obedience are holons, parts of a larger whole that frames our lives as vowed women religious. In what follows, we will view the evangelical counsels through a hermeneutical lens of catholicity, so as to explore the implications of encountering the vows as intercultural, unitive, and evolutionary.

25. Pope Paul VI, Decree on the Adaptation and Renewal of Religious Life (*Perfectae Caritatis*), October 28, 1965, 2e.

26. While "poverty, chastity, and obedience" are the common terms, some suggest various other names. For example, Schneiders advocates that "chastity" is more properly described as "consecrated celibacy," which she argues "is at the very heart of Religious Life. . . . Neither Religious poverty nor obedience constitute a state of life; they are aspects of a state of life constituted by the free choice of nonmarriage for the sake of the kingdom." Sandra M. Schneiders, *Selling All: Commitment, Consecrated Celibacy, and Community in Catholic Religious Life* (New York: Paulist Press, 2001), 125.

27. David Bohm, *Wholeness and the Implicate Order* (London: Routledge, 1980), xiv.

28. Delio, *Making All Things New*, 121.

### "Let Anyone Accept This Who Can" (Matt 19:12)— Invitation Not Mandate

The first Christmas after I had made my temporary vows, my father and I were walking through a crowded department store when an item caught my eye. It was a heating pad that could be warmed in a microwave, appropriately called a "bed-buddy." "I could use a bed-buddy," I said as we walked by. My father, who had not noticed the display, responded, "You should have thought of that before you entered the convent!"

From the outside, the vows can be viewed as restrictive, even punitive. They don't make sense to many, especially non-Catholics. But for those of us who have made vows, have staked our life on this form of life, we experience the evangelical counsels differently. We chose consecrated life because it is deeply rooted in the example and teaching of Jesus, and

> is a gift of God the Father to his Church through the Holy Spirit. By the profession of the evangelical counsels *the characteristic features of Jesus*—the chaste, poor and obedient one—*are made constantly "visible" in the midst of the world* and the eyes of the faithful are directed towards the mystery of the Kingdom of God already at work in history, even as it awaits its full realization in heaven.[29]

Canon 575 states something similar: "The evangelical counsels, based on the teaching and examples of Christ the Teacher, are a divine gift which the Church has received from the Lord and preserves always through His grace." The church recognizes that the ability to live the vows is a gift of the Holy Spirit, and thus, not a mandate for all believers. And these vows are clearly constitutive of the life.

> The counsels are, as it were, the main support of the religious life, since they express in a significant and complete way the evangelical radicalism which characterizes it. In effect, through the profession of

---

29. Pope John Paul II, Apostolic Exhortation on the Consecrated Life and its Mission in the Church and in the World (*Vita Consecrata*), March 25, 1996, 1; italics in the original.

the evangelical counsels made in the Church, the religious wishes "to be set free from hindrances that could hold [her] back from loving God ardently and worshipping [God] perfectly and . . . to consecrate [her]self in a more thoroughgoing way to the service of God."[30]

The Vatican documents recognize that each vow is individually significant while remaining a part of the larger context that is the evangelical counsels.

> These [vows] touch the human person at the level of the three essential spheres of [her] existence and relationships: affectivity, possession, and power. . . . The faithful exercise of them fosters the development of the person, spiritual freedom, purification of the heart, fervor of charity, and it helps a religious to cooperate in the construction of human society.[31]

We can argue that each vow is complete and effective in itself, separate from the other two. For example, diocesan priests promise chastity and vow obedience to their bishop but do not take a vow of poverty. But in the language of catholicity, the three vows of poverty, chastity, and obedience are also holons—parts of a larger whole, reflecting different aspects of Jesus' life that we are to emulate, since Jesus "is modeling what the Reign of God looks like as he announces it. So must we. Our lives are to be Good News for all: for us, for our communities, for all those with whom we interact, and to all places that are in need of this good news."[32] Understanding the evangelical counsels as intercultural, unitive, and evolutionary creates a way of witnessing to the Good News in an unfinished universe.

---

30. Congregation for Institutes of Consecrated Life and Societies of Apostolic Life, "Directives on Formation in Religious Institutes," February 2, 1990, 12.32, https://www.vatican.va/roman_curia/congregations/ccscrlife/documents/rc_con_ccscrlife_doc_02021990_directives-on-formation_en.html.

31. Congregation for Institutes of Consecrated Life and Societies of Apostolic Life, 12.33–34.

32. Maria Cimperman, *Religious Life for Our World: Creating Communities of Hope* (Maryknoll, NY: Orbis Books, 2020), 45.

### Intercultural

As we noted in our discussion on social location, we all are the mutable sum total of heritage, education, geography, experience, etc. In a word, we are not the same. Perhaps at some time in the history of religious life, a congregation's members were more monolithic, but, as the ethnic and racial diversity of the newer entrants indicate, that level of commonality has passed. Additionally, by virtue of their generational experiences, how Vatican II sisters view religious life and the evangelical counsels can be decidedly different from how post Vatican II sisters view the life. As used in this analysis, interculturality speaks not only of differences in culture and ethnicity, but also differences in generations and orienting ecclesiology. To engage in interculturality is to be willing to *cross over* from one's own perspective so as to *cross into* another's experience with the intent of then *creating* a new shared space. As Anthony Gittins explains:

> This is a culture in the making and, paradoxically, everyone within the new community will be an outsider to [this shared space], but each is able to become a participating outsider bringing his or her particular culture to the emerging reality.[33]

Through the focal point of interculturality, we can see the validity of a plethora of perspectives. Far from diluting our corporate understanding of, say, the vow of poverty, the diversity among our perspectives invites a deeper conversation that can lead to consensus. We can take our cue from the evangelists Matthew and Luke, who both include a beatitude about the poor but have decidedly different understandings of poverty. Matthew sees those who are poor in spirit as blessed (Matt 5:3) while Luke offers no qualifiers. It is simply "the poor" who are blessed (Luke 6:20).

Our own experience of want and need affects how we understand the vow of poverty. A decade ago, when we no longer had institutional convents available, a group of us younger sisters were advocating that the congregation consider purchasing a house in which we could live in community under one roof and avoid the costs of setting up separate apartments. The prioress at the time was not in

---

33. Gittins, *Living Mission Interculturally*, 23.

favor of this, leading some of us to wonder how valued community life really was. Only over time were we able to see that our personal experiences led to this stalemate. As a child, our prioress had only lived in rental properties; home buying being beyond her family's financial capacity. For we youngers, our parents considered home buying an important financial anchor, and renting was "throwing money down the drain."

The generational differences also come to play in our conversations (or silence) about the vow of celibacy. As various surveys and personal discussions have revealed, today's entrants come to the life having had a variety of sexual experiences, a broader understanding of gender, and numerous sustaining friendships outside the congregation. "Our human sexuality is God's gift, a fundamental dimension of who we are. Returning that gift to God in consecrated chastity makes better lovers of us."[34] Approaching the vow of celibacy through an intercultural lens also allows for an appreciation of how women from different cultural backgrounds and ethnicities experience and demonstrate affectivity. As with the vow of poverty, one size—or rather one expression of the vow of celibacy—does not fit all.

This is no less true than with the different interpretations of the vow of obedience. Sister Christine Danel, the superior general of the Xavière Sisters, examined the implications of culture. "Our manner of living in obedience is founded on the expression of what one has to say. Now, the connection between the word and the subject is not always the same among different cultures," she stated.[35]

Only when we are willing to cross over and into a new shared space are we truly able to understand how together we might live the vows. But Anthony Gittins offers a warning. While our diversity should be acknowledged and valued, it shouldn't rule the day.

> In the context of a would-be intercultural community, however, we must be careful. Differences distinguish one individual from another, even identical twins. But pushing differences too far— that is, by

34. Margaret Scott, "Greening the Vows: *Laudato Si'* and Religious Life," *The Way* 54 (2015): 86.

35. Nicolas Senèze, "Nuns Confronted with Power and the Vow of Obedience," *La-Croix International* (May 13, 2019), https://international.la-croix.com/news/religion /nuns-confronted-with-power-and-the-vow-of-obedience/10084.

defending our right to be different— might easily cause us to fall into an unhealthy and destructive individualism . . . We need to recognize that the unity of God the Creator is actualized and expressed quite clearly—and indeed ostentatiously—in the diversity of creation, without claiming thereby a license to defend our differences at the expense of community living and a community project or commitment.[36]

## Unitive

If interculturality speaks to how the vows can be perceived through our different cultural and generational lens, then the unitive aspect of our hermeneutic of catholicity addresses what the vows affect. As Sandra Schneiders writes:

> Profession itself and each of its three vows conduce to the spiritual journey into God of the person herself (what I have called the God-quest), to her participation in a certain kind of community life, and to her commitment to promoting the Reign of God.[37]

Poverty, chastity, and obedience individually and together encourage the individual toward personal wholeness: a simplicity of life, a freedom for relationships, an attentive listening to the divine and the manifestation of the divine in the created world. As we are made whole in our living of the evangelical counsels, we become a more viable member of community. A healthy, holy, and wholesome individual in a thriving, prayerful community, cannot but be a more vital force on behalf of the reign of God.

> Each of the three vows . . . has been understood at one time or another as the primary mediator of the God-quest that is at the heart of Religious Life. Negatively, the practice of purity of heart, renunciation of material goods, or the sacrifice of self-will disposed the Religious for growth in union with Christ. Positively, exclusive and wholehearted love of Christ, total reliance on providence, and active union of will with the will of God embodied, expressed, and fostered that union. Whichever aspect of profession was emphasized in a particular form of Religious Life or a particular order or con-

36. Gittins, *Living Mission Interculturally*, 148.
37. Schneiders, *Selling All*, 138.

gregation, the unitive function of the vows is their most intimate and personal dimension.[38]

This unitive aspect of the vows is whole-making not only for ourselves but for all of creation. Thus "consecrated people are called to open their hearts and minds, their whole being, to a cosmic world-view, to a holistic approach to life."[39] Our vow of poverty challenges us to stand in solidarity with all who are without what they need to live and thrive. As Scott recognizes:

> Consecrated poverty reminds us that everything is gift and places us in a relationship of cosmic reciprocity with the whole web of ecosystems and its recycling of resources that continually transforms death into new life.[40]

Likewise, our vow of chastity urges us to reach out in relationship to others and Earth. Our vow of obedience invites a deep listening to where the voice of God is urging us forward. Through the lens of catholicity, the vows function to counter division and to witness to wholeness.

> Traditionally the spirituality of consecration for vowed men and women has been built on a dualistic foundation that both fragmented and spiritualised the following of the chaste, poor and obedient Christ. It compartmentalised the three vows, tending to diminish their dynamic integration and complementarity. Theology today is moving towards a much more ecological, holistic approach to reality. It is against this holistic background that we need to reimagine religious life as an organic form of life, and contextualise the consecration of religious women and men, passionately in love with Jesus Christ.[41]

### Evolutionary

We—indeed, all of creation—are a work in progress. We should not be surprised, then, that our understanding of the evangelical counsels is likewise evolving. Interculturality speaks to how we

38. Schneiders, 112.
39. Scott, "Greening the Vows," 85.
40. Scott, 89.
41. Scott, 84.

view the vows. The unitive aspect of a hermeneutic of catholicity addresses how those vows function. And the evolutionary aspect reminds us that the vows are eschatological in their orientation. The vows point ahead to the fulfillment of God's reign. They are visible manifestations of our belief in God's faithfulness. As such, when we profess our vows, we ourselves become signposts pointing toward the realization of the reign of God, which Teilhard de Chardin described as Christogenesis or the Omega Point.

But the vows are also deeply attentive to the nowing of God's reign. The Greek word translated as "obedience" is *hupakoē*—"giving ear" or "listening to." To what was Jesus listening? How is the voice of God heard beyond the moments of theophany? Like God who observed the misery of the Hebrews in Egypt and "heard their cry" (Exod 3:7), Jesus saw and heard the suffering of his day and felt compassion for them (Mark 1:42, 6:34, 8:2; Matt 14:14; Luke 7:13; 10:33). He attended to the birds of the air, the sheep in the fold, and flowers of the field.

> Consider the lilies, how they grow: they neither toil nor spin; yet I tell you, even Solomon in all his glory was not clothed like one of these. (Luke 12:27)

Through obedience—an attentiveness, an appreciation, an ability to see in the created world the work of God—a path toward the divine opens to all of us. As abundantly evident in the gospels, true obedience to God's will is not blind, lock-step adherence to dogma, doctrine, emerging spirituality or even one's superior. Evolutionary obedience in the manner of Jesus, the obedience that we women religious vow to hold, is a deep listening to the divine heartbeat embodied and emergent in the very cosmos.

## Conclusion

At our profession, after the prioress reads each description of the evangelical counsels, the sister announces "Yes, this is what I chose." The meaning of poverty, chastity, and obedience within 1950s religious life would be radically altered in the following seven decades. Indeed, even the "what"—the apostolic life in community to which one said "Yes, this is what I chose"—would be transformed. But this yes isn't simply to the vows or the way of life. It is to something larger, more encompassing—it is to love, both as a noun and as a verb. If the vows shape how we live, love is the goal and manner by which we live.

> Consecration expresses a commitment to mirror the life of Jesus of Nazareth, imitating his way of life and his love: a love that empties itself in solidarity with all people, especially the smallest, the least and the forgotten.[42]

Interculturality, union, and evolution speak to how the vows are perceived, what the vows do, and where the vows are leading. Thus, through the hermeneutical lens of catholicity the evangelical counsels can be rescued from a limited historical interpretation and revitalized for an intercultural, intergenerational community that sets its heart on the realization of the reign of God.

While we most often think of ourselves as "living the vows" and not necessarily having a specific point-in-time encounter with them, there are moments in our religious lives when we do stop and ponder them. Think first profession, final vows, jubilee, or moments of crisis. The hermeneutic of catholicity invites just such an encounter in which we explore the intercultural, unitive, and evolutionary nature of the evangelical counsels. This brings us to the conclusion of our hermeneutical cycle: integration. In light of attending to our social location, and interpreting the vows through a hermeneutic of catholicity, what's the take-away? How do I integrate my new/ renewed understanding of these formative elements within my lived experience of religious life? But that question is itself a new starting point. As we discussed earlier in this chapter, the hermeneutical cycle is just that: cyclic. We return to our social location and the cycle of interpretation begins anew because each time we endeavor to reflect and interpret we do so from a new vantage point.

By drawing from the nexus of theology and emerging science, we can fashion a hermeneutic of catholicity through which to view poverty, chastity, and obedience. The trifocals of interculturality, union, and evolution allow us to focus on what is the essential element of

---

42. Scott, 87.

our lives as consecrated religious. Through this view of the vows, we can uphold diversity while also discerning between essence and cultural assimilation. We can grow in personal, communal, and ministerial wholeness and holiness. And we become both a witness to and a confirmation of the emergent reign of God.

# Chapter Nine

## *"For All the Earth"* *(1 Cor 10:26)*

## Mission and the Reign of God

### Introduction

A few years ago, the fad was to wear silicone wristbands stamped with a particular issue: pink ones for breast cancer awareness; red for AIDS awareness; yellow ones for LiveStrong. A popular one among teen-agers read: WWJD—What would Jesus do? The purpose of the accessory wasn't so much to advertise an awareness of the Gospel as it was to remind the wearer that when faced with a difficult situation she or he should ask that question—What would Jesus do?—before responding. As we turn from the vows as shaping and distinguishing our religious lives toward what we do as women religious, the question is a good one: What would Jesus do? Whether you hold a high Christology or a lower one, as vowed religious women we are obliged to ask this question. But in light of our growing understanding of cosmology and evolution, another question demands an answer: *Why* would Jesus do what he did? How do we understand Jesus' motivation for mission in an unfinished and emerging universe? Once we ponder that question, we are left with yet another: "What is ours to do today?"

### *Why Would Jesus Do What He Did?*

The first gospel written by the evangelist known as Mark makes quite clear the when, where, what, and why of Jesus' ministry.

> In those days Jesus came from Nazareth of Galilee and was baptized by John in the Jordan. And just as he was coming up out of the water, he saw the heavens torn apart and the Spirit descending like a dove on him. And a voice came from heaven, "You are my Son, the Beloved; with you I am well pleased." (Mark 1:9-11)

> Now after John was arrested, Jesus came to Galilee, proclaiming the good news of God, and saying, "The time is fulfilled, and the kingdom of God has come near; repent, and believe in the good news." (Mark 1:14-15)

At his baptism, Jesus has a profound spiritual experience in which he comes to recognize that he is God's beloved son. After John's arrest, something signals to Jesus that now he must act on his sonship, taking up the work of his father, "proclaiming the good news of God." The Greek reads *to euaggelion tou theou*, the gospel of God. As Mark presents it, Jesus does not proclaim the gospel of Jesus but the gospel of God. The apostle Paul had made this explicit in his letter to the Romans: "Paul, a servant of Jesus Christ, called to be an apostle, set apart for the gospel of God" (Rom 1:1).

What is this gospel, the Good News, of God? Drawing from the Hebrew Scriptures—the Scriptures Jesus knew—the Good News is that God is faithful to God's promises. But what are those promises? The first occurs in Genesis 9:8-17:

> Then God said to Noah and to his sons with him, "As for me, I am establishing my covenant with you and your descendants after you, and with every living creature that is with you, the birds, the domestic animals, and every animal of the earth with you, as many as came out of the ark. I establish my covenant with you, that never again shall all flesh be cut off by the waters of a flood, and never again shall there be a flood to destroy the earth." God said, "This is the sign of the covenant that I make between me and you and every living creature that is with you, for all future generations: I have set my bow in the clouds, and it shall be a sign of the covenant between me and the earth. When I bring clouds over the earth and the bow is seen in the clouds, I will remember my covenant that is between me and you and every living creature of all flesh; and the waters shall never again become a flood to destroy all flesh. When the bow is in the clouds, I will see it and remember the everlasting

covenant between God and every living creature of all flesh that is on the earth." God said to Noah, "This is the sign of the covenant that I have established between me and all flesh that is on the earth."

God makes a covenant with the created world. Nine times the phrases, "every living creature" (vv. 10, 12, 15, 16) and "all flesh" (v. 11, 15 [twice], 16, 17) are repeated. With the first introduction in verse 10, God makes clear what is included in "every living creature": "the birds, the domestic animals, and every animal of the earth with you." The covenant also extends to "the earth" (v. 13). "This is kind of amazing. God makes an everlasting covenant with every living creature of all kinds of flesh, whether furred, feathered, or finned, establishing a covenant 'between me and all flesh that is on the earth.' "[1] The very first unilateral commitment God makes is with all the creatures of Earth—not only the human ones—and with Earth itself, reaffirming what had been stated at the very dawn of God's creative acts: "God saw everything that [God] had made, and indeed, it was very good" (Gen 1:31). As Dianne Bergant, CSA, acknowledges, "This connectedness of all natural creation is found in other passages of the Old Testament, suggesting that the theme was not limited to one or two periods of Israelite history."[2]

Later, God will make a covenant with a specific family of Abraham and Sarah (Gen 12:1-3), with Moses and the people (Exod 19 and 24) and with King David and his heirs (2 Sam 7:8-17). The prophet Jeremiah will speak of a new covenant that God will write in our hearts:

> It will not be like the covenant that I made with their ancestors when I took them by the hand to bring them out of the land of Egypt—a covenant that they broke, though I was their husband, says the LORD. But this is the covenant that I will make with the house of Israel after those days, says the LORD: I will put my law within them, and I will write it on their hearts; and I will be their God, and they shall be my people. (Jer 31:32-33)

1. Elizabeth A. Johnson, *Creation and the Cross: The Mercy of God for a Planet in Peril* (Maryknoll, NY: Orbis Books, 2018), 165.
2. Dianne Bergant, *A New Heaven, A New Earth: The Bible and Catholicity* (Maryknoll, NY: Orbis Books, 2016), 10.

The Hebrew term, *hesed* captures the breadth and depth of God's commitment to relationship and stalwart dependability. It appears 249 times in the Old Testament, often translated as "steadfast love" as in this passage from Isaiah.

> This is like the days of Noah to me:
>     Just as I swore that the waters of Noah
>     would never again go over the earth,
> so I have sworn that I will not be angry with you
>     and will not rebuke you.
> For the mountains may depart
>     and the hills be removed,
> but my *steadfast love* shall not depart from you,
>     and my covenant of peace shall not be removed,
>     says the Lord, who has compassion on you.
>
> (Isa 54:9-10; italics added)

When we come to the New Testament, God's compassionate love is incarnated in Jesus, and God's faithfulness is everlasting. "What we learn about God from Jesus is not contrary to what had already been revealed about the loving-kindness and fidelity of God through the history and scriptures of Israel."[3] The apostle Paul states directly in 1 Corinthians 1:9: "God is faithful," *pistos ho theos*. This divine *hesed* and *pistis* when viewed through the lens of eschatology becomes the coming reign of God.

> Whereas originally the prophets had held out a vision of a renewed and restored land and people in this world, over time these ancient prophecies were seen as intimations of a far more radical change, when God would not only restore Israel, but would defeat all the manifestations of chaos and evil that plagued not just Israel but the whole world. These expectations were especially important in times of persecution, when faithful Jews needed assurances that their fidelity and even martyrdom were seen and cherished by God, who would reward them, not in this life but in the next.[4]

---

3. Johnson, *Creation and the Cross*, 182.

4. Barbara E. Bowe, *Biblical Foundations of Spirituality: Touching a Finger to the Flame* (Lanham, MD: Rowman & Littlefield, 2017), 132, 142.

The Gospel of Mark is clearly imbued with this sense of eschatology, and the Marcan Jesus is portrayed as the messianic Son of Man (Mark 2:10, 28; 8:31, 38; 9:12, 31; 10:33, 45; 13:26; 14:21, 41, 62; 15:30) who announces the in-breaking moment of the reign of God. The Greek is *kairos* and connotes a rightness of time, the critical moment to act. Everything Jesus does in the Gospel of Mark is designed to affirm his authority as the Son of Man (Mark 2:10) and to confirm the *kairos* of God's reign: the spirit-possessed are freed (Mark 1:23-27; 5:2-19; 9:17-27), the sick and infirmed are healed (1:30-31; 3:1-6; 5:25-34; 6:54-56; 7:29-30), the lepers cleansed (1:40-45), the paralyzed walk (2:3-12), tax collectors and sinners are welcomed (2:15), the sea is calmed and mastered (4:37-39; 6:48-51); the dead resuscitated (5:35-42), the hungry are fed (6:35-44 8:2-9), the deaf hear (7:32-35), and the blind see (8:22-26; 10:46-52). Jesus put his actions in context: "For the Son of Man came not to be served but to serve, and to give his life a ransom for many" (Mark 10:45). Little wonder, the centurion at the cross declares at Jesus' death: "Truly this man was God's son!" (Mark 15:39).

### Signifying a Larger Reality

The actions of Jesus were not an end in themselves. Rather, they served as signifiers, pointing to that which could not be seen or even fully understood, that which was now and not yet—the reign of God. In many respects, the sacraments of the church work similarly. As Thomas Aquinas stated:

> A sacrament is a sign that commemorates what precedes it—Christ's Passion; demonstrates what is accomplished in us through Christ's Passion—grace; and prefigures what that Passion pledges to us—future glory.[5]

The *Catechism of the Catholic Church* recognizes the connection between the life and ministry of Jesus and the seven sacraments.

> Jesus' words and actions during his hidden life and public ministry were already salvific, for they anticipated the power of his Paschal

5. Thomas Aquinas, *Summa Theologiae* III, 60.3.

mystery . . . The mysteries of Christ's life are the foundations of what he would henceforth dispense in the sacraments . . . Sacraments are . . . actions of the Holy Spirit at work in his Body, the Church. They are "the masterworks of God" in the new and everlasting covenant. (1115–1116)

The purpose of the sacraments is to build up the body of Christ and "because they are signs they also instruct" (1123). The seven sacraments have been variously organized, so that the sacraments of initiation include baptism, confirmation, Eucharist; the sacraments of healing are reconciliation and anointing of the sick; and the sacraments of service are marriage and holy orders. But the service denoted in the latter is described as "directed towards the salvation of others; if they contribute as well to personal salvation, it is through service to others that they do so. They confer a particular mission in the Church and serve to build up the People of God" (1534). Of interest to us is the lack of a sacrament of service available to everyone, regardless of whether they are married or ordained. If we look carefully, we see that it is within the sacrament of baptism that all of the faithful are "incorporated into the Church and made sharers in her mission" (1213). Like Jesus' activities of healing, feeding, freeing, and preaching, our ministerial efforts are not an end in themselves. Rather, they are signifiers of the mission to which we—by virtue of our baptism—are committed.

### An Evolutionary Vision of the Reign of God

Reading the gospels through an evolutionary lens, we find that creation itself was a source of inspiration for Jesus. Of the sayings of Jesus most often deemed authentic, Jesus' go-to metaphors are drawn from the natural world. Jesus speaks about seeds and soil (Mark 4:3-8), the birds of the air that don't work and yet are fed (Luke 12:24; Matt 6:26), a misfortunate ox in a well (Luke 14:4), the potential of mustard seeds (Mark 4:30-32; Luke 13:18-19; Matt 13:31-32), the couture of a field of lilies (Luke 12:27; Matt 6:28-30), the value of sparrows (Luke 12:6; Matt 10:29), hungry dogs at dinner time (Mark 7:27-28; Matt 15:26-27), consoling dogs (Luke 16:21), and sheep—lots and lots of sheep. There are sheep without shepherds (Mark 6:34; Matt 9:36), sheep among wolves (Matt 10:16,

John 10:12), the value of sheep (Matt 12:12), lost sheep (Matt 15:24; 18:12; Luke 15:4), the difference between sheep and goats (Matt 25:32), scattered sheep (Mark 14:27; Matt 26:31), sacrificial sheep (John 2:14), giving one's life for the sheep (John 10:15), obedient sheep (John 10:27), and feeding sheep (John 21:17).

While these multiple metaphors drawn from nature might have worked well in an agrarian society, Jesus himself was no farmer. Or fisherperson, for that matter. Jesus is described as a carpenter (Mark 6:3) from Nazareth (Mark 1:9), a small Jewish village not far from the city of Sepphoris. And yet, this Jesus "gave ear" to the wider created world around him. He paid attention and saw a direct connection between the work of nature and the providence of God.

> The kingdom of God is as if someone would scatter seed on the ground, and would sleep and rise night and day, and the seed would sprout and grow, he does not know how. The earth produces of itself, first the stalk, then the head, then the full grain in the head. But when the grain is ripe, at once he goes in with his sickle, because the harvest has come. (Mark 4:26-29)

As his parables attest, the reign of God that Jesus preached is both rooted in creation and yet still evolving. Jesus understood and acted on his unique role in stimulating the in-breaking of that reign (Mark 10:45). Jesus' death doesn't herald the completion of the reign. Rather, Jesus describes his departure as "preparing a place" for his disciples so that "where I am, there you may be also" (John 14:3). As Acts of the Apostles opens, the disciples desire to know if now—with his resurrection—Jesus will restore the kingdom? "It is not for you to know the times or periods" (Acts 1:7). The biblical canon ends awaiting a vision still unfulfilled of a new heaven and a new earth (Rev 21:1).

The now and not yet of the reign of God is similar to Teilhard de Chardin's understanding of the process toward Christogenesis and the Omega Point, that point at which humans individually and communally find their end and fulfillment.[6] "Teilhard described

6. Pierre Teilhard de Chardin, *The Phenomenon of Man* (New York: Harper & Row, 1961), 262.

evolution as Christogenesis, where God within and God ahead is the same God (Omega) who is coming to birth in the physical universe; incarnation and evolution are united."[7] As Teilhard de Chardin presented, the Gospel call means "returning to the world with new vision and a deeper conviction to take hold of Christ in the heart of matter and to further Christ in the universality of his incarnation."[8] Through a theological lens, "the object of evolution is that God should become manifest in the world and the world should attain its final unification in God."[9] Only then is the reign of God complete. In light of God's covenant in Genesis 9, this final unification will include all of creation. Thus, while addressed to human beings first by the incarnate one and later by his disciples, the Gospel is also Good News for the created world. How else could we understand Romans 8?

> For the creation waits with eager longing for the revealing of the children of God; for the creation was subjected to futility, not of its own will but by the will of the one who subjected it, in hope that the creation itself will be set free from its bondage to decay and will obtain the freedom of the glory of the children of God. We know that the whole creation has been groaning in labor pains until now. (Rom 8:19-22)

The thriving of creatures and creation is the realization of the Good News, since "every creature with its relationships is held in existence by the same vivifying Giver of life; and in the end all will be gathered into the new heavens and the new earth."[10] In her book, *Creation and the Cross*, Elizabeth Johnson, CSJ, describes God's relationship with creation as one of accompaniment.

> Bringing creation into the picture, it is not hard to see how such an accompaniment theology can also embrace the natural world. Today's science has made abundantly clear that deep relationality runs

---

7. Delio, *Making All Things New: Catholicity, Cosmology, Consciousness* (Maryknoll, NY: Orbis Books, 2015), 177.

8. Delio, 94.

9. Delio, 96.

10. Dawn M. Nothwehr, "For the Salvation of the Cosmos: The Church's Mission of Ecojustice," *International Bulletin of Mission Research* 43 (2019): 75.

through the whole cosmos. Thanks to the evolution of life, human beings are genetically related in kinship to all other species on our planet, and this whole living community is composed of chemical materials available from debris left by the death of a previous generation of stars. As John Muir wrote, "When we try to pick out anything by itself, we find it hitched to everything else in the Universe." So when an early Christian hymn sings that Christ is "the firstborn of all creation," and again, "the firstborn of the dead," (Col 1:15-18), we can see not only the human dead but the dead of all creation, every species, included.[11]

It is precisely because of these relationships and the interconnection among all of creation, that Johnson urges a theology of accompaniment in which we are converted from anthropocentrism to a planetary solidarity.[12]

The reign of God viewed through Teilhard de Chardin's evolutionary Christogenesis and Johnson's theology of accompaniment provokes a new understanding of mission and therefore ministry in an unfinished universe, an understanding that recognizes the cost of complexity, the need for a new ethic that supports our evolving sense of mission, and a clear statement of direction.

## The Cost of Complexity

Walking along a beach in north Florida, I came upon a smack of jellyfish in the process of being blithely tossed upon the sand. By the looks of the forerunners, it was not going to end well for the jellyfish. While they seem to have muscles and a nervous system, they don't have a brain. Or apparently the ability to go against the tide. The oldest discovered jellyfish fossil dates to 500 million years ago, but its predecessor may have existed 600 million years ago, and some scientists propose it was the first animal. The fifty or so gelatinous blobs slowly baking in the sun did not invoke any feelings of familiarity. I gave them a wide berth.

But not too far down the beach was a stranded starfish. I was immediately moved to rescue it. Is it because it has an echinoderm

11. Johnson, *Creation and the Cross*, 159.
12. Johnson, xiii.

instead of amorphous gelatin? Was it because the starfish and I are closer on the evolutionary ladder? Perhaps it was that a starfish had never stung me. Not so Mr. Jellyfish.

As I reflect on these two sea creatures and their demise, I am reminded of Darwin's recognition that pain and death are inevitable aspects of evolution.

> The story of life on earth is a marvelous tale of new forms emerging from old. The diversity of life that so beguiles us today is the outcome of a long struggle in which organic life keeps breaking through to life forms that are more complex and beautiful. But the cost is terrible. Over thousands of millennia new species arise, thrive, and go extinct. Billions and billions of sentient creatures with nervous systems suffer unto death. Yes, new life comes from death. But this does not lessen the hard truth that pain and death are woven into the very fabric of life's evolutionary history on earth.[13]

In her article, "In the Travail of the Cosmos: God and the Suffering in the Evolving Universe," Gloria Schaab, SSJ, reminds us that evolution creates "situations which are often termed 'natural evil' and which provoke difficult questions about God in an evolving and suffering universe."[14] This natural aspect of pain and death isn't so much a question of theodicy (how can God allow suffering in God's creation) as much as it is an invitation to take "the evolutionary function of affliction at face value and [seek] to reflect on its workings in view of the God of Love made know in revelation."[15]

Schaab discusses three perspectives on how to understand God's actions in light of this "natural evil."[16] The first, she attributes to Anglican priest and mathematical physicist John Polkinghorne, who proposes that God empties himself of divine attributes (kenosis) "in

---

13. Johnson, *Creation and the Cross*, 188.

14. Gloria L. Schaab, "In the Travail of the Cosmos: God and Suffering in the Evolving Universe," *Heythrop Journal* 58, no. 1 (January 2017): 92.

15. Elizabeth A. Johnson, *Ask the Beasts: Darwin and the God of Love* (London: Bloomsbury, 2014), 17.

16. While "natural evil" is a category in theology, it should not be interpreted as if nature itself is actively seeking to do evil, but that death and destruction can have natural causes.

order to allow creation and its creatures the true freedom to be and to act according to their God-given natures. This God does so with absolute freedom out of infinite love for finite creatures."[17]

The second perspective is derived from the work of another Anglican theologian and biochemist, Arthur Peacocke, who argues that in addition to thinking of God as "being" (who God is), we should also recognize that God is "becoming" (how God acts in the world).

> [The] processes of creation are immensely costly to God in a way dimly shadowed by and reflected in the ordinary experience of the costliness of creativity in multiple aspects of human creativity—whether it be in giving birth, in artistic creation, or in creating and maintain[ing] human social structures . . . Now, as we reflect on the processes of creation through biological evolution, we can begin to understand that this . . . involved God's costly, suffering involvement in them on behalf of their ultimate fruition.[18]

Finally, Schaab presents another image of God acting within the evolving and suffering cosmos, drawing from the work of Elizabeth Johnson and the Scriptures.

> If God is creating and nurturing the world within the divine being—transcendently, incarnately, and immanently—then God must be conceived as experiencing the world's suffering within Godself, rather than outside Godself. Pregnant with an evolving yet suffering cosmos, God can heal and transform suffering through the love and creativity that characterize the Trinity.[19]

To develop a trinitarian theology of divine suffering, Schaab explores the images of "she who is," *shekhinah*, and *sophia*, concluding that "each one pulses with a specific form of creative suffering with and for creation and its creatures."[20] The cosmos isn't suffering alone. It is literally enwombed by God.

---

17. Schaab, "In the Travail of the Cosmos," 97.

18. A. R. Peacocke, *Paths from Science Towards God: The End of All Our Exploring* (Oxford: Oneworld, 2002), 86–87.

19. Schaab, "In the Travail of the Cosmos," 102.

20. Schaab, 102.

And so back to my smack of dying jellyfish and lone rescued starfish. If the evolutionists are correct (pain and death are part of life) and if the theologians are correct (God is in the midst of that suffering), how are we, Earth thinking, to minister in this evolutionary process? Or as Francis of Assisi is remembered as asking, "What is mine to do?"

### Creating an Evolutionary Ethic

In the evolutionary process, pain, death, and mass extinction are troubling yet necessary companions of innovation, life, and complexity. Nonetheless, these "natural evils" leave a wake of suffering in their path. But not all pain, death, and extinction in creation is actually the result of evolution. Well, not directly. It would seem that human beings, the so-called pinnacle of the evolutionary process, are actively engaging in cosmocide, the wanton destruction of the created world.

Case in point:

- In last 500 years, 322 animals have gone extinct, which scientists attribute to human causes.

- By September 2019, 2.2 million acres of the Amazon basin were burned, nearly all of the 121,000 fires had human origins—farmers setting fires to clear the land.

- After years of climate change-induced drought, in the Fall of 2019 and early 2020, more than 16 million acres, the size of the state of West Virginia, went up in flames in Australia. Lightning strikes on brutally dry land caused most of fires, but at least 24 persons were arrested for having ignited some fires.

- An estimated billion animals lost their lives in the fires that ravaged New South Wales and Victoria.

- The year 2020 saw similar destruction in the United States where more than 4.6 million acres were destroyed by fires in California, Oregon, and Washington State. Meanwhile, the naming of hurricanes exhausted the 26-letter English alphabet. "Delta" became the fourth major storm to pummel Texas, Louisiana, and Alabama. Both the fires and the hurricanes resulted from climate change and human mismanagement.

Indeed, the researchers and scholars are correct in their assessment that we are living in a new geological epoch. For the past 12,000 years, we have been in the Holocene, the period that began after the last ice age. But now, say the scientists, we live in the Anthropocene, which describes the geological epoch in which human actions impact planetary systems. Sam Mickey explains that, "The Anthropocene is named after humans because it is a time when humans have massive, Earth-changing impacts, altering the chemistry of the atmosphere (climate change), changing DNA (genetic modification), and depositing non-biodegradable plastic, Styrofoam, and radioactive materials around the planet."[21]

As I continue this research on the implications of science and theology, I am shaken out of my academic silo and shamed by my lethargic activism. New theological thinking drawn from new scientific discoveries should lead to new modes of behavior. In other words, theology cannot be divorced from ethics. What we think about God should have implications for how we act as children of God. And evolutionary biologist Julian Huxley argued it is our destiny to act on behalf of the cosmos:

> [Humankind] is that part of reality in which and through which the cosmic process has become conscious and has begun to comprehend itself. [Our] supreme task is to increase that conscious comprehension and to apply it as fully as possible to guide the course of events.[22]

In light of this evolutionary consciousness (our advancing awareness of our place in the cosmos and interrelationship with all creation), we need to move beyond simply "thinking globally and acting locally." Rather, as Mickey proposes, we should engage in "Whole Earth thinking," which sounds a lot like working toward the reign of God.

> [Whole Earth thinking] calls for dangerous dreams of emancipation, dreams of freedom from the destructive refrains of domination and oppression. It calls for a vision of a more peaceful, just, and

---

21. Sam Mickey, *Whole Earth Thinking and Planetary Coexistence* (New York: Routledge, 2016), 6.

22. Julian Huxley, *Religion without Revelation* (London: Max Parrish, 1959), 236.

sustainable Earth community, a vision of participatory ecological democracy.[23]

Perhaps the first step to Whole Earth thinking is to pay attention. The fires in the Amazon, the drought in Australia, the floods in the United States, the typhoons in the Philippines, the volcanic eruptions in New Zealand aren't happening to those people and that land over there. We are "those people" and the interconnectivity of all creation means we share in the suffering. St. Paul's words have never been more true: "We know that the whole creation has been groaning in labor pains until now" (Rom 8:22).

What does an ethic of the New Cosmology and evolutionary consciousness look like? Beyond paying attention, how do we engage in Whole Earth thinking? While using different vocabulary, this is precisely the challenge presented by Pope Francis in his encyclical *Laudato Si'*:

> It is our humble conviction that the divine and the human meet in the slightest detail in the seamless garment of God's creation, in the last speck of dust of our planet. . . . In this universe, shaped by open and intercommunicating systems, we can discern countless forms of relationship and participation. This leads us to think of the whole as open to God's transcendence, within which it develops. Faith allows us to interpret the meaning and the mysterious beauty of what is unfolding. We are free to apply our intelligence towards things evolving positively, or towards adding new ills, new causes of suffering and real setbacks. This is what makes for the excitement and drama of human history, in which freedom, growth, salvation and love can blossom, or lead towards decadence and mutual destruction. The work of the Church seeks not only to remind everyone of the duty to care for nature, but at the same time "she must above all protect [hu]mankind from self-destruction."[24]

The encyclical was well-received in ecumenical, interreligious, and scientific communities, though not by all. When the American Presi-

---

23. Mickey, *Whole Earth Thinking*, 147.
24. Pope Francis, On Care for our Common Home (*Laudato Si'*), 9, 79.

dent and climate change denier, Donald Trump, met with the Pope in 2017, the pontiff gifted the president with his own signed copy. The 192-page work called for a "broad cultural revolution." James Martin, SJ, enumerated ten significant aspects of the document:

1. *The spiritual perspective is now part of the discussion on the environment.* "The encyclical firmly grounds the discussion in a spiritual perspective and invites others to listen to a religious point of view, particularly its understanding of creation as a holy and precious gift from God to be reverenced by all men and women."

2. *The poor are disproportionately affected by climate change.* "The pope states that focus on the poor is one the central themes of the encyclical, and he provides many baneful examples of the effects of climate change, whose 'worse impacts' are felt by those living in the developing countries."

3. *Less is more.* "*Laudato Si'* also diagnoses a society of 'extreme consumerism' in which people are unable to resist what the market places before them, the earth is despoiled and billions are left impoverished (No. 203)."

4. *Catholic social teaching now includes teaching on the environment.* "Against those who argue that a papal encyclical on the environment has no real authority, Pope Francis explicitly states that *Laudato Si'* 'is now added to the body of the Church's social teaching.' (No. 15)."

5. *Discussions about ecology can be grounded in the Bible and church tradition.* "In a masterful overview, Pope Francis traces the theme of love for creation through both the Old and New Testaments. He reminds us, for example, that God, in Jesus Christ, became not only human, but part of the natural world."

6. *Everything is connected—including the economy.* "Pope Francis links a 'magical conception of the market,' which privileges profit over the impact on the poor, with the abuse of the environment (No. 190)."

7. *Scientific research on the environment is to be praised and used.* "As the other great Catholic social encyclicals analyzed such questions as capitalism, unions and fair wages, *Laudato Si'* draws upon both church teaching and contemporary findings from other fields—particularly science, in this case—to help modern-day people reflect on these questions."

8. *Widespread indifference and selfishness worsen environmental problems.* "In the world of *Laudato Si'* there is no room for selfishness or indifference. One cannot care for the rest of nature 'if our hearts lack tenderness, compassion and concern for our fellow human beings' (No. 91)."

9. *Global dialogue and solidarity are needed.* "The pope calls into dialogue and debate 'all people' about our 'common home' (No. 62, 155). A global dialogue is also needed because there are 'no uniform recipes.' "

10. *A change of heart is required.* "We can awaken our hearts and move towards an 'ecological conversion' in which we see the intimate connection between God and all beings, and more readily listen to the 'cry of the earth and the cry of the poor' (No. 49)."[25]

As Amy Hereford, CSJ, notes in *Beyond the Crossroads: Religious Life in the 21st Century*, *Laudato Si'* frequently uses "Our Common Home" as both a metaphor and a reality. The term "points to the deep unity of all creation, and the important connection that we all share as part of the natural community."[26] Drawing on the work of scientists and environmentalists, Pope Francis writes:

> We need only take a frank look at the facts to see that our common home is falling into serious disrepair. Hope would have us recognize that there is always a way out, that we can always redirect our steps, that we can always do something to solve our problems. Still, we

25. James Martin, SJ, "Top Ten Takeaways from 'Laudato Si,' " *America* (June 18, 2015), https://www.americamagazine.org/faith/2015/06/18/top-ten-takeaways-laudato-si.

26. Amy Hereford, CSJ, *Beyond the Crossroads: Religious Life in the 21st Century* (Maryknoll, NY: Orbis Books, 2019), 2.

can see signs that things are now reaching a breaking point, due to the rapid pace of change and degradation; these are evident in large-scale natural disasters as well as social and even financial crises, for the world's problems cannot be analyzed or explained in isolation. There are regions now at high risk and, aside from all doomsday predictions, the present world system is certainly unsustainable from a number of points of view, for we have stopped thinking about the goals of human activity. "If we scan the regions of our planet, we immediately see that humanity has disappointed God's expectations" [Citing Pope John Paul II, "General Audience," January 17, 2001].[27]

Whether we call it, "Whole Earth thinking" or "care for our common home," the natural evil that accompanies evolution and creation is being accelerated and amplified by rampaging social and moral evil. It is not only Pope Francis who urges action. Earth itself cries out.

> These situations have caused sister earth, along with all the abandoned of our world, to cry out, pleading that we take another course. Never have we so hurt and mistreated our common home as we have in the last two hundred years. Yet we are called to be instruments of God our Father, so that our planet might be what he desired when he created it and correspond with his plan for peace, beauty and fullness.[28]

In the nineteenth and twentieth centuries, the emergence of apostolic women's religious congregations was a direct response to the crises of the industrial revolution, immigration, illnesses, and wars, a response filtered through a particular theology of religious life. Some two hundred years later, our theological understandings have changed, the needs diversified, but the manner of meeting those needs still calls for commitment, flexibility, and creativity. As Pope John Paul II encouraged, "You have not only a glorious history to remember and to recount, but also *a great history still to be accomplished! Look to the future, where the Spirit is sending you in order to do even greater things.*"[29] We are no longer building institutions;

---

27. *Laudato Si'*, 61.
28. *Laudato Si'*, 53.
29. Pope John Paul II, *Vita Consecrata*, 110.

we are cleaning up our common home. Not to save our souls, but to save our planet.

## Mission for an Unfinished Universe

Religious life ought to promote growth in the Church by way of attraction. The Church must be attractive. Wake up the world! Be witnesses of a different way of doing things, of acting, of living! It is possible to live differently in this world.[30]

Within two years of his meeting at the Union of Superiors General (USG), Pope Francis would initiate the Year of Consecrated Life (November 30, 2014 – February 2, 2016) and promulgate his encyclical on the environment (May 24, 2015). The timing is not coincidental.

The encyclical constitutes an invitation for vowed religious to respectfully and courageously enter into a dialogue with other persons of good will. The fruits of scientific research and contributions from varied faith traditions can move our pluralistic society toward a consensus on the urgent need for action. The common good will be enhanced as religious give voice to the poor and marginalized. Finally, by their actions, they will offer a prophetic witness on the value of interpersonal communion and an ecologically sensitive relationship with all creation.[31]

With *Laudato Si'*, the mission of God, the mission of the church, and the mission of religious are now consciously tied to the care of our common home. Whereas under Pope Benedict XVI mission had focused on conversion and transmission of the faith, under Pope Francis the purpose, motivation, and goal of mission has been revised.[32]

---

30. Pope Francis, Papal meeting with USG, November 29, 2013.

31. Timothy Scott, CSB, "*Laudato Si'* and Vowed Religious," *Canadian Religious Conference Bulletin* (Fall 2015): 4.

32. William P. Gregory, "Pope Francis' Effort to Revitalize Catholic Mission," *International Bulletin of Mission Research* 43 (2019): 7–19.

Mission clarification requires knowing the God of all creation. Mission motivation originates in humans knowing their true identity as ones loved by God *within and through* creation. Mission correction consists in heeding revelation from the "Book of Creation."[33]

As Dawn Nothwehr, OSF, writes, "The point is that Gospel salvation includes human well-being and the well-being of all of creation."[34] What does a mission of accompaniment look like in an evolutionary, unfinished universe? Whom or what do we accompany? Our growing awareness of our place within the larger created world has broadened our concerns beyond human society. We are compelled to do "Whole Earth thinking" and to see how the devastation of Earth has direct effect on those who are marginalized and impoverished. In *Laudato Si'*, Pope Francis makes the point that those who are poor most often suffer from the degradation of our common home:

> In the present condition of global society, where injustices abound and growing numbers of people are deprived of basic human rights and considered expendable, the principle of the common good immediately becomes, logically and inevitably, a summons to solidarity and a preferential option for the poorest of our brothers and sisters. This option entails recognizing the implications of the universal destination of the world's goods, but, as I mentioned in the Apostolic Exhortation *Evangelii Gaudium*, it demands before all else an appreciation of the immense dignity of the poor in the light of our deepest convictions as believers. We need only look around us to see that, today, this option is in fact an ethical imperative essential for effectively attaining the common good. (158)

As apostolic congregations, our ministries are often on behalf of those in need. Reflecting on the challenges of *Laudato Si'*, Timothy Scott, CSB, recognized that

> religious often live and serve on the periphery; in places where the environment is often degraded; in urban slums and places lacking safe drinking water or public spaces. The international character of

---

33. Nothwehr, "For the Salvation of the Cosmos," 68.
34. Nothwehr, 70.

many of our communities means that we have an awareness of the particular challenges of life in the developing world, where economic exploitation is often rampant. In the first instance, we need to bring that awareness of life at the margins to the forefront within our own communities and then to the broader society.[35]

The Good News of God is that Earth and all of its creatures have an advocate. It is us.

### Charism and Ministry for our Common Home

As a scene from the documentary *Band of Sisters*[36] opens, it's still dark out. Very dark. Mercy Sisters JoAnn Persch and Pat Murphy leave their suburban home for Broadview, Illinois, the setting of the US Immigration Deportation Center. What began as a spontaneous act of compassion in 2007 grew into the Interfaith Committee for Detained Immigrants. Rain or shine, the sisters and other volunteers stand outside and pray for those being deported. As Sr. JoAnn recalls:

> Since that day in 2007 we have a small staff, but over 200 volunteers have responded to the call of our immigrant sisters and brothers through our programs. These are men and women of 16 different faiths. We operate out of the principles that every man, woman and child is a human being, created in the image and likeness of God, who deserves to be treated with dignity and respect and who has a right to quality of life and safety for themselves and their families.[37]

The charism of the mercy imbues these two sisters with a deep sense of compassion born out in ministry to those who are in need. From the house on Baggot Street and the care and education of young women and girls to the myriad manifestations of mercy today, the congregational charism is unabated.

---

35. Scott, "*Laudato Si'* and Vowed Religious."

36. *Band of Sisters*, directed by Mary Fishman (Chicago: 2012), https://www.imdb.com/title/tt2405212.

37. JoAnn Persch, RSM, "Humans, Not Criminals: Seeking Alternatives to Family Detention," *Sisters of Mercy blog* (September 15, 2015).

The word "charism" comes from the Greek *charis*, which is often translated as "grace" or "favor." We learn from St. Paul that at baptism we receive the gifts of the Holy Spirit. They are a down payment on the fullness of the reign of God. Paul also calls these "fruits" and they include love, joy, peace, patience, kindness, generosity, faithfulness (Gal 5:22). Though these gifts differ, they are all from the same spirit (1 Cor 12:14). By virtue of our baptism, we, too, have a particular grace or charism given to us by the Spirit. Now lest we go the way of the Corinthians who argued over who had the "best" charismatic gifts, Paul reminds us that spiritual gifts are for the good of the whole (1 Cor 12:1-11; 14:14-25).

At profession, our particular gifts are joined with the corporate charism of our congregations, a charism that is not exclusive to our community but one that we recognize is deeply a part of our identity. It is to this charism that we commit ourselves, not to specific ministerial manifestations of that charism. As Pope Francis advised, we need "to strengthen . . . the charism of the Congregation, without mistaking it for the apostolic work which is carried out. The first remains, the second will pass. The charism . . . is creative, always looking for new paths."[38] Despite diminishment from age and a reduction in numbers, the closing of institutional ministries, and the societal upheaval that questions whether religion is even necessary, apostolic religious life continues. Reflecting on the Year of Consecrated Life, the Bishop Emeritus of Limerick, Donal Murray, noted:

> That underlying charism continues even when particular ministries can no longer be carried on as strongly as they were or when they are no longer necessary, or no longer possible. When that happens we need to look again to our beginnings to understand what our charism may be asking of us today.[39]

As the story of JoAnn Persch, RSM, and Pat Murphy, RSM, abundantly shows, a congregation's charism, as a gift of the Holy Spirit, is flexible, responsive, and energizing.

---

38. Pope Francis, Meeting with the USG, November 29, 2013.

39. Donal Murray, "Glorious and Unfinished—the Year of Consecrated Life," *The Furrow* 66 (2015): 316.

> Our question is not whether we can apply the legacy of our past
> to the context of today, but how the Holy Spirit, who inspired the
> founders and foundresses, the same Spirit who is with us and in us,
> is inspiring us to live that legacy.[40]

As Murray suggests, our challenge is to live our legacy in the present
with passion.

> It means believing that the same Christ, the same Spirit, the same
> vocation, that inspired our predecessors is calling us now to be awake
> and watchful. The gifts and charisms that marked the beginnings of
> your institutes of consecrated life are alive today by the same power
> of the same Spirit who awakened them in the first place.[41]

Indeed, the Spirit is active and, just as Paul encouraged the Corinthians that their individual gifts were for the good of the whole,
so, too, the charisms of individual congregations must be brought
together for the good of our common home.

### Crossing Congregational Boundaries

Even imbued with our charisms, how could we women religious
hope to contribute to the realization of the reign of God when the
challenges are so daunting, the costs too high, and our numbers so
small? Jesus seems to have anticipated our question with an insightful parable: "The kingdom of heaven is like yeast that a woman
took and mixed in with three measures of flour until all of it was
leavened" (Matt 13:33; Luke 13:20-21). We are no longer the foot
soldiers of the church, an army of sisters flooding the parochial
classrooms. Nor do we need to be. Rather, as Jesus argued, we are
to be leaven. And as the leaven is mixed with flour, we are to join
our efforts with others. Speaking about the Year of Consecrated
Life, Pope Francis stated:

> I also hope for a growth in communion between the members of
> different Institutes. Might this Year be an occasion for us to step out
> more courageously from the confines of our respective Institutes and

---

40. Murray, 312.
41. Murray, 314.

to work together, at the local and global levels, on projects involving formation, evangelization, and social action? This would make for a more effective prophetic witness. Communion and the encounter between different charisms and vocations can open up a path of hope. No one contributes to the future in isolation, by his or her efforts alone, but by seeing himself or herself as part of a true communion which is constantly open to encounter, dialogue, attentive listening and mutual assistance. Such a communion inoculates us from the disease of self-absorption.[42]

Collaboration among religious institutions is not new. The Sister Formation Conference, the forerunner of the Religious Formation Conference, was founded in 1954 to assure that sisters were appropriately prepared for their ministries. Following Vatican II, a remarkable collaboration among religious communities of men led to the creation of Catholic Theological Union in Chicago and Washington Theological Union in DC, both schools of theology and ministry that served multiple congregations. In the 1980s, collaborative novitiates and novitiate programs brought newer members together across the divide of congregational boundaries. And in the 1990s, a grassroots organization of sisters under the age of fifty formed Giving Voice. As their purpose statement describes:

> We seek to live our vocations rooted in our congregational charisms and grounded in God's hope for the future of religious life. We seek to connect with one another to strengthen our commitment, deepen our fidelity to religious life, foster connections that sustain our vocations, and create ways to live religious life in the present and into the future.[43]

Desirous of a book on religious life that spoke to their own Post-Vatican experience, members of Giving Voice authored, *In Our Own Words: Religious Life in a Changing World*,[44] itself a product

---

42. Pope Francis, "Apostolic Letter to All Consecrated People on the Occasion of the Year of Consecrated Life," II.3.

43. For more information see https://giving-voice.org/mission-vision.

44. Juliet Mousseau and Sarah Kohles, eds., *In Our Own Words: Religious Life in a Changing World* (Collegeville, MN: Liturgical Press, 2018).

of collaboration, common prayer, and collegial conversations. As Mary Therese Perez, OP, writes:

> We know that religious life today thrives in a setting of collaboration. Crossing the boundaries of orders and congregations, contemporary women religious live a global sisterhood, "created by partnerships— not only in what we do, in our works, but also in our relationships— how we think, plan, organize, learn, believe, and hope."[45]

Joining efforts and combining resources has led to justice initiatives to address endemic and global issues such as human trafficking, immigration, and environmental degradation. And most of these efforts began with grassroots efforts to respond to the emerging needs.

In 2009, an international network of religious congregations in seventy countries formed Talitha Kum to facilitate collaboration and activities against trafficking persons. Similarly, Sister Margaret Nacke, CSJ, was moved by "the millions whose lives have been relegated to commodity status, to slavery, and live in a world darkened by the selfishness and greed of those whose own lives are without light."[46] In 2013, she advocated for and helped start US Catholic Sisters Against Human Trafficking (USCSAHT), a collaborative, faith-based national network that offers education, supports access to survivor services, and engages in advocacy to eradicate modern-day slavery.[47] She describes these often unseen victims in our society:

> They are children who will never see the inside of a classroom because they work like "little adults" day in and day out, harvesting the cocoa for chocolate they will never taste. They are young men who cannot dream of a better life because every moment is governed by the number of fish they catch in waters far away from their homelands. They are older men who work in the depths of the earth, mining coal that will warm the homes they will never visit.

---

45. Mary Therese Perez, OP, "Local and Global: Charism of Religious Life Today," in *In Our Own Words*, ed. Mousseau and Kohles, 68. Perez cites Rosemary Nassif, "Supporting the Emergence of Global Sisterhood" (presentation, Plenary Assembly of International Union of Superiors General, Rome, Italy, May 9–13, 2016).

46. *Peace and Earth Blog*, "A Call to Be Light-Bearers," blog entry by Sister Margaret Nacke, CSJ, December 16, 2016, http://saccvi.blogspot.com/2016/12/a-call-to-be-light -bearers.html.

47. For more information see https://sistersagainsttrafficking.org.

These slaves are women who will never stand in their own kitchens and prepare meals for their children because they are in servitude in other kitchens to masters or mistresses whose consciences do not allow an opening for the light of human respect.[48]

Similarly, many of the thousands seeking asylum in the United States are themselves searching for a life raft of human respect. When Pope Francis participated in a virtual papal audience in 2015, he was introduced to Missionary of Jesus Sister Norma Pimentel, who operates a welcome center at Sacred Heart Church in McAllen, Texas, and serves as the Executive Director of Catholic Charities of the Rio Grande Valley.

After listening to the stories of the mothers and children in the center, Pope Francis asked to speak with Sister Norma. "I want to thank you," Francis said. "And through you to thank all the sisters of religious orders in the US for the work that you have done and that you do in the United States. It's great. I congratulate you. Be courageous. Move forward." And then to everyone's surprise and Sister Norma's delight, he added, "I'll tell you one other thing. Is it inappropriate for the Pope to say this? I love you all very much."[49]

That one moment of papal affirmation came during an overwhelming wave of unaccompanied minors from Central America, which began in 2014. Sister Norma and others who work along the border sent out urgent requests for volunteers, a call heard and amplified by Leadership Conference of Women Religious (LCWR). Since it began sending out requests for funds and volunteers to serve at respite centers on the US/Mexico border, more than one thousand religious have responded. "Sisters have provided legal, medical and educational support as well as responded to immediate needs," said Sr. Ann Scholz, a School Sister of Notre Dame and the associate director for mission for LCWR.[50]

48. Nacke, "A Call to Be Light-Bearers."

49. Teri Whitcraft, "Pope Francis to Texas Nun Norma Pimentel: 'I Love You All Very Much,'" ABC News (September 4, 2015), https://abcnews.go.com/US/pope-francis -texas-nun-norma-pimentel-love/story?id=33517481.

50. Tracy L. Barnett, "In a Village of Tents, Refugees Make a Life as They Wait on US Asylum," Global Sisters Report (March 2, 2020), https://www.globalsistersreport .org/news/social-justice/news/village-tents-refugees-make-life-they-wait-us-asylum.

Launched on the occasion of the Jubilee of the International Union of Superiors General (UISG; 1965–2015), the Migrant Project in Sicily established three intercongregational, international, and intercultural community houses, in which the sisters become "a bridge between the migrants who come ashore in Sicily and the people of the area, in order to build a true integration." The project's coordinator Sr. Elisabetta Flick comments, "We go on tip-toe, respecting the richness of listening to the needs in order to then build, together with our local partners, an ad-hoc project that respects the rights and dignity of those arriving in our country. We wish to be a credible witness that it is possible for different cultures, nationalities and languages to live together, if we are united by a common mission and moved by the one Spirit who acts and is present in each of us and in the world."[51]

While the collaborative work of sisters on behalf of those who are impoverished and marginalized meets immediate and pressing needs, other joint ventures take the long view. On June 18, 2020, the fifth anniversary of *Laudato Si'*, a new initiative to promote sustainable development was announced—not by the movers and shakers of some Fortune 500 company. Rather, sixteen US congregations of Dominican sisters joined with the firm of Morgan Stanley to establish a new investment funds initiative aimed at financing solutions to address climate change and assist communities worldwide most at risk. "The sisters provided initial seeding of $46.6 million in 2018 for the funds, which with additional capital investments have grown to $130 million. The money will be directed toward global projects pursuing solutions to climate change as well as achieving the United Nations Sustainable Development Goals."[52]

The climate funds initiative is a "fundamental response" to Pope Francis' call in *Laudato Si'*. As Adrian Dominican Sister Elise Garcia, OP, noted, Pope Francis' "sense of wanting to have an integrated approach to combating poverty, restoring dignity to the underprivi-

---

51. Barnett.

52. Brian Roewe, "Dominican Sisters Commit $46 Million to Seed New Climate Solutions Funds," *National Catholic Reporter* (June 18, 2020), https://www.ncronline.org/news/earthbeat/dominican-sisters-commit-46-million-seed-new-climate-solutions-funds.

leged, and at the same time protecting nature . . . is precisely what the Climate Solutions Fund aims to address." [53]

Pope John Paul II stated, we have "a great history still to be accomplished."[54] Initiatives like US Catholic Sisters Against Human Trafficking and Talitha Kum, collaborative efforts on behalf of migrants and immigrants, and the Climate Solutions Fund demonstrate that through our collaborative ministerial efforts, we creatively contribute to the reign of God and thus live into that "great history" together.

## Conclusion

As Dominican Sisters of Sinsinawa, we are fond of quoting our founder, Venerable Fr. Samuel Mazzuchelli, OP, who urged, "Let us set out for any place where the work is great and difficult, but where also with the help of the one who sends us, we shall open the way for the Gospel!" But in the twenty-first century, as an apostolic congregation, we, like many of you, aren't always sure to which of the numerous "places" we should go.

Some five decades ago, a novice had a pretty good idea of what ministry she would do upon her profession of vows. She had joined either a teaching order or a nursing order, so she would teach or nurse. Enter Vatican II, the civil rights movements, and widespread cultural changes. A congregation's founding ministry had set its identity and was often confused with its charism. As fewer members continued serving in sponsored institutions, many sisters wondered, "Who are we if we aren't in teaching anymore?" Reflecting on her post Vatican II vocation, Benedictine Sister Joan Chittister offered a helpful reminder: "The new vision says that religious are not called to be a labor force but a leaven, a caring, calling presence that moves quickly into new needs."[55] The congregation's mission is larger than its ministerial expression of that mission.

53. Roewe.

54. Pope John Paul II, *Vita Consecrata*, 110.

55. Joan D. Chittister, "No Time for Tying Cats," in *Midwives of the Future: American Sisters Tell Their Story*, ed. Ann Patrick Ward (Kansas City, MO: Leaven, 1985), 19.

And that mission—as proclaimed by Jesus of Nazareth and continued by the church—is to work toward the realization of the reign of God. Precisely because we live in an unfinished universe, the reign of God remains the horizon event for which we yearn. The slow work of evolution confirms that we are moving toward the Omega Point, the unification of all of creation with the Creator. An emergent vision of mission and ministry for an unfinished universe follows its own timeline. But the reality of death and suffering as an effect of evolution and as a result of human sin reminds us that there is work to be done. Today.

Our understanding of cosmology, evolution, and theology should affect why, how, and what we do in ministry, which Maldari defines as "human work energized by the Holy Spirit."[56] No longer is the "why" limited to only human concerns. Pope Francis' call to preserve our "common home" challenges us to see the dawning of the reign of God with new eyes. *Laudato Si'* becomes a charter that redirects our efforts, so that mission moves from an anthropocentric concern for evangelization and conversion to a cosmic accompaniment, care, and advocacy for all of creation. The "how" of our ministry is directly related to the particular charism gifted to our congregation by the Holy Spirit, a charism most readily seen in our founders and foundresses, but no less evident in our members today—if we look. We should ask "How can our charism be put to the service of all of creation?" And with that answer we should measure our ministerial activities. Finally, "what are we to do" might be better phrased as "what we ought not to do." No longer can individual congregations afford to act alone. Perhaps the demographics and institutional diminishment are simply reminders that ministry in an emerging universe must be collaborative. The integrity of all of creation surely reminds us that we are most effective when we are most connected. Thus, when we consider where the mission of God, our congregational charisms, and the needs of our common home intersect, we find our answer to the question, "Why, how and what is ours to do?" in an emerging universe.

---

56. Donald C. Maldari, SJ, *Christian Ministry in the Divine Milieu: Catholicity, Evolution, and the Reign of God* (Maryknoll, NY: Orbis, 2019), 46.

# Conclusion

# *Community as the Holy Preaching*

> The future belongs to those who give the next generation reason to hope.
>
> —Pierre Teilhard de Chardin, SJ

"Where's Jesus?" It all started with that question. And a deep concern that the enthusiasm for the New Cosmology and its related concepts would cause a rift between those sisters who held a traditional belief and those who advocated for the emerging theology. As one survey respondent wrote:

> What concerns me is when [Jesus Christ and the New Cosmology] are seen as mutually exclusive. One can be very excited about the new universe story and passionate about Jesus. I hope as our awareness grows, we hold on to the core of our faith and bring that into conversation with all our new learning.

Anecdotally, I heard these concerns, and as I began this research, I shared them. I am a biblical scholar, after all. I was deeply worried that the New Cosmology would leave the Bible behind. However, what I discovered is that the problem is not necessarily that new theological understandings can unseat our traditional views but that an enthusiastic but cursory knowledge of science can lead to uncritical theological thinking. The first section of this book, "Chapter of Faults," began by discussing the results of a survey that

234 The Heavens Are Telling the Glory of God

invited cohorts of women religious to share their views on the New Cosmology and religious life. Of those who identified their age, the participants could be divided among three age cohorts: 31 percent of sisters were 25–44 years of age; 31 percent of sisters were 45–64 years of age; and 38 percent of sisters were 65 years of age and older. Each age cohort had various levels of familiarity with the New Cosmology and its related concepts. The differences in familiarity may reflect why those age groups with less familiarity were often most critical of the theology and concerned about its implications for their faith. Chapters 2 and 3 then explored the roots of difference among the age cohorts by investigating generational characteristics and formative experiences of the church. Despite our common vows and our love of our congregational mission and charism, we are not the same. And that diversity helps to explain partially why sisters of different age cohorts view emerging theology differently.

By acknowledging our diversity, we had done the preliminary work that prepared us to enter into a chapter of affairs. In chapters 4–6, the findings from the scientific trinity of cosmology, quantum mechanics, and evolution offered a new lens through which to view the Divine Trinity of Creator, Incarnate One, and Holy Spirit. Far from "throwing the baby Jesus out with the cosmological bathwater,"[1] emerging science and traditional theology proved to be strange but companionable bedfellows. Science presents the facts (as they are currently known) and theology reflects on the deeper religious meaning of those facts. To the question "Where is Jesus?," reflection on cosmology confirmed the Franciscan tenet that "Christ is the redeeming and fulfilling center of the universe. Christ does not save us *from* creation; rather, Christ is the reason *for* creation."[2] To the question of "Where is Jesus?" the answer is: everywhere.

As the survey of women religious showed, despite the unsettlement, misunderstandings, and in some cases downright dislike of this theological perspective, many recognized the potential that the New Cosmology could offer religious life.

---

1. Rhonda Miska articulated this helpful distillation of the root concern at the beginning of this project.
2. Ilia Delio, *Christ in Evolution* (Maryknoll, NY: Orbis Books, 2008), 6.

Especially as we see the demographic changes in religious life in the US and Europe, I find it helpful and hopeful to reframe what some call diminishment into the evolution into something new.

The section "Chapter of Elections" discussed the implications of the discoveries of science for religious life, with the hope of encouraging an "evolution into something new," as one survey participant stated. The three significant areas of our religious lives—formation, the vows, and mission—must be revisited and rethought in light of our emerging and evolving reality. We may read and discuss theology and science, but that doesn't always translate to changes in our institutional lives. If we take seriously the science of emergence, how might formation for an emergent future allow for a more creative, evolutionary, and engaging mode of incorporating new members? A hermeneutic of catholicity that integrates the role of interculturality, the unitive nature of all creation, and the evolutionary trajectory toward Omega/God offers a lens through which to interpret the elements of our consecrated lives, especially the evangelical counsels. Finally, we have "a great history still to be accomplished" but it will not look like our past. Pope Francis urges us to take the challenges of *Laudato Si'* to heart. We must engage in mission for our common home. Mission that requires "whole earth thinking" and collaborative action.

What we think about the New Cosmology, what we know about science and the implications for theology, and how we can integrate emerging theology into our institutional life and mission are important steps toward a new chapter in the evolving future of religious life. But, as my sixth-grade teacher was wont to say: "Show don't tell." Darwin used the image of an entangled bank to describe the intricacy and interconnection of all of life. It was a visible, tangible witness to the complexity underlying beauty and order.

> There is a grandeur in this view of life, with its several powers, having been originally breathed into a few forms or into one; and that, whilst this planet has gone cycling on according to the fixed law of gravity, from so simple a beginning endless forms most beautiful and most wonderful have been, and are being, evolved.[3]

3. Darwin, *The Annotated Origin: A Facsimile of the First Edition of "On the Origin of Species,"* ed. James Costa (Cambridge, MA: Harvard University Press, 2009), 489–90.

It many respects, our life in community is the entangled bank of our beliefs, hopes, and dreams for religious life. It speaks of the unity of charism, our common search for the divine, and/or the completion of one form and the emergence of another. To paraphrase a familiar adage, "Evolution begins at home." How might our integration of science and theology become visible in the entangled bank of our community life?

## The Entangled Bank of Community

Reflecting on the Rule of St. Augustine, I was struck by French Augustinian André Sève's insight that the Rule means we are a community of friends in search of God. His words point to the importance of creating community, and the importance of our ongoing search for God in our lives. In our often-fragmented culture, there are many who would resonate with that goal of a common search for the transcendent.[4]

I have to admit that when I have read the Rule of St. Augustine, "a community of friends" on a "common search for the transcendent" is not what first comes to mind. Nonetheless, the sentiment does provoke the question, what should our living in community look like if we take the findings of science, emerging theology, and the signs of the times seriously? If culture and consciousness are both evolving, how might the culture of community and our collective consciousness more accurately be reflective of this unfolding reality? My modest proposal is that our community life should be essential, emergent, and expansive. But first, as Aquinas is purported to have said, "seldom affirm, never deny, always distinguish." While there are many different ways of defining "community," I am advocating for community living under one roof. Those who hold a different definition may find some helpful insights in what follows, but the authenticity of the witness that I will describe is rooted in the day-to-day struggle to become "a community of friends" on "a common search for the transcendent."

4. Susan Smith, "Whither Religious Life? Reflections from New Zealand," *Global Sisters Report* (August 5, 2020), https://www.globalsistersreport.org/news/whither-religious -life-reflections-new-zealand.

## Essential

> I trust that, rather than living in some Utopia, you will find ways to create "alternate spaces," where the Gospel of self-giving, fraternity, embracing differences, and love of one another can thrive . . . [These spaces] should increasingly be the leaven for a society inspired by the Gospel, a "city on a hill," which testifies to the truth and the power of Jesus' words.[5]

Pope Francis doesn't beat around the bush. In his letter announcing the Year of Consecrated Life he clearly stated his expectations. We religious are to create spaces in which "the Gospel of self-giving, fraternity, embracing differences, and love of one another can thrive." In a word, he is calling us to the ideals presented in our documents. We are—literally—to live the dream. Or at the very least, to try to.

"The first purpose for which you have been formed into one community is to dwell peacefully in the convent and to be of one heart and mind in God."[6] The Rule of St. Augustine takes inspiration from the Acts of the Apostles, particularly those sections that describe the community of disciples living together (Acts 4:32). In a world in chaos, fractured by sin, selfishness, pride, and greed, the goal of a group of unrelated adult women dwelling in peace is, indeed, a profound witness. And essential to creating that peace is setting common, realistic, and healthy expectations. Imagine a conversation at the local level in which a community reads, prays, and discerns how the gospel in light of *Laudato Si'* might direct their common life? Or a conversation that acknowledges our theological differences and how that is expressed in our common prayer—without judgment or "fraternal" correction.

A future of religious life must provide for a communal living that meets the essential needs of its members while witnessing to what essential values it holds. And foundation to that future is space.

5. Pope Francis, "Apostolic Letter to All Consecrated People on the Occasion of the Year of Consecrated Life," II.3, http://www.vatican.va/content/francesco/en/apost_letters /documents/papa-francesco_lettera-ap_20141121_lettera-consacrati.html.

6. Barbara Beyenka, OP, "Translation of the Rule of St. Augustine," in *The Rule, Constitution, Statutes, and Enactments* (Sinsinawa, WI: Sinsinawa Dominicans, 1990, revised 2012).

Recently, a sister who had served in leadership admitted that in planning for its future, the congregation had made some financial decisions that were now stifling any possibility for living together as community. They had opted to tear down their motherhouse and constructed an apartment building with individual units. The sisters had lovely separate living spaces, but there was no common kitchen, chapel, or community room. But as younger women enter, many of them describe living in community as an important aspect of their discernment. As the Center for Applied Research in the Apostolate's Report on Recent Vocations to Religious Life (2020) stated,

> As in 2009, praying together, living together, and sharing meals with other members are particularly important aspects of community life to most newer members of religious institutes, with more than eight in ten reporting each of these aspects as "very" important.[7]

The enthusiasm for "living under one roof" is particularly high among Millennials. "Most new members prefer to live in large (eight or more members) or medium (four to seven members) communities rather than alone or in communities of two or three. This trend, identified in 2009, has shown slight increases in 2019."[8] Given these trends, if congregations hope to have a future, it is essential that they have space in which that future can thrive.

### Emergent

If you are what you should be, you will set [the world] on fire.

—Catherine of Siena[9]

One of the elements of emergence theory is that what emerges is ontologically connected to what precedes it. As discussed in chapter

---

7. Mary L. Gautier and Thu T. Do, "Recent Vocations to Religious Life: A Report for the National Religious Vocation Conference" (Washington, DC: Center for Applied Research in the Apostolate, March 2020), 110.

8. Gautier and Do, 114.

9. The original says "you will set fire to all Italy." St. Catherine of Siena, "Letter to Stefano Maconi," in *St Catherine of Siena as Seen in her Letters*, trans. Vida D. Scudder (New York: E.P. Dutton, 1905), 305.

7, "the higher emergent levels (e.g. living organisms) include the lower levels (e.g. inorganic chemistry), on which they are based."[10] Nested ontological hierarchies imply that an emergent novelty has a history, a connection to what has developed prior, and builds on that. In our discussion on emergence, we focused on the emergent disciple and formation programs, but the concepts can be effectively applied to common life.

Local communities are not lone outposts, divorced from the congregation. In most cases, convents are connected to congregational ministries, or houses of sisters are established in areas where the sisters serve. In addition to ministerial connections to particular neighborhoods, there are also subtle cords that tie us to our congregations. I have visited numerous local communities of Mercy sisters in several different countries. Without fail, hanging on a wall there is a picture of Catherine McAuley and often a photo of the original house on Baggot Street.

The local community is a distillation of the congregation's history, hopes, values, and vision. It is a nested hierarchy of charism visible at the local level. And the theory of emergence states that in the third-order, emergence is evolutionary, where the novelty is passed on to the next generation. We might imagine that a local community that successfully meets its essential needs and purpose is now able to evolve to meet the emerging needs of its wider environment, bearing witness to Catherine of Siena's words: "If you are what you should be, you will set [the world] on fire." Our community life will become a visible witness of the gospel within our neighborhood. As Kaye Ashe, OP, wrote:

> When relationships—with others; with the cosmos; and with the source of all life, truth, beauty, and love—go well, everything flourishes. It's up to us together to envision a world in which our wide web of relationships becomes ever more life affirming and to act in accord with our vision.

10. Niels Henrik Gregersen, "Emergency and Complexity," in *The Oxford Handbook of Religion and Science*, ed. Philip Clayton and Zachary Simpson (New York: Oxford University Press, 2006), 767.

## Expansive

Enlarge the site of your tent,
   and let the curtains of your habitations be stretched out;
do not hold back; lengthen your cords
   and strengthen your stakes.

                                   —Isaiah 54:2

The prophet known as Second Isaiah announces an oracle of hope to people in exile. But it isn't enough to simply rejoice at God's coming salvation; Israel in exile is to actively prepare for the fulfillment of the prophecy. "Enlarge the site of your tent, and let the curtains of your habitation be stretched out, do not hold back; lengthen your cords and strengthen your stakes" (Isa 54:2). The realization of Israel's hope will come from an unlikely redeemer: Cyrus the Persian (Isa 44:23–45:8). Walter Brueggemann describes how untenable this might have seemed to Isaiah's audience.

> That old prophet had just told the exiled Jews that they would be saved by a *goi*, by the Gentle, Cyrus the Persian. This was God's new way to save God's chosen people. Apparently some of the Jews said, "No, we will not be saved by a *goi*. We refuse that rescue and will wait for a good Jewish Messiah."[11]

As we envision a new chapter for religious life that upholds the value of community, we are eager to "enlarge the site of our tent" so to speak, but we might be as surprised as were the Jews in exile by who actually enters into our expanded abode. As Soli Salgado writes of the national Nuns and Nones conversations:

> As a growing share of younger people consider themselves "nones," referring to the box they check next to religion, many religious congregations in the U.S. have been aging and diminishing in size and scope of ministry. But to the sisters involved in Nuns and Nones,

---

11. Walter Brueggemann, "Getting Smashed for Jesus," *Time* (May 25, 2014), https://time.com/110732/sermon-series-getting-smashed-for-jesus.

these flipped numbers between surprisingly similar groups have become an invitation for a creative evolution.[12]

Some of the conversations have led to sharing physical space. The sisters at Mercy Center in Burlingame, California, invited a few millennial Nones to share the grounds as part of a pilot program. "Even if there weren't empty buildings sitting around, there would still be a desire to find a locus, a place where this sharing across generations could happen,"[13] commented Carol Zinn, SSJ, who participated in the first Nuns and Nones conversation in 2016.

The Formation Project, founded by Casper ter Kuile and Angie Thurston, is another program designed to serve as a "novitiate for millennials." As Mary Dacey, of the Sisters of St. Joseph of Philadelphia described the program:

> It's all the elements of religious formation that we experienced as sisters. The difference here is that it's online and for people who are married, single, LGBT, from any denomination—could be atheist. But the critical piece here is a desire for deepening spiritual life.[14]

In tune with the Spirit, women religious are responding to the emerging needs of a new generation that doesn't necessarily adhere to institutional religions or even hold theistic beliefs. Such expansive endeavors are built on a commitment by women religious to be in the conversation. To be open to exploring new avenues in which the gospel and the congregation's charism can evolve.

Assisi Community in Washington, DC, is another example of an expansive mode of intentional communal living. In 1986, four Catholic anti-war advocates purchased a row house there to live among those suffering from poverty.

---

12. Soli Salgado, "Nuns and Nones: A Modern Religious Community," *Global Sisters Report* (February 7, 2019), https://www.globalsistersreport.org/news/trends/nuns-and-nones-modern-religious-community-55831.

13. Salgado.

14. Salgado.

Violence, racism, ego—this is typical fodder at Assisi House, one of the city's oldest intentional communities, which these days consists of 13 people ages 4 to 81 sharing morning prayer, nightly meals, one kitchen and a mission statement calling them to "live faithfully the Gospel call to work for a more just and peaceful world."[15]

As one of the founders, Joe Nagle, OFM, described, "This isn't just a nice way to live together, or a more convenient way, or even a way to be politically active. This has to do with the divine, how we're expected to live."[16] Since its founding, more than a hundred men and women have lived at Assisi House. Regardless of their faith tradition, orientation, or place of employment, they commit to the hard work of building community.

As we ponder the various expansive modes of communal life, we actually have recourse to the past. "The Holy Preaching" was the term used by Saint Dominic to describe a multiple-membered community. The first foundation of St. Dominic was a community of women who had been converted from heresy and were no longer welcome in their family homes. But very soon, that community included friars and lay members. As Barbara Beaumont, OP, describes:

> So here we have as elements of Dominic's newness of vision, preachers and sisters living on the same site, in a process of becoming. He was obviously prepared to live with the possible ambiguities and difficulties inherent in such a situation. But this isn't all, for almost immediately, that is to say as early as August 8 1207, there is incontrovertible evidence for the presence of lay people living and working alongside the preachers and the converted ladies at Prouilhe. Indeed such an enterprise as the Holy Preaching was becoming would clearly need help with the various tasks associated with subsistence agriculture and housekeeping. Dominic accepted these people who

15. Michelle Boorstein, "D.C.'s 'International Communities' Put Strangers in a House Joined by Core Values," *The Washington Post* (August 31, 2013), https://www.washingtonpost.com/local/dcs-intentional-communities-put-strangers-in-a-house-joined-by-core-values/2013/08/31/7b1c01f4-0f3d-11e3-bdf6-e4fc677d94a1_story.html.

16. Boorstein.

gave themselves to the community of the Holy Preaching, very much in the manner of Benedictine oblates.[17]

When we consider how our community life can be expansive, we should take heart that we've done this before. And life in community itself can become a "holy preaching."

## Trust in the Slow Work of God

There is precious wisdom to be culled from women religious and how they live out a committed life together. Newly emerging models of community are inevitable. I trust the committed life is evolving and will continue to evolve. The question I ponder today is what commitment might look like for all of us in the midst of this massive, disruptive global transition. How might the current crisis be a catalyst to push that evolution forward, opening hearts and minds to new possibilities?[18]

Our community life can be essential, emergent, and expansive if we are willing to attend to the signs of the times and do the hard work such a life requires. It is not for the faint of heart. Our very diversity—cultural, generational, theological—means that every community must actively engage in intercultural living. As Pope Francis writes in *Fratelli Tutti*, "We need only have a pure and simple desire to be a people, a community, constant and tireless in the effort to include, integrate and lift up the fallen."[19] Though Pope Francis is speaking of the larger society in which we live, his example of the Good Samaritan also speaks to our vowed life in community.

---

17. Barbara Beaumont, OP, "The Coming of the Preacher," presentation, International Commissions of the Dominican Order, Prouilhe, France, April 2006, http://www .domlife.org/800/BeaumondOP_Prouilhe_2006.htm.

18. Quincy Howard, OP, "Religious Vows Offer Wisdom as We Experience This Epic Uncertainty," *Global Sisters Report* (May 22, 2020), https://www.globalsisters report.org/news/coronavirus/column/religious-vows-offer-wisdom-we-experience-epic -uncertainty.

19. Pope Francis, On Fraternity and Social Friendship (*Fratelli Tutti*), 77, http://www .vatican.va/content/francesco/en/encyclicals/documents/papa-francesco_20201003 _enciclica-fratelli-tutti.html.

"Life exists where there is bonding, communion, fraternity; and life is stronger than death when it is built on true relationships and bonds of fidelity."[20]

Indeed, this endeavor to explore the impact of emerging science and theology on our vowed lives has been an exercise in communion, sisterhood, and fidelity. Where is Jesus in the New Cosmology? We conclude this conversation on the emerging future of religious life recognizing that it's not that we come up with the same answer, but that we search together.

> The search—
> for self,
> for wisdom,
> for love,
> for truth,
> for justice,
> for God—
> is strenuous and unending.
> We need good companions
> in order to persevere in it.
> In good company,
> in a community of conviction,
> the quest never loses its
> relevance,
> its urgency,
> or its savor.
> —Kaye Ashe, OP

20. Pope Francis, "Angelus" (November 10, 2019), *L'Osservatore Romano* (November 11–12, 2019): 8.

# Afterword

Wiping my sweaty hands on my jeans and trying to ignore the twist in my gut, I entered the room to meet the president of the Sisters of St. Francis for the first time. I was told she wanted to speak with me before I submitted my application for candidacy in the community. I remember her words—probably because my senses were heightened by nerves. She had two pieces of advice she wanted to share with me before I began this journey into religious life. The second was: "Trust the process."

I had no idea what she meant. I also had no idea how many times I would come back to these words. In fact, I've learned their meaning again and again as I've lived religious life. We women religious have been invited to "trust the process" many times. We've had to trust the process of entering into the deep, personal work of the novitiate. We have learned to trust the process of negotiating the liminal space of changing ministries and moving into new communities. We are now learning to trust that the processes and structures of religious life as we have known them are evolving into something new. Within these pages, Laurie has invited us to trust the process of naming and claiming the evolution of our theology in light of science. We are called to form ourselves into "emergent disciples" who are ready to engage the signs of these times.

The real gift of Laurie's work is her generational apologetics approach in which she invites the generations that make up religious life to actually hear each other's insights and concerns about the so-called "new" cosmology. She effectively removes the hurdles of miscommunication around this subject. She also addresses the concerns of those who seek the particularity of the Jesus story within the New Cosmology by interpreting Scripture alongside scientific insight. By beginning with delving into each generation's formative experiences of church and science, this book tackles the lacuna of previous conversations about New Cosmology. As we gain a greater appreciation for one another's perspectives, we find a starting point for a larger engagement of the implications of our cosmological vision across religious life. Thus, Laurie's substantial contribution to the New Cosmology conversation enables us to set aside our initial reaction to the subject—whether it be delight or a groan—so that we can deepen our collective integration of its meaning into our lives.

Inviting people to discover a common understanding and articulation of the relationship between science and theology is useful. It allows us women religious to harness our power by naming our theology afresh as we respond to the needs of today. The very process of learning to bridge the gaps in our experiences and understanding of New Cosmology in religious life serves as excellent practice for aiding us in communicating relevant theology grounded in scientific insight to the average person in the pews and beyond. If we can effectively communicate amongst ourselves what it means to embrace an updated theology informed by scientific discovery, we have a better chance of sharing these concepts with a larger world.

This leads me to recall the first piece of advice the president gave me before I entered the community: "Remain faithful to prayer. No matter what happens, if you have a strong prayer life, you will be okay."

This was a piece of advice I could understand. Relationship with God and others is evident in prayer as we turn our hearts and intentions toward the expansive energy of God.

I find that I am especially fascinated by the profound relationality of the scientific concept of entanglement. All the subatomic particles that make up my person are entangled with other particles scattered throughout the universe—including the particles that make up my family, my own Franciscan community, all those who say yes to religious life, people who profoundly disagree with everything I stand for, mountains on the other side of the world, and more.

Therefore, I am in a fundamental relationship with so many others, those I am aware of and beyond, indeed all of creation! Just as Francis of Assisi understood himself to be a sibling of all creation, we too are connected across difference and conflicts. It may take an expanding universe to make enough room to work out some of our political and religious differences! Yet, it is encouraging to reflect on the growing complexity of the universe as weaving us into a whole, even when my limited imagination cannot fathom how a resolution could ever come about. Somehow, some way, this divine and all-encompassing entanglement is in process, moving us toward greater complexity and unity.

As women religious, we know that prayer is key for nurturing our relationship with God and each other. However, Laurie further posits that intercessory prayer works precisely because the subatomic particles that entangle us with the cosmos have free will in our unfinished universe. Remaining faithful to prayer means remaining faithful to our relationship with all the subatomic particles that make up creation.

An integrated, grounded theology that includes Jesus has the potential to yield a new confidence in us, rooting us in our own specific traditions even as we embrace our place in the cosmos as the little and powerful leavening we are called to be.

As we continue to ponder Laurie's contribution to the conversation, we might consider:

- How do we engage in the paradox of experiencing smaller numbers of women religious in an expanding universe?

- What will we elect to do together?

- How does confidence in all that is emerging in these times change our perspectives? What happens if we do indeed trust the process?

Sarah Kohles, OSF

Discussion and Reflection Questions are available at
https://litpress.org/discussion/the-heavens.

# Glossary of Terms

In order to have fruitful conversation and meaningful dialogue on any topic, there needs to be a shared understanding among interlocuters around the definition of key terms and concepts. Much conflict, or perceived conflict, is rooted in a lack of shared understanding of the terms by dialogue partners. The following glossary, while not exhaustive, provides the definitions or connotations of terms to allow for a better conversation on the role of Jesus in the New Cosmology.[1]

## Catholicity
From the Greek, *kata* (according to) and *holos* (whole), so creating a sense of the whole, or "whole-making." The most common definition refers to the quality or state of being Catholic. As it is used in the New Cosmology, "the word catholicity was coined to describe a consciousness of the whole cosmos, the whole physical order of things to which the human was connected but distinct from; cosmos was the source for guiding human action."[2]

## Christogenesis
Pierre Teilhard de Chardin coined the term "Christogenesis" as the fourth and final stage of development (after cosmogenesis, biogenesis, and noogenesis).[3] For Teilhard de Chardin "*someone* and not something is coming to birth at the heart of evolution. He used the

---

1. The bulk of the research and writing of this glossary was prepared by Rhonda Miska, project research assistant.

2. Ilia Delio, *Making All Things New: Catholicity, Cosmology, Consciousness* (Maryknoll, NY: Orbis Books, 2015), 8.

3. Pierre Teilhard de Chardin, *The Phenomenon of Man* (New York: Harper & Row, 1961).

term *Christogenesis* to indicate that evolution is, from the point of Christian faith, the birth of the cosmic Person."[4] For Teilhard, Christogenesis is "literally the birthing of Christ."[5]

## Consciousness

According to the Oxford English Dictionary, consciousness is defined as "the state of being able to use your senses and mental powers to understand what is happening." Teilhard de Chardin describes consciousness as "'Every kind of psyche, from the most rudimentary forms of interior perception conceivable to the human phenomenon of reflective consciousness'. Consciousness is first grasped as our experience as human beings, the 'I' looking inside itself."[6] Delio proposes that the definition of consciousness can be expanded to include not just humans but systems. "A system is conscious if it can communicate or process information that, in turn, serves as its organizational function. Anything capable of self-organizing possesses a level of consciousness."[7]

## Cosmic Christ

The Cosmic Christ is the fulfilled potentiality seeded in the creation, germinated in the human Jesus, and blossomed in evolutionary consciousness. "The whole concept of evolution has liberated Christ from the limits of the man Jesus and enabled us to locate Christ at the heart of creation: the primacy of God's love, the exemplar of creation, the centrating principle of evolution, and the Omega point of an evolutionary universe."[8]

## Cosmology

From two Greek words: *kosmos* (the world, the universe) and suffix *logos* (study of). "The aim of cosmology is to understand the large-scale structure and overall evolution of the universe. It involves both

4. Ilia Delio, *The Unbearable Wholeness of Being: God, Evolution, and the Power of Love* (Maryknoll, NY: Orbis Books, 2013), 124.

5. Delio, xxii.

6. Francois Euvé, SJ, "Humanity Reveals the World," in *From Teilhard to Omega: Co-Creating an Unfinished Universe*, ed. Ilia Delio (Maryknoll, NY: Orbis Books, 2014), 72.

7. Delio, *Making All Things New*, 65.

8. Ilia Delio, *Christ in Evolution* (Maryknoll, NY: Orbis Books, 2008), 174.

observations—classifying and cataloguing the various contents of the universe—and models to explain these observations."[9]

## Creation

Creation is "the living world in light of its relation to the God who creates it. Language of creation signals that this finite world is pervaded with the 'absolute presence' of the living God who empowers its advance in the beginning, continuing now, and moving into the future."[10] As a concept, creation is connected to but distinct from "nature," "the environment," or "the natural world" since creation is "a specifically theological term the use of which signals that the natural world studied by science is being viewed through the lens of religious belief."[11]

## Emergence

"In an ordinary sense the term 'emergence' connotes something coming out of hiding, coming into view for the first time. Evolutionary scientists use it to describe the spontaneous appearance of unprecedented new biological forms."[12] In emergence, the whole is more than the sum of the parts, and what emerges is markedly new. "Emergent properties are those that arise out of some subsystem but are not reducible to that system. Emergence is about more than but not altogether other than . . . Emergence means that the world exhibits a recurrent pattern of novelty and irreducibility."[13]

## Entanglement

Schrödinger described entanglement as occurring "when two systems, of which we know the states by their respective representatives, enter into temporary physical interaction due to known forces between them, and when after a time of mutual influence the systems

---

9. Bernard Carr, "Cosmology and Religion," in *The Oxford Handbook of Religion and Science*, ed. Philip Clayton (Oxford: Oxford University Press, 2008), 139.

10. Elizabeth A. Johnson, *Ask the Beasts: Darwin and the God of Love* (London: Bloomsbury, 2014), 5.

11. Johnson, 4.

12. Johnson, 175.

13. Philip Clayton, *Mind and Emergence: From Quantum to Consciousness* (Oxford; New York: Oxford University Press, 2004), 39.

separate again, then they can no longer be described in the same way as before, viz. by endowing each of them with a representative of its own."[14] Entanglement of quantum states of particles means that a measurement of one particle affects the state of the entangled particle, even at a distance. Notably Einstein called this "spooky action at a distance." See nonlocality.

## Evolution

Evolution describes the biological development of all organizations from less complex to more complex species, a development governed by natural law. "Far from being a mere speculation, [the theory of evolution] is based on a solid and growing body of empirical evidence . . . [I]ts insight into how and why a vast diversity of plants and animals have come to exist on earth, both now and in the past as revealed by the fossil record, has become a central organizing principle of the study of biology on every continent."[15]

## Evolutionary Consciousness

The term "evolutionary consciousness" refers to the growth in evolutionary complexity that leads to awareness. "Correlated with this movement towards complexity is the movement towards higher levels of consciousness. The whole process has included several critical moments or thresholds at which leaps to new levels have been made. Such thresholds were the emergence of life on earth and then the emergence of rational self-consciousness in human beings."[16]

## Holon

The term, "holon," was coined to describe the reality that all individual elements in a living system are actually part of a larger whole, so that "a holon is simultaneously a whole and a part."[17]

---

14. Erwin Schrödinger, "Discussion of Probability Relations Between Separated Systems," *Proceedings of the Cambridge Philosophical Society* 31 (1935): 555.

15. Johnson, *Ask the Beasts*, 13.

16. "Teilhard de Chardin, Pierre," in *The Oxford Dictionary of the Christian Church*, ed. F. L. Cross and E. A. Livingstone (New York: Oxford University Press, 2005).

17. Delio, *Making All Things New*, 121.

## Integrity of All Creation

"Integrity of all creation" reflects the vision put forth in *Laudato Si'* for "integral ecology" based on the deep interconnected and interrelated reality of all human and non-human elements of creation. The term "integrity of all creation" has been added to the terms "justice and peace" (sometimes abbreviated "JPIC") in the names of church, diocesan, and other ministerial offices. This reflects the growing consciousness that, from a Christian perspective, work for justice and peace cannot be separated from "care for our common home."

## New Cosmology

The New Cosmology integrates scientific facts, including discoveries about the expanding universe and evolution, and proposes that creation is ongoing and—building on the work of Teilhard de Chardin—emerging into greater complexity. Related to the New Cosmology is the "new universe story," articulated by Thomas Berry, Brian Swimme, and other 20th- and 21st-century thinkers who focus on the 13.8 billion year unfolding history of the universe. The following are generally considered elements of the New Cosmology: the Big Bang (the Universe has a beginning); the Universe is expanding; the Universe will eventually "die"; all of creation is interrelated; our consciousness is evolving.

## Nonlocality

Nonlocality, a result of entanglement, is a term used in quantum physics to describe how an "atom's measured attributes are determined not just by events happening at the actual measurement site but by events arbitrarily distant including events outside the light cone, that is, events so far away that to reach the measurement site their influence must travel faster than light."[18]

## Noosphere

The noosphere is the "level of shared consciousness that transcends boundaries of religion, culture, or ethnicity. It is a sphere of collective

---

18. Delio, *The Unbearable Wholeness of Being*, 27.

consciousness"[19] According to Teilhard de Chardin, as evolution continues toward the Omega Point, the noosphere "will reach collectively its point of convergence—at 'the end of the world.'"[20]

## Omega Point

The Omega Point is a term created by Teilhard de Chardin to describe "the limit point, the unification towards which all evolution has been moving and which, with human cooperation, will continue to move."[21] Chardin describes the Omega as "the meeting-point between the Universe arrived at the limit of centration and another Centre that is deeper still, a self-subsistent Centre and absolutely ultimate Principle of irreversibility and personalization: the only true Omega."[22]

## Quantum Theory

Quantum theory "took its name from the initial simple but puzzling observation that atoms absorbed and emitted energy only in certain discrete amounts called *quanta* after the Latin *quantus* for 'how much?'"[23] Quantum mechanics focuses on the behavior of light and matter at the subatomic level. Unlike Newtonian physics, cause and effect do not seem to function at the quantum level. Rather here either position or the wavelength of a particle may be measured, but not both, allowing "prediction of the probability but not the exact value of observable events."[24]

19. Delio, *Making All Things New: Catholicity, Cosmology, Consciousness*, 110.

20. Teilhard de Chardin, *The Phenomenon of Man*, 272.

21. Patrick H. Byrne, "The Integral Visions of Teilhard and Lonergan: Science, the Universe, Humanity, and God," in *From Teilhard to Omega: Co-Creating an Unfinished Universe*, ed. Ilia Delio (Marknoll, NY: Orbis Books, 2014), 88.

22. Teilhard de Chardin, *Man's Place in Nature* (New York: Harper & Row, 1966), 121.

23. Dennis Overbye, *Lonely Hearts of the Cosmos* (Boston: Back Bay Books, 1999), 109.

24. Ian G. Barbour, *Religion and Science. Historical and Contemporary Issues* (New York: HarperCollins, 1997), 359.

# Bibliography

Abbott, Brenda. "Eric Doyle OFM: Blessed John Duns Scotus, Teilhard de Chardin and a Cosmos in Evolution." *Franciscan Studies* 75 (2017): 497–525.

Abrams, Nancy Ellen. *The New Universe and the Human Future: How a Shared Cosmology Could Transform the World.* New Haven, CT: Yale University Press, 2011.

Agullo, Ivan, and Parampreet Sing. "Quantum Cosmology: A Brief Review." In *100 Years of General Relativity*, edited by A. Ashtekar and J. Pullin, 183–240. Hackensack, NJ: World Scientific, 2017.

Amos, Clare. "The Genesis of Reconciliation: The Reconciliation of Genesis." *Mission Studies* 23 (2006): 9–26.

Ashley, J. Matthew. "Reading the Universe Story Theologically: The Contribution of a Biblical Narrative Imagination." *Theological Studies* 71 (2010): 870–902.

Ayala, Francisco J. "Evolution, Biological." In *Encyclopedia of Science and Religion*, edited by J. Wentzel Vrede van Huyssteen, 1:291–98. New York: Macmillan, 2003.

Barbour, Ian G. *Religion and Science. Historical and Contemporary Issues.* New York: HarperCollins, 1997.

Barbour, Ian G. *Religion in the Age of Science.* San Francisco: Harper & Row, 1990.

Barringer, Felicity. "Ideas & Trends; What IS Youth Coming To?" *New York Times*, August 19, 1990.

Barrow, John D. "The Evolution of the Universe." *New Literary History* 22 (1991): 835–56.

Belben, Tim. "Quantum Creation? Cosmologists Are Coming up with Some Strange Theories about the Origin of the Universe. Can Christian Theology Keep Pace?" *Modern Believing* 51 (2010): 47–54.

Belenkiy, Ari. "Alexander Friedmann and the Origins of Modern Cosmology." *Physics Today* 65 (2012): 38–43.

Bergant, Dianne. *A New Heaven, A New Earth: The Bible and Catholicity.* Maryknoll, NY: Orbis Books, 2016.

Bergant, Dianne. "'In the Image of God' but What Is the Image?" In *Forget Not God's Benefits (Ps 103:2): A Festschrift in Honor of Leslie J. Hoppe, OFM,* edited by Barbara E. Reid, 10–24. Washington, DC: Catholic Biblical Association, 2022.

Berry, Thomas. *The Dream of the Earth.* San Francisco: Sierra Club Books, 1988.

Berry, Thomas. *The Great Work: Our Way into the Future.* 1st ed. New York: Bell Tower, 1999.

Berry, Thomas. *The New Story.* Chambersburg, PA: Anima Books, 1978.

Berry, Thomas. "Wonderworld as Wasteworld: The Earth in Deficit." *Cross Currents* 35 (1985): 408–22.

Berry, Thomas, Anne Lonergan, Caroline Richards, and Gregory Baum, eds. *Thomas Berry and the New Cosmology.* Mystic, CT: Twenty-Third Publications, 1987.

Bevere, Allan R. "Cosmos Dissolved or Made New?: Cosmology, Polkinghorne and Christian Liturgy." *Liturgy* 28 (October 2013): 28–40.

Bohm, David. *Wholeness and the Implicate Order.* London: Routledge, 1980.

Bowe, Barbara E. *Biblical Foundations of Spirituality: Touching a Finger to the Flame.* Lanham, MD: Rowman & Littlefield, 2017.

Brennan, Patrick McKinley. "Subsidiarity in the Tradition of Catholic Social Doctrine." In *Global Perspectives on Subsidiarity,* edited by Michelle Evans and Augusto Zimmermann, 29–48. Ius Gentium: Comparative Perspectives on Law and Justice. Dordrecht: Springer, 2014.

Bude, Heinz. "Qualitative Research." In *A Companion to Qualitative Research,* edited by Uwe Flick, Ernst von Kardoff, and Ines Steinke, translated by Bryan Jenner, English., 108–12. London: Sage Publications, 2004.

Byrne, Patrick H. "The Integral Visions of Teilhard and Lonergan: Science, the Universe, Humanity, and God." In *From Teilhard to Omega: Co-Creating an Unfinished Universe,* edited by Ilia Delio, 83–110. Maryknoll, NY: Orbis Books, 2014.

Capra, Fritjof. *The Tao of Physics.* Berkeley, CA: Shambala, 1975.

Carlson, Elwood, *The Lucky Few: Between the Greatest Generation and the Baby Boom.* Springer, 2008.

Carr, Bernard, "Cosmology and Religion." In *The Oxford Handbook of Religion and Science,* edited by Philip Clayton, Philip, 139–54. Oxford: Oxford University Press, 2008.

Carr, Paul H. "A Theology for Evolution: Haught, Teilhard, and Tillich." *Zygon* 40 (September 2005): 733–38.

Carvalhaes, Cláudio. "We Are All Immigrants! Imago Dei, Citizenship, and The Im/Possibility of Hospitality." *Practical Matters Journal* (Spring 2018): 181–97.

Castelli, Elizabeth. "Virginity and Its Meaning for Women's Sexuality in Early Christianity." *Journal of Feminist Studies in Religion* 2 (1986): 61–88.

Catherine of Siena, "Letter to Stefano Maconi," in *St Catherine of Siena as Seen in her Letters,* translated by Vida D. Scudder. New York: E.P. Dutton, 1905.

Chaisson, Eric J. "A Singular Universe of Many Singularities: Cultural Evolution in a Cosmic Context." In *Singularity Hypotheses: A Scientific and Philosophical Assessment,* edited by A. H. Eden, J. H. Moor, J. H. Soraker, and E. Steinhart, 413–440. Berlin: Springer, 2012.

Chittister, Joan D. "No Time for Tying Cats." In *Midwives of the Future: American Sisters Tell Their Story,* edited by Ann Patrick Ward. Kansas City, MO: Leaven, 1985.

Cimperman, Maria. *Religious Life for Our World: Creating Communities of Hope.* Maryknoll, NY: Orbis Books, 2020.

Cimperman, Maria. *Social Analysis for the 21st Century.* Maryknoll, NY: Orbis Books, 2015.

Clayton, Philip. *Mind and Emergence: From Quantum to Consciousness.* New York: Oxford University Press, 2004.

Corning, Peter A. "The Re-Emergence of Emergence, and the Causal Role of Synergy in Emergent Evolution," *Synthese* 185 (2012): 295-317.

Council of Major Superiors of Women Religious. *The Foundations of Religious Life: Revisiting the Vision.* Notre Dame, IN: Ave Maria Press, 2009.

Cousins, Ewert H. *Christ of the 21st Century.* Chicago: Franciscan Herald Press, 1978.

D'Antonio, William V., James D. Davidson, Dean R. Hoge, and Mary L. Gautier. *American Catholics Today: New Realities of Their Faith and Their Church.* Lanham, MD: Rowman & Littlefield, 2007.

Darwin, Charles. *The Annotated Origin: A Facsimile of the First Edition of "On the Origin of Species,"* edited by James Costa. Cambridge, MA: Harvard University Press, 2009.

Darwin, Charles. *The Descent of Man.* London: John Murray, 1871.

Deacon, Terrence. "The Hierarchical Logic of Emergence: Untangling the Interdependence of Evolution and Self-Organization." In *Evolution and Learning: The Baldwin Effect Reconsidered,* edited by Bruce H. Weber and David J. Depew, 273–308. Cambridge, MA: MIT Press, 2003.

Debono, Marc-Williams. "From Perception to Consciousness: An Epistemic Vision of Evolutionary Processes." *Leonardo* 37 (2004): 243–48.

Delgado, Melvin. *Baby Boomers of Color: Implications for Social Work Policy and Practice*. New York: Columbia University Press, 2015.

Delio, Ilia. *Christ in Evolution*. Maryknoll, NY: Orbis Books, 2008.

Delio, Ilia. "Godhead or God Ahead? Rethinking the Trinity in Light of Emergence." In *God, Grace & Creation*, edited by Philip J. Rossi, 3–22. Maryknoll, NY: Orbis Books, 2010.

Delio, Ilia. *Making All Things New: Catholicity, Cosmology, Consciousness*. Maryknoll, NY: Orbis Books, 2015.

Delio, Ilia. *The Unbearable Wholeness of Being: God, Evolution, and the Power of Love*. Maryknoll, NY: Orbis Books, 2013.

Delio, Ilia. "Transhumanism or Ultrahumanism? Teilhard de Chardin on Technology, Religion, and Evolution." *Theology and Science Journal* 10 (May 2012): 153–66.

Dinges, D. William and Ilia Delio, OSF. "Teilhard de Chardin and the New Spirituality." In *From Teilhard to Omega: Co-Creating an Unfinished Universe*, 166–83. Maryknoll, NY: Orbis Books, 2014.

Doi, Joanne Jaruko. "Interculturality: A Foundation for U.S. Mission." In *The Gift of Mission: Yesterday, Today, Tomorrow: The Maryknoll Centennial Symposium*, edited by James H. Kroeger, 204–208. Maryknoll, NY: Orbis Books, 2013.

Duffy, SSJ, Kathleen. "Sophia: Catalyst for Creative Union and Divine Love." In *From Teilhard to Omega: Co-Creating an Unfinished Universe*, 24–36. Maryknoll, NY: Orbis Books, 2014.

Dugan, Katherine. "#Adoration: Holy Hour Devotions and Millennial Twenty-First Century Catholic Identity." *U.S. Catholic Historian* 36 (Winter 2018): 103–27.

Duve, Christian de. *Singularities: Landmarks on the Pathways of Life*. Cambridge: Cambridge University Press, 2005.

Edwards, Denis. "A Relational and Evolving Universe Unfolding within the Dynamism of the Divine Communion." In *In Whom We Live and Move and Have Our Being*, edited by Philip Clayton and A. R. Peacocke, 199–210. Grand Rapids, MI: Eerdmans, 2008.

Edwards, Denis. *Earth Revealing—Earth Healing: Ecology and Christian Theology*. Collegeville, MN: Liturgical Press, 2001.

Edwards, Denis. *How God Acts Creation, Redemption, and Special Divine Action*. Theology and the Sciences. Minneapolis: Fortress Press, 2010.

Edwards, Denis. *Jesus and the Cosmos*. New York: Paulist Press, 1991.

Einstein, Albert, Boris Podolsky, and Nathan Rosen. "Can Quantum Mechanical Description of Physical Reality Be Considered Complete?" *Physical Review* 47 (May 15, 1935).

Ellard, Peter. *The Sacred Cosmos: Theological, Philosophical, and Scientific Conversations in the Twelfth-Century School of Chartres*. Scranton, PA: University of Scranton, 2007.

Ellyard, David. *Sky Watch: A Guide to the Southern Skies*. Crows Nest, NSW: Australian Broadcast Corporation, 1988.

Erickson, Tamara. *What's Next, Gen X? Keeping Up, Moving Ahead and Getting the Career You Want*. Boston: Harvard Business School Publishing, 2010.

Euvé, SJ, Francois. "Humanity Reveals the World." In *From Teilhard to Omega: Co-Creating an Unfinished Universe*, edited by Ilia Delio, 67–80. Maryknoll, NY: Orbis Books, 2014.

Francois, CSJP, Susan Rose. "Religious Life in a Time of Fog." In *In Our Own Words: Religious Life in a Changing World*, edited by Juliet Mousseau and Sarah Kohles, 182–203. Collegeville, MN: Liturgical Press, 2018.

Frank, Adam. *The Constant Fire: Beyond the Science vs. Religion Debate*. Berkeley, CA: University of California Press, 2009.

Frohlich, Mary. *Breathed into Wholeness: Catholicity and the Rhythms of the Spirit*. Maryknoll, NY: Orbis Books, 2019.

Gautier, Mary L., and Thu T. Do. "Recent Vocations to Religious Life: A Report for the National Religious Vocation Conference." Washington, DC: Center for Applied Research in the Apostolate, March 2020.

Gervais, Christine L. M. *Beyond the Altar: Women Religious, Patriarchal Power, and the Church*. Waterloo, ON: Wilfrid Laurier University Press, 2019.

Gillis, Chester. *Roman Catholicism in America*. New York: Columbia University Press, 1999.

Gittins, CSSp, Anthony J. *Living Mission Interculturally: Faith, Culture, and the Renewal of Praxis*. Collegeville, MN: Liturgical Press, 2015.

Grabinski, C. Joanne. "Cohorts of the Future." *New Directions for Adult and Continuing Education* 77 (Spring 1998): 73–84.

Greenwood, Kyle. *Scripture and Cosmology: Reading the Bible Between the Ancient World and Modern Science*. Downers Grove, IL: IVP Press, 2015.

Gregersen, Niels. "The Cross of Christ in an Evolutionary World." *Dialog: A Journal of Theology* 40 (2001): 192–207.

Gregersen, Niels Henrik. "Emergency and Complexity." In *The Oxford Handbook of Religion and Science*, edited by Philip Clayton and Zachary Simpson, 767–82. New York: Oxford University Press, 2006.

Gregory, William P. "Pope Francis' Effort to Revitalize Catholic Mission." *International Bulletin of Mission Research* 43 (2019): 7–19.

Griffiths, Bede. *Return to the Center*. Springfield, IL: Templegate, 1976.

Grumett, David, and Paul Bentley. "Teilhard De Chardin, Original Sin, and the Six Propositions." *Zygon: Journal of Religion & Science* 53 (June 2018): 303–330.

Guth, Alan H. "The Inflationary Universe." In *Cosmology: Historical, Literary, Philosophical, Religious, and Scientific Perspectives*, 411–45. New York: Garland Publishing, 1993.

Haight, SJ, Roger. *Faith and Evolution: A Grace-Filled Naturalism*. Maryknoll, NY: Orbis Books, 2019.

Halvorson, Hans, and Helge Kragh. "Cosmology and Theology." In *The Stanford Encyclopedia of Philosophy*, edited by Edward N. Zalta, Spring 2019. Metaphysics Research Lab, Stanford University, 2019. https://plato.stanford.edu/archives/spr2019/entries/cosmology-theology.

Halvorson, Hans, and Helge Kragh. "Physical Cosmology." In *The Routledge Companion to Theism*, edited by Charles Taliaferro, Victoria S. Harrison, and Steward Goetz, 241–55. New York: Routledge, 2003.

Haught, John F. *Christianity and Science: Toward a Theology of Nature*. Maryknoll, NY: Orbis Books, 2007.

Haught, John F. *God After Darwin: A Theology of Evolution*. 2nd edition. New York: Routledge, 2018.

Haught, John F. *Making Sense of Evolution: Darwin, God, and the Drama of Life*. Westminster John Knox Press, 2010.

Haught, John F. "Teilhard de Chardin: Theology for an Unfinished Universe." In *From Teilhard to Omega: Co-Creating an Unfinished Universe*, edited by Ilia Delio, 7–23. Maryknoll, NY: Orbis Books, 2014.

Haught, John F. *The New Cosmic Story: Inside Our Awakening Universe*. New Haven, CT: Yale University Press, 2017.

Hawking, S. W. *A Brief History of Time: From the Big Bang to Black Holes*. Bantam Books, 1988.

Hayes, OFM, Zachary. "Christ, Word of God and Exemplar of Humanity: The Roots of Franciscan Christocentrism and Its Implications for Today." *The Cord* 46 (1996): 3–17.

Hayes, OFM, Zachary. *A Window to the Divine*. Quincy, IL: Franciscan Press, 1997.

Hayes, OFM, Zachary. "New Cosmology for a New Millennium." *New Theology Review* 12 (August 1999): 29–39.

Hereford, CSJ, Amy. *Beyond the Crossroads: Religious Life in the 21st Century*. Maryknoll, NY: Orbis Books, 2019.

Honner, SJ, John. "Unity-in-Difference: Karl Rahner and Niels Bohr." *Theological Studies* 46 (1985): 480–506.

Horan, Daniel P. *Catholicity and Emerging Personhood: A Contemporary Theological Anthropology.* Maryknoll, NY: Orbis Books, 2019.

Howe, Neil, and William Strauss. *Millennials Rising: The Next Great Generation.* New York: Random House, 2000.

Huxley, Julian. *Religion without Revelation.* London: Max Parrish, 1959.

Ingram, Richard E. "A New Cosmology." *Studies: An Irish Quarterly Review* 39 (1950): 445–52.

Isasi-Diaz, Ada Maria. *Mujerista Theology: A Theology for the Twenty-First Century.* Maryknoll, NY: Orbis Books, 1996.

Jackson, J. B. C. "Ecological Extinction and Evolution in the Brave New Ocean." *Proceedings of the National Academy of Sciences* 105 (2008): 11458–65.

Jasper, David. *A Short Introduction to Hermeneutics.* Louisville, KY: Westminster John Knox Press, 2004.

Johnson, Elizabeth A. *Ask the Beasts: Darwin and the God of Love.* London: Bloomsbury, 2014.

Johnson, Elizabeth A. *Creation and the Cross: The Mercy of God for a Planet in Peril.* Maryknoll, NY: Orbis Books, 2018.

Johnson, Elizabeth A. *Quest for the Living God: Mapping Frontiers in the Theology of God.* New York: Continuum, 2007.

Johnson, Elizabeth A. *Women, Earth, and Creator Spirit.* New York: Paulist Press, 1993.

Johnson, SNDdeN, Mary, Patricia Wittberg, SC, and Mary L. Gautier. *New Generations of Catholic Sisters: The Challenge of Diversity.* Oxford: Oxford University Press, 2014.

Kaas, Jon H. "The Evolution of the Neocortex from Early Mammals to Modern Humans." *Phi Kappa Phi Forum* 85 (Spring 2005): 11–14.

Katz, Stephen. "Generation X: A Critical Sociological Perspective." *Generations: Journal of the American Society on Aging.* 41 (Fall 2017): 12–19.

Kulandaisamy, OSM, Denis. "The Biblical Understanding of the Evangelical Counsels." *Vaiharai* 20 (June 2015): 1–25.

Küster, Volker. *The Many Faces of Jesus Christ: Intercultural Christology.* Maryknoll, NY: Orbis Books, 2001.

Larson, Brendon. "The Role of Scientism in Myth-Making for the Anthropocene." *Journal for the Study of Religion, Nature and Culture* 9 (2015): 185–91.

Le, Loan. *Religious Life: A Reflective Examination of Its Charism and Mission for Today.* Cambridge: Cambridge Scholars Publishing, 2016.

Lemaître, Georges. *The Primeval Atom: An Essay on Cosmogony.* New York: Van Nostrand, 1950.

Liderbach, Daniel. *The Numinous Universe*. New York: Paulist Press, 1989.

Lonergan, Bernard. *A Second Collection*. Edited by William Ryan and Bernard Tyrrell. Toronto: Toronto University Press, 1996.

Luminet, Jean-Pierre. "The Rise of Big Bang Models, from Myth to Theory and Observation." In *Proceedings Antropogenesi, Dall'Energia al Fenomeno Umano*, edited by E. Magno A. Pavan, 1–15. Portogruaro, Italy, 2008.

MacHaffie, Barbara J. *Her Story: Women in Christian Tradition*. Minneapolis: Fortress Press, 2006.

Maldari, SJ, Donald C. *Christian Ministry in the Divine Milieu: Catholicity, Evolution, and the Reign of God*. Maryknoll, NY: Orbis, 2019.

McCarthy, Margaret Cain, and Mary Ann Zollmann, eds. *Power of Sisterhood: Women Religious Tell the Story of the Apostolic Visitation*. Lanham, MD: University Press of America, 2014.

Mickey, Sam. *Whole Earth Thinking and Planetary Coexistence*. New York: Routledge, 2016.

Moltmann, Jürgen. *God in Creation: A New Theology of Creation and the Spirit of God*. San Francisco: Harper & Row, 1985.

Moltmann, Jürgen. *The Spirit of Life: A Universal Affirmation*. Minneapolis: Fortress Press, 1992.

Mora, Camilo, Derek P. Tittensor, Sina Adl, Alastair G. B. Simpson, and Boris Worm. "How Many Species Are There on Earth and in the Ocean?" *PLoS Biology* 9 (August 2011). https://www.ncbi.nlm.nih.gov/pmc/articles/PMC3160336.

Morgan, C. Lloyd. *Emergent Evolution*. New York: Henry Holt, 1923.

Morris, Simon Conway. "Evolution and the Inevitability of Intelligent Life." In *The Cambridge Companion to Science and Religion*, edited by Peter Harrison, 148–72. Cambridge: Cambridge University Press, 2010.

Mousseau, Juliet, and Sarah Kohles, eds. *In Our Own Words: Religious Life in a Changing World*. Collegeville, MN: Liturgical Press, 2018.

Mowbray, Kenneth, and Ian Tattersall. "Evolution, Human." In *Encyclopedia of Science and Religion*, edited by J. Wentzel Vrede van Huyssteen, 298–301. New York: Macmillan, 2003.

Murphy, Nancy. "Divine Action, Emergence and Scientific Explanation." In *The Cambridge Companion to Science and Religion*, edited by Peter Harrison, 244–59. Cambridge: Cambridge University Press, 2010.

Murray, Donal. "Glorious and Unfinished—the Year of Consecrated Life." *The Furrow* 66 (2015): 311–19.

Nanko, Carmen Marie. "Elbows on the Table: The Ethics of Doing Theology, Reflections from a U.S. Hispanic Perspective." *Journal of Hispanic/Latino Theology* 10 (February 2003): 52–77.

Nanko-Fernández, Carmen Marie. *Theologizing En Espanglish*. Maryknoll, NY: Orbis Books, 2010.

New Strategist Press. *American Generations: Who They Are & How They Live*. East Patchogue, NY: New Strategist Press, 2018.

Newell, Catherine L. "From Conflict to Wonder: Recent Literature in Science and Religion." *Religious Studies Review* 44 (December 2018): 389–93.

Nothwehr, Dawn M. "For the Salvation of the Cosmos: The Church's Mission of Ecojustice." *International Bulletin of Mission Research* 43 (2019): 68–81.

Nouwen, Henri J.M. *The Wound Healer: Ministry in Contemporary Society*. New York: Doubleday, 1972.

Oakes, Kaya. "Faithless Generation? In Search of Other Gen-X Catholics." *Commonweal* (October 10, 2013). https://www.commonwealmagazine .org/faithless-generation.

O'Brien, RSM, Sister Mary Judith, and Sister Mary Nika Schaumber, RSM. "Conclusion." In *The Foundations of Religious Life: Revisiting the Vision*, edited by Council of Major Superiors of Women Religious, 177–209. Notre Dame, IN: Ave Maria Press, 2009.

O'Toole, James M. *The Faithful: A History of Catholics in America*. Cambridge, MA: Harvard University Press, 2008.

Overbye, Dennis. *Lonely Hearts of the Cosmos: The Story of the Scientific Quest for the Secret of the Universe*. Boston: Back Bay Books, 1999.

Panikkar, Raimon. *Christophany: The Fullness of Man*. Translated by Alfred DiLascia. Maryknoll, NY: Orbis Books, 2004.

Peacocke, A. R. *Paths from Science Towards God: The End of All Our Exploring*. Oxford: Oneworld, 2002.

Peacocke, Arthur. "Theology and Science Today." In *Cosmos as Creation*, edited by Ted Peters. Nashville, TN: Abingdon Press, 1989.

Pearce, Ben K. D., Andrew S. Tupper, Ralph E. Pudritz, and Paul G. Higgs. "Constraining the Time Interval for the Origin of Life on Earth." *Astrobiology* 18 (2018): 343–64.

Pennington, Jonathan T., and Sean M. McDonough. *Cosmology and New Testament Theology*. Library of New Testament Studies: 355. London: T & T Clark, 2008.

Perez, OP, Mary Therese. "Local and Global: Charism of Religious Life Today." In *In Our Own Words: Religious Life in a Changing World*, edited by Juliet Mousseau and Sarah Kohles, 67–81. Collegeville, MN: Liturgical Press, 2018.

Peters, Ted, ed. *Cosmos as Creation: Theology and Science in Consonance.* Nashville, TN: Abingdon Press, 1989.

Peters, Ted. *God as Trinity: Relationality and Temporality in the Divine Life.* Louisville, KY: Westminster John Knox Press, 1993.

Pigliucci, Massimo. "What, If Anything, Is an Evolutionary Novelty?" *Philosophy of Science* 75 (2008): 887–98.

Polkinghorne, J. C. *Belief in God in an Age of Science.* Terry Lectures. Yale University Press, 1998.

Polkinghorne, John. *Quantum Theory: A Very Short Introduction.* Oxford: Oxford University Press, 2002.

Powe, Jr., F. Douglas. *New Wine New Wineskins: How African America Congregations Can Reach New Generations.* Nashville: Abingdon Press, 2012.

Price, Elizabeth Box. "Christian Nurture and the New Cosmology." *Religious Education* 103, no. 1 (January 2008): 84–101.

Rahner, Karl. *Foundations of Christian Faith: An Introduction to the Idea of Christianity.* Seabury Press, 1978.

Rauscher, Elizabeth A. "Non-Locality as a Fundamental Principle of Reality: Bell's Theorem and Space-like Interconnectedness." *Cosmos and History: The Journal of Natural and Social Philosophy* 13 (2017): 204–16.

Reid, Barbara E. *Wisdom's Feast: An Invitation to Feminist Interpretation of the Scriptures.* Grand Rapids, MI: Eerdmans, 2016.

Reid, OP, Barbara E. "The What, Why, and How of Feminist Biblical Interpretation." *The Bible Today* (2019): 135–41.

Rolston, Holmes. *Three Big Bangs: Matter-Energy, Life, Mind.* New York: Columbia University Press, 2011.

Ruse, Michael. "Evolution." In *Encyclopedia of Science and Religion,* 1:279–81. New York: Macmillan, 2003.

Russell, Robert J. *Cosmology: From Alpha to Omega. The Creative Mutual Interaction of Theology and Science.* Theology and the Sciences. Minneapolis: Fortress Press, 2008.

Russell, Robert John. "Cosmology and Eschatology." In *The Oxford Handbook of Eschatology,* edited by Jerry L. Walls, 563–80. Oxford: Oxford University Press, 2008.

Russell, Robert John. "Eschatology and Scientific Cosmology: From Deadlock to Interaction." *Zygon: Journal of Religion & Science* 47 (December 2012): 997–1014.

Russell, Robert John. "Resurrection, Eschatology, and the Challenge of Big Bang Cosmology." *Interpretation: A Journal of Bible & Theology* 70 (January 2016): 48.

Russo, Mario A. "Soteriology, Eschatology and Cosmology: Resolving the Dissonance and Providing a Lens." *Science & Christian Belief* 31 (April 2019): 26–40.

Ryan, Robin. *Jesus and Salvation: Soundings in the Christian Tradition and Contemporary Theology.* Collegeville, MN: Liturgical Press, 2015.

Sakho, Ibrahima. *Introduction to Quantum Mechanics. 1, Thermal Radiation and Experimental Facts Regarding the Quantization of Matter.* Hoboken, NJ: Wiley, 2019.

Schaab, Gloria L. "In the Travail of the Cosmos: God and Suffering in the Evolving Universe." *Heythrop Journal* 58 (January 2017): 91–107.

Schaefer, Judith K. *The Evolution of a Vow: Obedience as Decision Making in Communion.* Zürich: Lit Verlag, 2008.

Schäfer, Lothar. "Quantum Reality and the Consciousness of the Universe: Quantum Reality, the Emergence of Complex Order from Virtual States, and the Importance of Consciousness in the Universe." *Zygon: Journal of Religion & Science* 41 (2006): 505–32.

Schneiders, Sandra. *Beyond Patching: Faith and Feminism in the Catholic Church.* Mahwah, NJ: Paulist Press, 1990.

Schneiders, Sandra M. *Selling All: Commitment, Consecrated Celibacy, and Community in Catholic Religious Life.* New York: Paulist Press, 2001.

Schneiders, Sandra M. *Written That You May Believe: Encountering Jesus in the Fourth Gospel.* New York: Crossroad Publishing, 1999.

Schreiter, CPPS, Robert J. "A New Modernity: Living and Believing in an Unstable World." *Melintas: An International Journal of Philosophy and Religion* 21 (2005): 143–87.

Schreiter, Robert J. *The New Catholicity: Theology between the Global and the Local.* Maryknoll, NY: Orbis Books, 1997.

Schrödinger, Erwin. "Discussion of Probability Relations Between Separated Systems." *Proceedings of the Cambridge Philosophical Society* 31 (1935): 55–563.

Scott, Margaret. "Greening the Vows: *Laudato Si'* and Religious Life." *The Way* 54 (2015): 83–93.

Segundo, Juan Luis. *An Evolutionary Approach to Jesus of Nazareth.* Edited and translated by John Drury. Maryknoll, NY: Orbis Books, 1988.

Silk, Joseph. *Horizons of Cosmology: Exploring Words Seen and Unseen.* West Conshohocken, PA: Templeton Press, 2009.

Silk, Joseph. *The Infinite Cosmos: Questions from the Frontiers of Cosmology*. Oxford: Oxford University Press, 2006.

Simmons, Ernest L. *The Entangled Trinity: Quantum Physics and Theology*. Minneapolis: Fortress Press, 2014.

Smith, Christian, Kyle Longest, Jonathan Hill, and Kari Christoffersen. *Young Catholic America: Emerging Adults In, Out of, and Gone from the Church*. New York: Oxford University Press, 2014.

Smut, J. C. *Holism and Evolution*. New York: Macmillan, 1926.

Spergel, David. "Cosmology Today." *Daedalus* 143 (2014): 125–33.

Stearns, Beverly Peterson, and Stephen C. Stearns. *Watching, from the Edge of Extinction*. New Haven, CT: Yale University Press, 1999.

Stenger, Victor J. *Quantum Gods: Creation, Chaos, and the Search for Cosmic Consciousness*. Amherst, NY: Prometheus Books, 2009.

Strauss, William, and Neil Howe. *Generations: The History of America's Future, 1584 to 2069*. New York: HarperCollins, 1991.

Suenens, Leon Joseph Cardinal. *The Nun in the World: Religious and the Apostolate*. Westminster, MD: The Newman Press, 1963.

Tate, W. Randolph. "Post Modern Interpretation." In *The Oxford Encyclopedia of Biblical Interpretation*, edited by Steven L. McKenzie. New York: Oxford University Press, 2013.

Teilhard de Chardin, Pierre. *Christianity and Evolution*. New York: Harcourt Brace Jovanovich, 1971.

Teilhard de Chardin, Pierre. *Human Energy*. Translated by J. M. Cohen. London: Collins, 1969.

Teilhard de Chardin, Pierre. *Man's Place in Nature*. New York: Harper & Row, 1966.

Teilhard de Chardin, Pierre. *The Future of Man*. New York: Doubleday, 1964.

Teilhard de Chardin, Pierre. *The Phenomenon of Man*. New York: Harper & Row, 1961.

Teilhard de Chardin, Pierre. *Writing in Time of War*. Translated by René Hague. New York: Harper & Row, 1968.

Tentler, Leslie Woodcock. *American Catholics: A History*. New Haven, CT: Yale University Press, 2020.

Trimmer, John D. "The Present Situation in Quantum Mechanics: A Translation of Schrödinger's 'Cat Paradox.'" *Proceedings of the American Philosophical Society* 124 (1980): 323–38.

Vahia, Mayank N. "Evolution of Science I: Evolution of Mind." *Current Science* 111 (November 2016): 1456–64.

Van Till, Howard J., Robert E. Snow, John H. Stek, and Davis A. Young. *Portraits of Creation: Biblical and Scientific Perspectives on the World's Formation.* Grand Rapids, MI: Eerdmans, 1990.

Velmans, Max. "The Evolution of Consciousness." *Contemporary Social Science: Journal of the Academy of Social Sciences* 7 (June 2012): 117–38.

Wadell, Paul J. *The Primacy of Love: Introduction to the Ethics of Thomas Aquinas.* Eugene, OR: Wipf & Stock, 2009.

Wagler, Ron. "The Anthropocene Mass Extinction: An Emerging Curriculum Theme for Science Educators." *The American Biology Teacher* 73 (February 2011): 78–83.

Ward, SLG, Benedicta, translator. *The Sayings of the Desert Fathers: The Alphabetical Collection.* Kalamazoo, MI: Cistercian Publications, 1975.

Wake, D. B., and V. T. Vredenburg. "Are We in the Midst of the Sixth Mass Extinction? A View from the World of Amphibians." *Proceedings of the National Academy of Sciences* 105 (2008): 11466–73.

Weaver, John David. "The New Cosmology—an Opportunity for the Gospel." *The Theological Educator* 51 (1995): 19–28.

Weaver, Mary Jo. "Who Are Conversative Catholics?" In *Being Right: Conversative Catholics in America*, edited by Mary Jo Weaver and R. Scott Appleby. Bloomington, IN: Indiana University Press, 1995.

Wilbur, Ken. *The Integral Vision: A Very Short Introduction to the Revolutionary Integral Approach to Life, God, the Universe, and Everything.* Boston: Shambhala, 2007.

Williams, Alex. "Improbable Singularities—Evolution Is Riddled with Them." *Journal of Creation* 29 (2015): 92–98.

Wilson, Edmund O. *The Diversity of Life.* New York: Norton, 1999.

Yang, Yang. "Social Inequalities in Happiness in the United States." *American Sociological Review* 73 (April 2008): 204–26.

Zhoudunming, Tu, Dmitri E. Kharzeev, and Thomas Ullrich. "Einstein-Podolsky-Rosen Paradox and Quantum Entanglement at Subnucleonic Scales." *Physical Review Letters* 124 (February 14, 2020). https://link.aps.org/doi/10.1103/PhysRevLett.124.062001.

# Scripture Index

# Subject Index